VARIANTS
7

The Journal of the European Society
for Textual Scholarship

ESTS Board Members

Barbara Bordalejo, UK
Herman Brinkman, The Netherlands
Burghard Dedner, Germany
Anne Mette Hansen, Denmark
João Dionisio, Portugal
Caroline Macé, Belgium
Rüdiger Nutt-Kofoth, Germany
Bodo Plachta, Germany
Peter Robinson, UK
Michael Stolz, Switzerland
Paulius V. Subačius, Lithuania
Dirk Van Hulle, Belgium
Wim Van Mierlo, UK

General Editor

Barbara Bordalejo

Associate Editor

Wim Van Mierlo

Textual Scholarship and the Canon

Edited by
Hans Walter Gabler, Peter Robinson
and Paulius V. Subačius

AMSTERDAM - NEW YORK, NY 2008

Cover image:
Sigune sitting in a tree (Bavarian State Library, Cgm 8470, Bl. 182v).

Cover design:
Pier Post

The paper on which this book is printed meets the requirements of "ISO 9706: 1994, Information and documentation - Paper for documents - Requirements for permanence".

ISBN: 978-90-420-3235-4
E-Book ISBN: 978-90-420-3236-1
ISSN: 1573-3084
©Editions Rodopi B.V., Amsterdam - New York, NY 2008
Printed in The Netherlands

Variants 7 (2008)

Textual Scholarship and the Canon

Edited by Hans Walter Gabler, Peter Robinson and Paulius V. Subačius

Peter Robinson
    Introduction   1

Mikas Vaicekauskas
    To Burn or To Republish?
        The Fate of the 18th–19th century Lithuanian Bestseller   9

Paulius V. Subačius
    Canonisation as Impediment to Textual Scholarship:
        Lithuanian Postcolonial Experiences   23

Paula Henrikson
    Canon and Classicity:
        Editing as Canonising in Swedish Romanticism   37

Gabriel Viehhauser
    On the Margin of the Canon:
        Editions, the "Whole" Text and the "Whole" Codex   57

Michael Stolz
    Medieval Canonicity and Rewriting:
        A Case Study of the Sigune-figure in Wolfram's *Parzival*   75

Rüdiger Nutt-Kofoth
    The Beißnerian Mode, the Zellerian Mode,
    and the Canonical Way of Modern Editing:
        Upheavals and Deviations in German Editorial
        Methodology – and its Historiography   95

Jesús Varela Zapata
   The Canon Beyond Academia:
      Alternative Sources of Canonicity in Twentieth-
      Century Literature in English   107

Nila Vázquez
   Drawbacks in the Process of Editing a
      Non-Canonical Chaucerian Text:
      The Case of Yonge Gamelyne of the
      Canterbury Tales   119

Luc Herman, John M. Krafft and Sharon B. Krafft
   Missing Link:
      The *V.* Galleys at the Morgan Library
      and the Harry Ransom Center   139

Hans Walter Gabler
   From Argument to Design:
      Editions in Books and Beyond the Book   159

Christian Benne
   Ossian: The Book History of an Anti-book   179

Reviews

Gillian Wright
   Peter Beal, comp. A *Dictionary of English
      Manuscript Terminology 1450-2000.*   203

Annika Bautz
   Paul Eggert, *Securing the Past: Conservation in Art,
      Architecture and Literature.*   205

Christine Collière-Whiteside
   Olga Anokhina and Sabine Pétillon, eds.
      Critique génétique: Concepts, methods, outils.   207

Oliver Pickering
   Siân Echard, *Printing the Middle Ages.*   210

Stephen B. Dobranski
   The 1671 Poems: "Paradise Regain'd" and
    "Samson Agonistes." Ed. Laura Lunger Knoppers.
    Vol. 2 of *The Complete Works of John Milton.*   212

Katie Halsey
   Janet Todd and Linda Bree (eds). *The Cambridge Edition*
    of the Works of Jane Austen: Later Manuscripts.   215

Chris Ackerley
   Dirk Van Hulle. *Manuscript Genetics:*
    Joyce's Know-How, Beckett's Nohow   218

Werner Gelderblom
   Musique Deoque: Un Archivio Digitale di Poesia Latina
    /A Digital Archive of Latin Poetry.   223

Notes on Contributors   225

Introduction

Peter Robinson

For textual scholars, as for everyone else in the academy, the words "canon", "canonical" and "canonicity" evoke a time when life seemed simpler, and perhaps even golden. Textual scholars were particularly well served by the notion of an accepted canon: a hierarchy of texts with a widely-accepted group of masterpieces at its apex, which (all agreed) needed to be provided with thorough, scholarly, exact, accurate, well-presented and (yes!) definitive editions. It seemed a happy compact. We all knew the works which were the foundation of our culture. We all knew that we as textual scholars had a core role to play, as a kind of priesthood purifying these works from corruption, so that readers might be made healthy by reading well-cleansed texts. Publishers, learned organizations, even governments, also had seats at this table. We all knew where we were. Or so the myth goes.

It can be argued that this always was a myth, and the disputes down the ages about what works are "canonical", and about just what the word means anyway, reveal that this consensus was ever only apparent, a matter of rhetoric rather than fact. Paula Henrikson's essay in this volume traces in illuminating detail the contortions of several generations of scholars in Sweden and elsewhere to arrive at a useful definition of "classic" (one might argue that a text could be "canonical" without being "classic" — but this argument would only serve to dramatize the cracks in the consensus) and then to fit modern texts into this frame. From a different angle, Nila Vazquez' article on the decidedly non-canonical *Tale of Yonge Gamelyn* shows how unhelpful notions of canonicity are for the editor of such a work (and of course, most works must be "non-canonical": if the term means anything at all, it must exclude most works).

But if the canon was always more to do with rhetoric than fact, at least it was a rhetoric to which most affected to subscribe. Not now. We live in an age as much post-canonical as post-modern. In place of the older conviction, that "canonicity" was somehow intrinsic to the work itself, independent of the circumstances of its making and reception, we have a quite new conviction, at least as widely held as the older conviction: that "canonicity" flows from the reception of the work, not the work itself. Thus, in place of the view that a canonical work endured beyond bronze and marble, its place in our regard forever fixed, we now see that the reputation of a work is completely formed by its readership. Further, we see that the circumstances of the making of a work can have a vital impact on its reception (Vaicekaukas), as can commercial pressures and academic fashions (Zapata), political changes in the surrounding landscape (Subacius), academic disputes about modes of editing (Nutt-Kofoth) and even the instability of the work itself, shown in large-scale divergences among the documents of the work (Stolz and Viehhauser).

It is appropriate to begin this volume with two essays dealing with issues of canonicity in Lithuania. The conference where most of the eight essays in this volume on the subject of the canon and editing were presented as conference papers was held in Vilnius, Lithuania in November 2007. The conference organizers chose the conference theme "Textual Scholarship and the Canon" just because it is such a problematic issue in Lithuania. The first essay in the volume, Mikas Vaicekaukas on the sometime Lithuanian best-seller *The Gate Open to Eternity*, might stand as a textbook counter-argument to the view that the worth of a work is intrinsic to itself, quite apart from its readership. The extraordinary vicissitudes of *The Gate Open to Eternity* explode this view completely. First, it achieved massive popularity within the first decades of its composition, being reprinted a full seventeen times in under a hundred years up to 1851. It had a huge popular appeal, written in a language close to the people, and containing an extraordinary mixture of styles, with tales and sermonizing side-by-side. This mixture of styles, and its status as a foundation literary work of its vernacular, puts one in mind of Dante and Chaucer, though without their formal rigour. As Paula Henrikson reminds us, formal sophistication was a key element in enlightenment attempts to define classicism, and by 1850 learned opinion in Lithuania had turned decisively against *The Gate Open to Eternity* ("should have been burnt long ago … meaningless ramblings presented as religious truth"). Partly this reflected literary snobbery, partly anti-Catholic sentiment. Yet the continuing popularity of *The Gate Open to Eternity* was not to be denied: even though it was not published, it continued to be widely copied, and Vaicekaukas tells a revealing tale of a Bishop who condemned it outright, and then prepared his own version of the work, fit (in his view) for the more sophisticated readers of the 1870s: "the reader had changed, so Valančius changed the entire work as well." But worse yet was to follow, as the Soviet rulers of Lithuania declared that *The Gate Open to Eternity* represented all that was wrong in the old order they sought to sweep away. The essay ends with a question: perhaps now, 250 years on, *The Gate Open to Eternity* might finally achieve a canonical status in a newly-understood Lithuanian national literature. So the wheel might turn full circle.

The following essay, by Paulius V. Subačius, complements the close focus of the Vaicekauska essay by looking at the broader movements in literary culture within Lithuania over the past 150 years. We note above how well in the West notions of canonicity fed into the prevailing model of western scholarship. But the situation was perfectly inverted in Lithuania: canonisation of texts actually stood in the way of textual scholarship. Subacius explains that this was a result of the distorting experiences first of colonialism, as the Soviet occupation imposed its own upside-down values on Lithuania, and then post-colonialism, where people in rebellion against the Soviet regime sought to invert Soviet values and hence achieved their own special version of the upside-down. This led to a disjunction of aims: popular editions of core Lithuanian texts must be published as quickly as possible, to re-inforce the new national culture; but because of this need for haste there is no time to provide the critical editions of these which are so badly needed. On the other hand: a very few critical editions are being produced , but of texts which hardly anyone reads.

These two essays illustrate the strange distortions which concepts of the canon have imposed upon academic discourse. The next article, by Paula Henrikson, traces the history of the concept of a "classic" from the sixteenth-century on across Europe, focussing on its appropriation by the Romantics and then by self-consciously national literary movements, particularly Sweden, from 1750 on. In complete contrast to Lithuania, this led to "a golden century of editorial scholarship" in Sweden, as surging currents of nationalism found validation in "national classics" and authorized the creation of "normative" texts, as the base for a coherent society nurtured on national scriptures. Henrikson's narrative stops at 1900, in retrospect (we can now see) a highpoint of canonical textual confidence: think, in England, of the Early English Text Society, based on the same glad certainties. But already, one can see the flaws in the façade: the embarrassing failures of Swedish writers to produce works which could be fairly reckoned as classics and a vociferous opposition to the Romantic/ Nationalist claims, leading to a need for scholars of that school to rewrite their national literary history.

The next two essays both use the textual tradition of Wolfram von Eschenbach's *Parzival* as the starting point for different critiques of the concept of canonicity. Viehhauser's article opens by citing a recent listing of Wolfram's *Parzival* as the one "book" from Middle High German which a cultured reader "must" read. The first irony is that "book" appears in quotation marks in the previous sentence: Wolfram explicitly disclaims the title of "book" for his work. Viehauser then proceeds to dismantle the relevance of a narrowly-understood "canonicity" to any discussion of Wolfram by examining the history of attempts to edit Wolfram. A canonical author needs a canonical text, and generations of editors sought to provide one. With little success: the simple facts of the textual tradition of Wolfram, as commonly for any popular text produced in the manuscript age, defy their reduction into a single text, in anything like a fixed form. There is no help for it: our canonical work turns out to have competing forms and an unstable text, leading directly to a need to acknowledge that we have to deal with (at the least) multiple canonised texts. Further, Viehhauser demonstrates that one cannot detach texts from the material documents in which they appear: thus (in theory) every text, in every document, might have a canonical status. At this point, we are in danger of losing the ability of canonicity to discriminate among competing works, and even competing forms of works. To this Viehhauser offers a pragmatic solution: a model of an edition which presents alternative "canonised" forms of the text (four, in the standard print format devised by the *Parzival* project), along with richly-detailed material evidence of each document (full sets of high-quality digital images in the electronic publication). The aim is to be both "representative" of the central canon, embodied in the four texts, and of its "margins", as seen in the full exposition of variants and of the material documents in the edition.

Stolz's article explores canonicity from a different angle: from close analysis of a few variants among the different texts of Wolfram's work, to explore what scribes actually did, and how this impacts on our notions of authorship, canonicity and re-writing. As does Viehhauser, and building on Karl Uitti, he finds that canonicity must embrace variation: here, the originary text itself and then what scribes do with the text. Stolz deals in detail with a few variants from Wolfram, relating to the Sigune figure. In one case, a simple scribal confusion of letters led to the extraordinary placement of Sigune in a tree, rather than under it; in others, we see scribes adapting, elaborating, and converting simple errors into imaginative tropes. In the process, they produced what we may see as new texts — but, as Stolz points out, there is every evidence that they scribes did not see themselves as producing new texts. They were working on a broad canvas, where the work we label Wolfram's *Parzival* is capable of multiple and protean expressions, to which they themselves might contribute. For Stolz, as for Viehhauser, the digital medium is an ideal means of exploring and exposing the *e pluribus unum* which is Wolfram's multi-faceted, multiply-expressed, work.

These last two essays show that a work may appear, from its earliest dissemination, in multiple canonized forms — and indeed, dissemination will create multiple forms. Nutt-Kofoth's essay sends the argument in a different direction: to look at the multiple forms of a work in its genetic phase, as it proceeds through authorial drafts towards a published work. This has become one of the most richly-tilled fields of textual scholarship in the last decades: so much so that different national modes of genetic editing have arisen, and even different models within the one community. Thus, we have "Zellerian" and "Beißnerian" modes of editing genetic texts of modern German authors, and Nutt-Kofoth details the oppositions between the two modes of editing, with their different stresses on abstracted text and material representation. While parts of the opposition seem to be the result of academic posturing, the tension reflects a division of purpose which lies at the heart of any editorial enterprise — between the pursuit of the "work" in its pure and purefied form, and the need to show the actual instantiation of the work in multiple stubbornly-difficult documents. Neither of these two modes could claim canonical status, still less the editions made according to their lights. Again, the "canonical" must accommodate many differing views.

Declarations of "canonicity" are claims for our attention: a demand that we read this work, not another; or that we read it a particular way; or that we edit it according to a prescribed manner. We can measure some kinds of attention, in terms of copies sold, prizes won, academic citations, even popular votes. This is the route taken by Zapata in his survey of sources of canonicity in twentieth-century literature in England. Zapata outlines the beginnings of a "modern canon" in Arnold and Leavis. However, his article stresses the role played by non-academic sources: popular polls and literary prizes, notably the Nobel Prize. The broad agreement of all these with one another, and with the "establishment" academic view of what constitutes the canon expressed by Harold Bloom, is striking: the same names appear over and over. He notes too the surprising influence of prize citations on academic publishing: in an inversion of how academics imagine themselves, it seems that popular opinion influences academic writings, not the other way about. Some elements of this overview are disquieting, if all too familiar: the massive influence of the prize culture on publishing, for example. His broad conclusion is firm: deny the canon as we might, there is a distinct set of authors and books which (even in this post-canonical age) hold "canonical" status. Further, academic culture is now a rather minor player in determining what books and authors are canonical. As we were in the last stages of preparing this volume, *Time* magazine put Jonathan Frantzen on its cover, on the occasion of the publication of his latest novel *Freedom* — which immediately leapt up the *New York Times* best-seller list, and into every airport bookstall. It took centuries for Shakespeare to become canonical: an author can now achieve this in a day.

The last essay in this section is by Vázquez, on the issues which arise when one edits a decidedly non-canonical text: in this case, the *Tale of Yonge Gamelyn*, found only in manuscripts of Geoffrey Chaucer's *Canterbury Tales* but universally regarded (though commonly without argument) as not by Chaucer, or indeed as part of the *Tales* at all. Her article is striking for its demonstration that editorial norms, developed for so long and with such sophistication for dealing with acknowledged canonical texts (such as the Canterbury Tales itself) are of very little utility when dealing with a non-canonical text. The standard recourses of editors of canonical texts — identify the text nearest the authorial original; or at least the "best text"; establish "best" readings on the grounds of stemmatics or of taste; express the text in a normalized spelling — are not available. We have no idea who, when or where the author was, and hardly any concept of what material he or she was working with, or what pathways the documents took before the tale appears in manuscripts written around 1400; among the manifest deficiencies of all the texts we have, the idea of a "best" text is irrelevant; in a text of notable poetic impurity, "best" readings are something of a nonsense; the spelling of all the witnesses is so unstable that there is no norm. To top this, the low status of the text appears to have tempted previous editors to produce texts which were sloppy even by their standards. In these circumstances, Vazquez's resort, to print a conspectus of the whole tradition and to settle for the modest aim of provision of "some information" about the *Tale* and its tradition, seems the best which can be achieved. There are interesting issues here, to do with pragmatism as theory, and about the dissolution of canonicity into variation. Perhaps we need a theory of editing which is not built from the heights on an older notion of canonical works, with an attempt to adapt it downwards to accommodate variation in all its guises, but which is built from the base, on an acceptance of variation in every text and then reaches up towards our sense of the works which might be constructed from the many.

***

This volume also includes three other essays not submitted as part of the "Textual Scholarship and the Canon" cluster. Herman, Krafft and Krafft's article on the galleys of Pynchon's *V.* explains the passage of Pynchon's first novel from authorial typescript to published novel. Parts of the article read like a detective story, in its meticulous reconstruction of events. Overall, it gives an extraordinary window into Pynchon's struggles with his own creation and into the remarkably impressive effort of his publisher (including no less than three in-house proofreaders — what first novel since has had such care?) to accommodate Pynchon. Alas, the venerable firm of J. B. Lippincott, founded in 1792, which saw this book through the press (and so, one could argue, changed the course of modern fiction, at least in America) is no more. After a series of corporate acquisitions it is part of the behemoth Wolters Kluwer, itself now part of something called Bridgestone Capital, and the Social Text is much diminished.

One may set this article alongside Nutt-Kofoth's discussion of differing modes of genetic editing: indeed, one might produce a genetic edition of *V.* based on the materials surveyed in this article, in Zellerian or Beißnerian or some other mode. But one doubts that any such edition, no matter how clear its exposition (including use of the most sophisticated digital presentation) would be as useful, as illuminating to any reader, as this article. Sometimes, the best edition really is an article. We note, with sadness, the passing of one of the co-authors, Sharon Krafft, between the acceptance of this article in final form and its publication: we trust that this article is a worthy memorial.

Gabler's article is an authoritative reflection, by one of the most experienced and influential scholarly editors of our time, on the rhetorical dimensions of editing, whereby an edition is a "multi-stranded argument" created by the editor. Gabler notes that the first printers were also editors. He observes also the intrinsic hypertext in early print volumes, and sees that these early editions are expressions, through rigorous design, of intellectual force. He traces this through many editions up to the present, to reach an ideal starting-point for a discussion of electronic editions as continuations, by many electronic means, of this tradition of purposeful editing. Gabler ends by calling for a conception of electronic editions not simply as accumulations of material (which indeed they have tended to become) but "genuinely relational webs of discourse." Here is a challenge many of us might take up.

This volume is completed by Benne's article on the extraordinary impact of Macpherson's *Ossian*. In self-congratulatory mode, we might reflect that this is exactly the kind of article *Variants* exists to publish: it combines elements of various kinds of history (book, literary, social and intellectual) with an arresting thesis, based on the closest examination of material documents. Benne sees the roots of modern hermeneutics not in print declarations, but in modern manuscript culture: in the specific forms which Ossian's texts take, in their paratextual and bibliographic codes. Here, textual scholarship meets book history meets intellectual history, and all are the better for it. It is a thesis which could scarcely have been imagined a few decades ago, and a measure of its success is the new light it brings on the famous use of Ossian in Goethe's *Sorrows of Young Werther*, and even on parts of *Werther* which do not reference Ossian directly. Thus, the whole point of the volume of Lessing which lies on Werther's desk after his suicide is exactly that is not *Ossian*.

* * *

Finally, readers familiar with earlier volumes of *Variants* will note a substantial innovation in this volume. On the initiative of the *Variants* general editor, we have moved to a full implementation of the "Chicago B" author/date bibliographic referencing. While this system is less widely used in the humanities than in the sciences, we think it leads to a clarity of exposition and ease of readership well suited to *Variants* articles.

To Burn or To Republish?

The Fate of the 18th–19th century Lithuanian Bestseller

Mikas Vaicekauskas

In the second half of the 18th — the first half of the 19th century, the most popular Catholic work of a non-practical nature in Lithuania was *Broma atverta ing viečnastį* (*The Gate Open to Eternity*), published in 1753 by the priest Mykolas Olševskis[1] (c. 1712 — c. 1779), a monk of the Order of Canons Regular of Penance (*Ordo Canonicorum Regularium Mendicantium S. Mariae de Metro de Poenitentia*). In Lithuanian literature this work is interesting from the points of view of socio-cultural functioning and of its own history. The work was written at the time when the language of Lithuanian fiction was not yet created; one can speak only of certain rudiments.[2] Therefore it should be seen as the central text of the period's Lithuanian literature written in Lithuanian.

Broma atverta ing viečnastį comprises spiritual readings and sermons, didactic stories ("priklodai") and examples, spiritual meditations, prayers and other pieces of religious writing on the theme of death. *Broma atverta ing viečnastį* is about God and heaven, hell and the devil, the human soul and eternal fate; the sermons are illustrated with episodes from the lives of the saints and other stories. The book is written in a language very similar to the spoken language well understood by the people, with numerous borrowings from Latin and Polish. It contains numerous Latin quotations from the Holy Scripture and works by religious writers. The work was written in accordance with the tradition and literary fashions of the period, in a blend of high and low styles, yet the book stood out in its expressive lower baroque style. It abounds in comparisons, contrasts, antitheses, metaphors, hyperboles, paradox, repetitions, and other figures of speech. The rudiments of *belles-lettres* narrative in the didactic stories and examples, as well as the didactic and religious content and its expression made *Broma*

---

[1] [Mykolas Olševskis], BROMA | ATWERTA | Ing | WIECZNASTI, | PAR | Atmi-nima paſkutiniu dayktu. | Su ſpaſabays Diſponawojma mir- | ſztanciu, ant ścieſliwa ſmercia. | *Su ſpaſabays ratawojma* duſiu *Ciśćiu kien-* | *tanciu. Teypogi ape kitus Artykuhus Wie-* | *ros Szwętos, ſu trumpays pamokſtays, ir pri-* | *kłodays, iſz pawożniu Authoriu iſzrinktays*. | Par Kuniga | MIKOŁA | OLSZEWSKI | Theologa Abſoluta Kanawnika Regu- | larna BB. MM. De paenitentia; ſu Me- | dytacyomis ant ciełos Nedieles. | Metuoſe nuog Uſzgimima JEZUSA P. 1753. | WILNIUY | Drukarnie J. K. M. Kunigu Franciſzkonu; VUB L$_R$ 1062 (Olševskis 1753).

[2] Meanwhile, literature in Latin and Polish was quite abundant in Lithuania.

atverta ing viečnasti popular among and understandable to the readership of the time. The work is characterised as "a cultural text of late Baroque marked with a strong impression of mediaeval ideals" (Tereškinas 1992). During the hundred years before its last publication in 1851 *Broma atverta ing viečnasti* was reprinted as many as seventeen times — in 1753, 1759, 1764, 1766, 1777, 1779, 1785, 1789, 1793, 1795, 1799, 1806, 1811, 1824, 1846, 1847, 1851. As can be seen from the sales registers of the printing houses, each reprint consisted of quite a number of copies.[3]

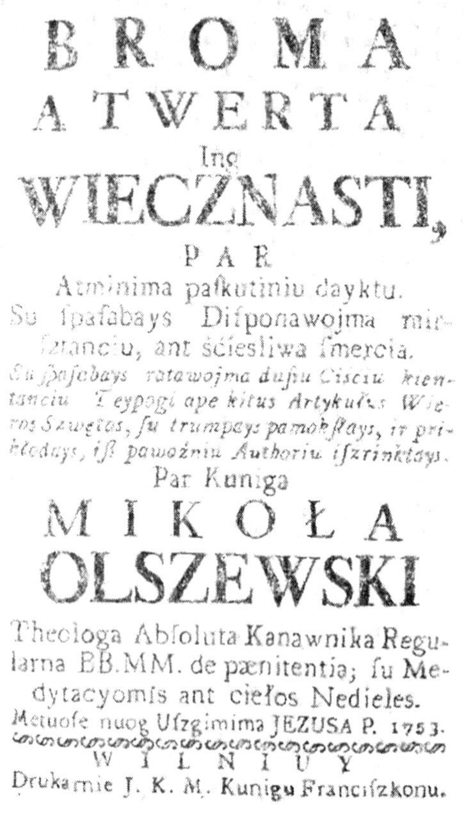

> BROMA
> ATWERTA
> Ing
> WIECZNASTI,
> PAR
> Atminima paſkutiniu dayktu.
> Su ſpaſabays Diſponawojma mir-
> ſzianciu, ant ścieſliwa ſmercia.
> Su paſabays ratawojma duſiu Ciſciu kien-
> tanciu. Teypogi ape kitus Artykułus Wie-
> ros Szwętos, ſu trumpays pamokſłays, iʃ pri-
> kładays, iſʒ pawożniu Authoriu iſzrinktays.
> Par Kuniga
> MIKOŁA
> OLSZEWSKI
> Theologa Abſoluta Kanawnika Regu-
> larna EB.MM. de pænitentia; ſu Me-
> dytacyomis ant cielos Nedieles.
> Metuoſe nuog Uſzgimima JEZUSA P. 1753.
> WILNIUY
> Drukarnie J. K. M. Kunigu Francisʒkonu.

Fig. 1. Title page of Mykolas Olševskis' *Broma atverta ing viečnasti* (1753).

The reprints of this work in the 17-18th centuries point to the fact that the need for *Broma atverta ing viečnasti* was constantly felt. There was,

---

[3] For instance, the estimations of Jurgis Lebedys based on the registers of the revenue for books sold and expenses show that from 1777 to 1784 (between the publications of *Broma atverta ing viečnasti* from 1777 to 1785) the printing house of Vilnius Academy sold 1345 copies of this book (Lebedys 1976, 99-100).

in 1864, another — the eighteenth indeed — attempt to publish it, but in order to publish a book of religious content the publisher had to obtain an approval from Church authorities for it. However, the Samogitian bishop Motiejus Valančius (1801–1875), the most influential 19th century Lithuanian cultural and public figure, did not grant this permission. In a letter addressed to the Vilnius Censorship Committee, he argued that "the book contained invented and somewhat silly stories that encouraged superstition among ordinary people."[4] It is possible that at that time Valančius had the idea of publishing a new and revised edition of *Broma atverta ing viečnastį*, but it could have been prevented by the ban on the press in Latin alphabet (the characters were banned in 1865–1904) in the whole territory of Russia-occupied Lithuania (Vaicekauskas 2005b).

It should also be noted, that in 1874, already under the ban on the Lithuanian press, Aleksandras Luotys (? — before 1899), an employee of one of the printing houses in St. Petersburg, copied two Lithuanian works — Valančius' *Trumpas katekizmas* (*A Short Catechism*, 1865) published in "grazhdanka" (Cyrillic Lithuanian), and *Broma atverta ing viečnastį* (the 1846 edition) — by hand and bound them as a book.[5] Although rare, such hand-written books were a known fact in the history of 19th century Lithuanian culture (Vaicekauskas 2009). The reason for copying these works could be the desire to possess a personal copy of the books at the time of the press ban: *Trumpas katekizmas* for practical purposes, and *Broma atverta ing viečnastį* — as an ageless and for some time no longer published spiritual work (Vaicekauskas 2003; Subačius 2006).

---

[4] Motiejus Valančius' letter to the Vilnius Censorship Committee No. 453, 1864 02 28, *LVIA*, f. 1671, ap. 4, b. 98, l. 223.

[5] [Aleksandras Luotys], *Trumpas Katechizmas. Awkcziawsej kraβta wyresnibei lejpant paraβitas diel kataliku jawnumenes i moksla lejdamus. Yβspawstas. Wilniui Yβspawsty dalejda. Metus 1874 Rugsieje 16 deina. Motiejus Walonczawskis Wiskups. Raβi Aleksandra Lowtis. Broma Atwerta ing Wiecznasty. Iszdowta par Kuniga Mikola Olszewski. Isz spausta Wilniow 1846 Metusy. Paraβi Aleksandra Lowtis 1874 Metusy M. S Peterborga*, *LLTI BR*, f. 1, b. 3468.

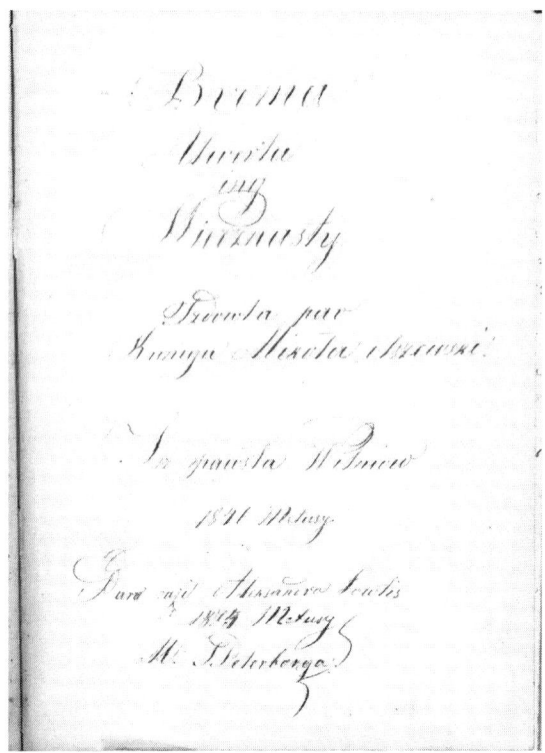

Fig. 2. Title page of Aleksandras Luotys' manuscript *Broma atverta ing viečnastį* (1874).

Although no longer in print, *Broma atverta ing viečnastį* maintained its popularity throughout the second half of the 19th century and until the early 20th century. But let us return to Bishop Valančius, who in the second half of his life was actively engaged in writing, editing and printing of highly popular didactic and religious books intended for ordinary believers, such as *Žyvatas Jėzaus Kristaus Viešpaties mūsų* (*The Life of Jesus Christ Our Lord*, 1853), *Žyvatai šventųjų* (*The Lives of the Saints*, 1858), *Vaikų knygelė* (*Children's Book*, 1868), *Paaugusių žmonių knygelė* (*Grownups' Book*, 1868), *Gyvenimas Švenčiausios Marijos Panos* (*The Life of the Holy Virgin Mary*, 1874). In 1874–1875, at the end of his life, being very ill and living in the shadow of approaching death, Valančius wrote his last book *Broma atidaryta ing viečnastį* (*The Gate Open to Eternity*), and it was the revised and expanded edition of 1851 *Broma atverta ing viečnastį*. However, he did not publish it: what have survived are the manuscript and its copy, and it has not been published so far.[6]

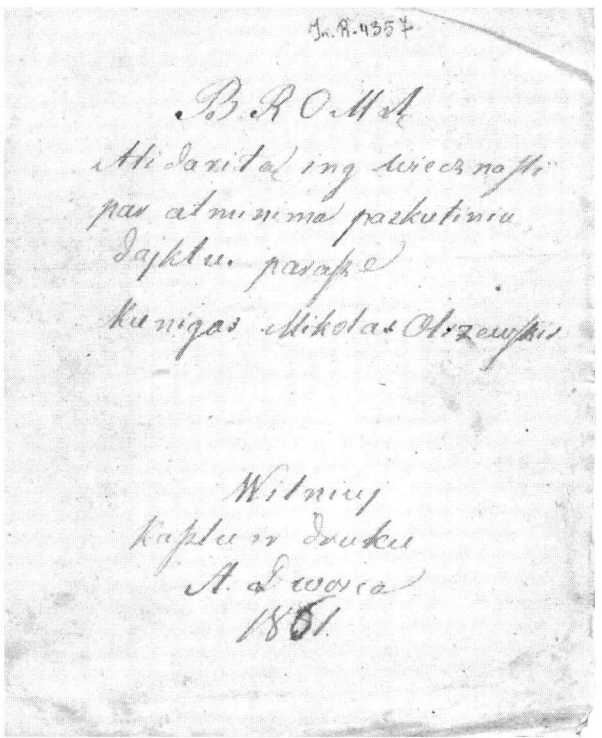

Fig. 3. Title page of Motiejus Valančius' manuscript *Broma atidaryta ing viečnastį* (1874–1875).

From the manuscript we can see what had been done. The style was changed and the language was edited taking into account the usage of the period. The didactic stories in particular were rewritten in the style characteristic of the bishop. The structure of the book was also slightly changed: in some places the text was shortened, in others — expanded and supplemented with notes and edifications. The didactic stories were made more relevant, expanded upon and actualised with Lithuanian material, such as the personages, the place and time of action. For example, instead of an ordinary monk, Valančius described Dominykas Šukevičius, a Bernardine monk from Tytuvėnai monastery in 1820:

[6] [Motiejus Valančius], *BROMĄ Atidaritą ing wiecznaſti par atminima paskutiniu dajktu, paraſze Kunigas Mikołas Olszewſkis*, LLTI BR, f. 1, b. 4357 [Valančius] 1874-1875); [Motiejus Valančius], *BROMĄ Atidaritą ing Wiecznasti par atminima paskutiniu dajktu. Parasze Kunigas Mikołas Olszewskis. Wilniuj Kasztu ir druku A. Dworca 1861*, [Copy], LLTI BR, f. 1, b. 4411.

Mikas Vaicekauskas To Burn or To Republish? 13

Mykolas Olševskis[1]	Motiejus Valančius[2]
Buwa wienas Zokaninkas jaunas, | tasay kientiedamas pakusas, norie|je pametys Zokana griszti ant swie|ta; kada tas pakusas pasaki senam | Zokaninkui, ansay atsaki: Sunau | żinok, jog asz jau tame Kloszto-|riuy giwenu metu 60. yr wienos | adinas nebuwau wałnas nug paku-|su, o tu nori tayp greytay atrasti | pakaju; tay girdiedamas anas Zo-|kaninkas, pradieje linksmay kine-||tiety[3] pakusas. [...])[4]	Priwedimas. Metusi 1820. Tituwienusi | istojes i Bernadinu zokana jaunas | Dominikas Szukiewicze, datire daug || pagundinimu, kuręms be parglitas | i gałwą lendąnt,[5] nuluda, kie-|tina pamesti zokana ir buti szejp|-|jau źmogumi. Wiena karta pametes[6] | ji didej nuskurdusi naujuku pardie-|tinis diewobajmingas Wasilkiewicze | kłause: kas tau ira? Bene sergi? Ko | nuludaj kajp neturis ko walgiti? Szis | atsakie: tejsibe tiewali jog nuludau, | ir źadu zokana pamefti. Tare pardie-|tinis: kodiel mełdamasis, jug tawi | milem? Atsakie Dominikas tejsibe | tieweli, bet apnika mani kajp wap-|sas pagundinimaj, kurejs negalu at-|siginti. Tare Wasilkiewicze: o pana | Szwętoi afz jau zokani esmi pęn-|kies defzimtis metu, pagundinimaj | tecziaus manęs neaplejda, o tu woz | su wienu koi i zokana iżęngiej ir || jau nori buti luosas nu pagundini-|mu? Iszkłauses to parspieima Do-|minikas, palika źokani ir kięntieje | pagundinimus kajp kiti.[7]

Table 1. Comparison of print and manuscript versions of *Broma atverta ing viečnastį* and *Broma atidaryta ing viečnastį*. See end of article for footnotes.

Fig. 4. Part of page 50 of Mykolas Olševski's *Broma atverta ing viečnastį* (1851).

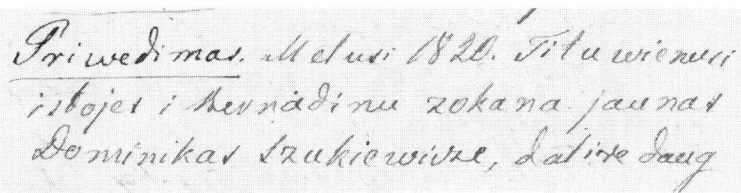

Fig. 5. Part of page 88 of Motiejus Valančius' manuscript of *Broma atidaryta ing viečnastį* (1874–1875).

He also added new stories of his own. They are written so as to make the readers at the time believe that they were real documented events that had taken place in a particular place in Lithuania in the not so distant past (Vaicekauskas 2005a). Valančius could have had several motives to undertake this work: the book was very popular, the subject of the book would never loose its actuality, and it had considerable spiritual benefit. In fact, he did the same that Olševskis had done in his own time. Sensing extremely well the needs of the readers, Valančius wrote a highly accessible work for them. From the first edition of *Broma atverta ing viečnastį* the reader had changed, so Valančius changed the entire work as well.

After the bishop's death in 1875 there was one attempt to publish Valančius' edition of *Broma atverta ing viečnastį*. In 1904, a meeting of the representatives of all three Lithuanian dioceses was held in Kaunas. The main objective of this meeting was to raise the level of education of the priests and the general public. Among such things as organizing the publishing of a Catholic newspaper, attending to the printing of religious literature, writing the history of the Catholic church, publishing of some of Valančius' books and the like, one of the items in the resolutions of the meeting included the instruction to the priest Juozas Tumas (1869–1933) to prepare Valančius' edition of *Broma atidaryta ing viečnastį* for publication ([Tumas] 1921). It was the first and so far the only attempt to publish the manuscript as part of the jubilee edition of Valančius' works that was organized in 1900. However, for reasons unknown this resolution was not carried out (Vaicekauskas 2008).

Despite *Broma atverta ing viečnastį* great popularity in poorly educated layers of society, from the early 19th century the work attracted considerable — and rather severe — criticism. Part of the Lithuanian cultural elite, mostly of a non-Catholic orientation, held a negative opinion about the book. *Broma atverta ing viečnastį* was criticised even after it was no longer reprinted, that is, in the late 19th and during the 20th century; this was very likely related to the wide circulation of this work among readers. The first review of *Broma atverta ing viečnastį* came from the philologist Kristijonas Gotlybas Milkus (1733–1807), a Lutheran priest from the Kingdom of Prussia. Referring to Lithuanian catholic writing in his *Anfangs-Gruende einer Littauischen Sprach-Lehre* (*Foundations of Lithuanian Grammar*, 1800), he presented three stories from *Broma atverta ing viečnastį* and thus commented on them: "From three last examples that have been given here as the best of the immense amount of the most absurd stories of monks that *Broma* is packed with, readers can get the impression how poor the enlightening literature of our Catholic neighbours is."[7] He looked at the work's didactic and spiritual value from the Protestant point of view. Milkus' view of the work was echoed by August Gotthilf Krause (1787–1855), a Lutheran priest and a historian of Lithuania Minor, in his book *Litthauen und dessen Bewohner in Hinficht der Abftammung, der volkshuemlichen Verwandtfchaft und Sprache* (*Lithuania and Its Residents from the Point of View of the Origin, National Kinship and Language*, 1834).[8] His commentary, too, was for a number of times mentioned and quoted in the studies on Lithuanian literature in 20th century.[9]

Rev. Liudvikas Adomas Jucevičius (1813–1846) was the first to review *Broma atverta ing viečnastį* in Lithuania. While still a Catholic priest (and an Orthodox believer from 1843), he gave one of the most radical comments on the work in his Polish manuscript of *Wiadomości biograficzne i literackie o*

---

[7] [Kristijonas Gotlybas Milkus], Anfangs-Gruende | einer | Littauifchen | Sprach-Lehre, | worinn zwar die | von dem juengern Ruhig | ehemals | herausgegebene Grammatik | zum Grunde gelegt, | aber mit ftarken Zufaetzen | und | neuen Ausarbeitungen | verbeffert und vermehrt worden | von | Chriftian Gottlieb Mielcke, | Cantor in Pillckallen. | Koenigsberg, 1800. | Druck und Verlag der Hartungfchen Hofbuchdruckerey, 168 ([Milkus] 1800).

[8] [Auguft Gotthilf Kraufe], Litthauen | und | dessen Bewohner | in Hinficht | der Abftammung, der volksthuemlichen | Verwandtfchaft und Sprache. | Ein gefchichtlicher Berfuch, | mit / Beziehung auf Ruhigs Betrachtung der | littauifchen Sprache, | herausgegeben | von | Auguft Gotthilf Kraufe, | Prediger. | Koenigsberg, 1834. | Druck und Verlag der Hartungfchen Hofbuchdrukkerei, 81 ([Kraufe] 1834).

[9] Leonas Gineitis, *Kristijonas Donelaitis ir jo epocha* (Gineitis 1964), 18; Leonas Gineitis, *Kristijonas Donelaitis ir jo epocha* (Gineitis 1990), 20; Leonas Gineitis, *Lietuvių literatūros istoriografija: Ligi 1940 m.* (Gineitis 1982, 85. A modern commentary on Milkus' view is given by Albinas Jovaišas: "[...] M. Olševskis belonged to Baroque culture and the clergy of a Catholic land, while K. G. Milkus was a person of enlightening ideas, a rationalist, and to some extent a pre-Romantic. And yet both K. G. Milkus and M. Olševskis are both right, each in his own way. K. G. Milkus is right in that, in one way or another, M. Olševskis' style was without a perspective, it gradually disappeared. Meanwhile, what K. G. Milkus propagated himself was later developed by the figures of Lithuanian culture and literature, by the nations spiritual leaders D. Poška, L. Rėza, S. Stanevičius, S. Daukantas and others. Their efforts determined the further cultural progress of the Lithuanian nation" (Ulčinaitė and Jovaišas 2003, 373–374).

uczonych żmudzinach (*Biographical and Literary Information on Learned Samogitians*, 1841): "This work [...] consists of prayers and examples from the lives of the saints; it is written totally uncritically and should have been burnt long ago due to lots of meaningless ramblings presented as religious truth" (Jucevičius 1975, 111).

The tradition of negative reviews was carried on by the fierce anti-cleric Jonas Šliūpas (1861–1944) in the late 19th century. In the review of the history of Lithuanian literature, *Lietuviškieji raštai ir raštininkai* (*Lithuanian Writings and Writers*, 1890) he pointed out that *Broma atverta ing viečnastį* was a thoroughly useless book, that it disordered people's minds, that priests started burning it, and that it was simply poison. He admitted, however, that readers were strongly attracted by its ascetic content (Šliūpas 1977, 51). Jonas Šliūpas' opinion about the work, and first of all its anti-religious aspect, served as a basis for some Lithuanian historians of culture and literature, especially during the Soviet period.

Initially criticism mostly concerned the content. However, in the first half of 20th century, following long years of Polonisation and Russification, the ban on the Lithuanian press, and with nationalist cultural tendencies prevalent in Lithuanian society, there emerged a new aspect in the evaluation of *Broma atverta ing viečnastį* — that of its style and language. According to Mykolas Biržiška (1882–1962) and Vincas Maciūnas (1909–2003), the key historians of Lithuanian literature at the time, Olševskis' work was a fact of the decline of the language, a writing of the poorest content brimming with barbarisms and macaronisms. However at the same time they pointed out that Olševskis' books, just like others, taught Lithuanian people to read, that they were intended for the barely educated layers of society and written in a language and style intelligible to them.[10]

Yet the worst times struck *Broma atverta ing viečnastį* in the Soviet period, when due to ideological reasons religious literature was neither researched nor tolerated. (Research in the history of the book was allowed but not encouraged.) The key text in the history of Lithuanian literature in that period was *Lietuvių literatūros istorija* (*The History of Lithuanian Literature*, 1957) prepared under the guidance of Kostas Korsakas (1909–1986), the main ideologist of the history of Lithuanian literature in the Soviet period. The

---

[10] Mykolas Biržiška, *Mūsų raštų istorija: 1547 m. — 1904 m.* (1920, 15); Mykolas Biržiška, *Mūsų raštų istorija*, I dalis: *Ligi 1864 m.* (1925, 35); Mykolas Biržiška, "Lietuvių literatūra Vilniaus universiteto metu," Mykolas Biržiška, *Iš mūsų kultūros ir literatūros istorijos* 1 (1931, 189); Vincas Maciūnas, *Senosios lietuvių literatūros istorija. Proza*, Paskaitų užrašai, 1938 02 05 — 05 28, *VUB RS*, Jurgio Lebedžio fondas, f. 133, b. 852, l. 38; Vincas Maciūnas, "Mūsų literatūros raidos etapai," Vincas Maciūnas, *Rinktiniai raštai*, ed. Jonas Šlekys, (Maciūnas 2003, 85–88; 86).

definitions and descriptions presented there set the Soviet-antireligious tone for the attitude that prevailed for a long time to come. It was argued that the stories of *Broma atverta ing viečnastį* distort reality and that they inculcate asceticism, spiritual servility, and the belief in miracles, devils, hell, heaven and the like. The book itself inflicted "grave damage not only by its obscurantist content but also by its language polluted with jargon and foreign words;" books like *Broma atverta ing viečnastį* "hinder ideological self-awareness of the people, inflicted considerable harm to Lithuanian culture, folklore and the development of the Lithuanian language." Such books clearly point to "Catholic obscurantism, the hostility of the Catholic clergy to the culture and education of Lithuanian people" (Korsakas and Lebedys 1957, 197). Similar opinions about *Broma atverta ing viečnastį* prevailed in Lithuanian Soviet encyclopaedias, literary histories, textbooks of literature, other sources and academic research into literature, language, history and culture (Kostas Korsakas, Jurgis Lebedys, Jonas Palionis, Leonas Gineitis, Zigmas Zinkevičius). Soviet ideology was added to the nationalist criticism of the first half of the 20th century. Everything — the author, the content, the language, and the style — was criticized and condemned. *Broma atverta ing viečnastį* title alone was employed to summarize and evaluate entire Catholic literature of the seventeenth-eighteenth centuries. It used to be called "religious literature to maintain the disintegrating capitalism," "the tool for the subjection of the people," "the Catholic reaction, the document of the hostility of the Catholic clergy to Lithuanian folk culture," "obscurantist literature." It was argued that *Broma atverta ing viečnastį* poisoned people's consciousness, cultivated superstition, blemished people's feeling of beauty, degraded the language and promoted the consolidation of the feudal-ecclesiastical jargon (Korsakas and Lebedys 1957, 127, 131; Palionis 1979, 106–07; Palionis 1995, 113–14; Gineitis 1964, 16–20; Gineitis 1990, 18–20; Lebedys 1977, 139–43; Zinkevičius 1990, 38).

Evaluation along such lines marked the entire Soviet period and first years of Independence. No attempt was made to articulate something new or at least take a more objective look at the work that had turned into a phenomenon. Thus in Soviet historiography of Lithuanian literature *Broma atverta ing viečnastį* became the canon — or, rather, the anti-canon — of ancient Lithuanian literature (16th–18th centuries), especially Lithuanian religious, Catholic literature.

How could it happen that this exceptionally popular and important work acquired the status of the anti-canon of national literature? Mykolas

Olševskis' *Broma atverta ing viečnastį* was intended for poorly educated layers of society; it did not stand out in its artistic qualities or originality, and just described this ever-relevant theme of death at the time when fictional literature written in Lithuanian practically did not exist. Readers of the period liked and understood it due to its spiritual and didactic content, thanks to the rudiments of a *belles-lettres* narrative, its style and linguistic expression. However, during national revival of the end of the 19th century, during the period of the nurturing of national culture in the first half of the 20th century, and in the period of Soviet occupation and coercive Soviet ideology it was treated as a text-book example of anti-national literature. And yet the number of reprints and the instances of the rewriting of *Broma atverta ing viečnastį* point to the fact that the work's popularity was not accidental. A more thorough socio-cultural and philological research would easily prove that *Broma atverta ing viečnastį* had links with European tradition of this particular genre, that it laid the foundation for Lithuanian didactic *belles-lettres*, and that it was the most-read book in its time. Will it not happen that 250 years after the first publication of the most controversial work in Lithuanian literature it will turn into the literary canon of its time?

Bibliography

Biržiška, Mykolas. 1931. "Lietuvių Literatūra Vilniaus Universiteto Metu." In Mykolas Biržiška *Iš Mūsų Kultūros Ir Literatūros Istorijos*. Kaunas: Vytauto Didžiojo universiteto Humanitarinių mokslų fakulteto leidinys.

———. 1925. *Mūsų Raštų Istorija, I Dalis: Ligi 1864 m*. Kaunas: Valstybės spaustuvė, Švietimo ministerijos Knygų leidimo komisijos leidinys.

———. 1920. *Mūsų Raštų Istorija: 1547 m. – 1904 m.*. Kaunas: "Švyturio" B-vė Kaune.

Gineitis, Leonas. 1990. *Kristijonas Donelaitis Ir Jo Epocha*. 2 ed. Vilnius: Vaga.

———. 1964. *Kristijonas Donelaitis Ir Jo Epocha*. Vilnius: Valstybinė politinės ir mokslinės literatūros leidykla.

———. 1982. *Lietuvių Literatūros Istoriografija: Ligi 1940 m*. Vilnius: Vaga.

Jucevičius, Liudvikas. 1975. *Mokyti Žemaičiai*. Edited by Meilė Lukšienė and Vytautas Raudeliūnas. Vilnius: Vaga.

Korsakas, Kostas, ed. 1957. *Lietuvių Literatūros Istorija 1: Feodalizmo Epocha*. Vilnius: Valstybinė politinės ir mokslinės literatūros leidykla.

Korsakas, Kostas, and Jurgis Lebedys, eds. 1957. *Lietuvių Literatūros Istorijos Chrestomatija. Feodalizmo Epocha*. Vilnius: Valstybinė grožinės literatūros leidykla.

[Krauſe, Auguſt Gotthilf]. 1834. *Litthauen Und Dessen Bewohner in Hinſicht Der Abſtammung, Der Volksthuemlichen Verwandtſchaft Und Sprache*. Koenigsberg: Hartungſchen Hofbuchdrukkerei.

Lebedys, Jurgis. 1976. *Lietuvių Kalba XVII–XVIII a. Viešajame Gyvenime*. Edited by Vanda Zaborskaitė. Vilnius: Mokslas.

———. 1977. *Senoji Lietuvių Literatūra*. Edited by Juozas Girdzijauskas. Vilnius: Mokslas.

Maciūnas, Vincas. 2003. "Mūsų Literatūros Raidos Etapai." In *Rinktiniai Raštai*. Edited by Jonas Šlekys. Vilnius: Lietuvių literatūros ir tautosakos institutas.

[Milkus, Kristijonas Gotlybas]. 1800. *Anfangs-Gruende Einer Littauiſchen Sprach-Lehre*. Koenigsberg: Hartungſchen Hofbuchdruckerey.

Olševskis, Mykolas. 1753. *Broma Atverta Ing Viečnastį*. Vilnius: J. K. M. Kunigu Franciſzkonu.

[Olševskis, Mykolas]. 1851. *Bromą Atidarytą Ing Viečnastį par atminima paskutiniu dajktu*. Vilnius: A. Dworca.

Palionis, Jonas. 1979. *Lietuvių Literatūrinės Kalbos Istorija*. Vilnius: Mokslas.

———. 1995. *Lietuvių Rašomosios Kalbos Istorija*. Vilnius: Mokslo ir enciklopedijų leidykla.

Šliūpas, Jonas. 1977. *Rinktiniai Raštai*. Edited by Kostas Doveika. Vilnius: Vaga.

Subačius, Giedrius. 2006. "Filologinis Aleksandro Luočio Salto: Трумпасъ Катехизмасъ (1865) Verčiamas *Trumpu Katechizmu* (1874)." *Baltistica* XL 1 (2):283-308.

Tereškinas, Artūras. 1992. "Stiliaus Ir Žanro Problemos M. Alšausko Ir K. Lukausko Pamoksluose." In *Senosios Literatūros Žanrai*, edited by Algis Samulionis, 104–63. Vilnius: Mokslo ir enciklopedijų leidykla, Lietuvių literatūros ir tautosakos institutas.

[Tumas, Juozas]. 1921. "[Kunigų Švietimo Rūpesčiai]." *Mūsų senovė* 1.2:119.

Ulčinaitė, Eugenija, and Albinas Jovaišas. 2003. *Lietuvių Literatūros Istorija: XIII–XVIII Amžiai*. Vilnius: Lietuvių literatūros ir tautosakos institutas.

Vaicekauskas, Mikas. 2009. "Lietuviška Rankraštinė Knyga Spaudos Draudimo Laikotarpiu." *Naujasis Židinys-Aidai* 1-2:20-28.

———. 2005a. "Paskutinė Valančiaus Knyga." In *Istorijos Rašymo Horizontai*, edited by Aušra Jurgutienė and Sigitas Narbutas, 266-94. Vilnius: Lietuvių literatūros ir tautosakos institutas.

———. 2005b. "Motiejaus Valančiaus draudimas perspausdinti Bromą (1864)." *Archivum Lithuanicum* 7:177-205.

———. 2008. "Sumanymas Išleisti Motiejaus Valančiaus *Bromą Atidarytą Ing Viečnastį* 1904 m." *Colloquia* 21:114-35.

———. 2003. "Valančius Ir Olševskis II, Arba Tikslinimai Ir Kiti Rankraščiai. 'Bromos Atvertos Ing Viečnastį' 250-osioms Išleidimo Metinėms." *Knygų aidai* 4:10-18.

[Valančius, Motiejus] [1874–1875]. *Bromą Atidaritą ing wiecznaſti par atminima paskutiniu dajktu*, LLTI BR, f. 1, b. 4357.

Zinkevičius, Zigmas. 1990. *Lietuvių Kalbos Istorija 4: Lietuvių Kalba XVIII–XIX a.* Vilnius: Mokslas.

Footnotes to Table 1

1   [Mykolas Olševskis], BROMA | ATWERTA | ING | WIECZNASTI | PAR ATMINIMA PASKUTINIUN DAYKTU. | Su spasabays Dysponawoima mirsztan-|ėziu, ant szcześliwa smerczia, yr rata-|woima Duśziu Czysciuy kientanéziu. | Teypogi apey Artykułus Wieros S. su trun-|pays Pamokſłays, yr Prikłodays, isz pawo-|żniun Authoriu iszrinktays. | par | KUNIGA MIKOŁA OLSZEWSKI | Theologa Absoluta Kanaunika Regular-|na BB. MM. *de poenit:* | *Su Medytacyjomis ant ciełos Nedielies.* | WILNIUJ. | Kasztu yr druku A. Dworca. | 1851, 50–51 ([Olševskis] 1851).

2   [Valančius 1874-1875] , 88–90.

3   Must be *kintiety*.

4   There was one monk who, tortured by temptations, wanted to abandon the order and return to the world. When he spoke of those temptations with an old monk, the latter said: "My son, I had been living in this monastery for sixty years, and for a single hour had I been free of temptations, while you want to find peace so quickly." Upon hearing this, the young man started enduring the temptations joyfully.

5   The word *kietina* is crossed out here.

6   Must be *pamates*.

7   An example. Dominykas Šukevičius, a young monk who entered a Bernardine monastery in Tytuvėnai in 1820, experienced numerous temptations, and while they were bothering his mind, he grew sad, made up his mind to leave the monastery and be an ordinary man. Once the supervisor of novices, pious Vasilkevičius, saw him very sad and asked him, "What is the matter with you? Are you ill? Why are you sad, as though you do not have anything to eat?" He said, "It is true, Father, I got sad and intend to leave the monastery." The supervisor said, "Why, pray, but we love you so much?" Dominykas answered, "It is true, Father, but temptations have besieged me like wasps, and I cannot keep them away." Vasilkevičius said, "O Holy Virgin, I have been in the monastery for fifty years and temptations do not leave me alone, while you have only put one foot in the monastery and want to be free of temptations?" Upon hearing this admonition, Dominykas remained in the monastery and endured temptations like everybody else.

Canonisation as Impediment to Textual Scholarship
Lithuanian Postcolonial Experiences

Paulius V. Subačius

In the past few decades textual scholarship in the West has not been helpful for establishing the canons of individual works. This has been the case because "the new developments in textual scholarship have one thing in common: they all question the concept of *one* critical text" (van Vliet 2006, 194). Theoreticians of editing are increasingly more in favour of the egalitarian approach to different texts that have acquired various historically determined forms. And yet, within the long-term perspective extending as far back as the Museum of Alexandria, it becomes clear that the need for establishing the canonical form of a work or dissatisfaction with existing canonical texts has been the principal driving forces of textual scholarship. Authoritative editions, in their turn, marked the course of the great European works and shaped the canons of national literature.

The term "canon" in the present paper describes the list of works relevant to any one country's literature and their hierarchy.[1] Reflection on the changes in the canon reveals the paradoxical situation of textual criticism in Soviet and post-Soviet Lithuania. This situation is in discord with the traditional image of the symbiotic relationship between the canon and textual scholarship. This has nothing to do with post-modern doubt concerning the possibility of the canon and its meaning (cf. Hernstein Smith 1988, 45-53) — rather the opposite. The present paper has two objectives: on the one hand to show how the canon of the nations of Central Europe, specifically in Lithuania, was rearranged in the context of dramatic political alterations and the mass dissemination of books; on the other, to survey that aspect of contemporary editorial strategies that likely relates to the colonial imprint on post-Soviet culture.

The historical context is necessary to explain how canonisation became an obstacle in the way of textual criticism in Lithuania. Therefore, let us turn briefly to the end of the 19th century. What were the most prominent

---

[1] "Originally the Canon meant the choice of books in our teaching institutions", – Harold Bloom remarks simply in his influential *The Western Canon: The Books and School of the Ages* (Bloom 1995, 15); the choice imply selection, hierarchy and consensus as to the meaning of literary value; we used "country's literature" in the place of more usual "national literature" with a view to texts written in various languages.

names and titles of the national literature? In Lithuania this question arose for the first time barely over a hundred years ago. The popular movement arising in the country occupied by tsarist Russia at that time was still engaged in the process of giving birth to the idea of national state. In the 1890's one of the figures prominent in that movement, the physician Jonas Šliūpas (1861-1944), published the first synoptic history of the Lithuanian literature in Lithuanian (Šliūpas 1890), and another of its active participants, Reverend Juozas Tumas (1869-1933) proposed the publication of the full works of Motiejus Valančius (1801-1875; Tumas 1899). The problem of textual criticism and textual authority was not even addressed at the time. After the declaration of Lithuanian independence in 1918 new school syllabi were put together in great haste. There was a great shortage of literary texts that could be included in them and thus canonised. Therefore, the rapid publication of *writings*, rather than their meticulous scholarly preparation, was the priority. Moreover, until the University of Lithuania opened in 1922 in Kaunas (the capital Vilnius was occupied by Poland at the time), there were no academic philological institutions in Lithuania.

Nevertheless, even at that stage the publications that were coming out even while trying to satisfy the needs of the gymnasia, managed to establish philological quality requirements. For example, the first anthology of old Lithuanian literature was compiled by Mykolas Biržiška, an authority in national bibliography (Biržiška 1927). This publication was characterised by the competence with which the texts were prepared for publication. Simultaneously, Biržiška made a ranked list of 16th to 18th century Lithuanian authors. Several anthologies of 19th century literary works and the publications of minor newly discovered manuscripts in the recently launched philological journals[2] reflected two functions: the formation of a national literary canon, on the one hand, and the cultivation of textual criticism, on the other. The works of Kristijonas Donelaitis, the founding father of Lithuanian *belles lettres*, were published four times (Biržiška 1918, 1921, 1927a; Ambrazevičius 1940). In the preparation of these publications older editions of the foreign scholars, Augustus Schleicher (1865) and Georg Nesselmann (1869), were used. The adherence to German philological tradition, as well as the assistance of German scholars and publishers, made possible the publication of several photographic reprints of the

---

[2] E.g. Augustinas Janulaitis (ed.) "Simono Daukanto laiškai" [The Letters of Simonas Daukantas] (1922); Vaclovas Biržiška (ed.) "Kunigo Cyprijono Nezabitauskio-Zabičio laiškai kun. Gailevičiui" [The Letters of Reverend Cyprijonas Nezabitauskis-Zabitis to Reverend Gailevičius] (1931); Kazys Alminauskis (ed.) "Vytauto skundas" [The Complaint of Vytautas] (1939).

older literature (e.g. Gerullis 1923, Specht 1929). They were in no way inferior to the best German facsimile editions of that time. However, the only elements of textual criticism that they contained were found in the introductions. Even more noteworthy is another circumstance: the sole audience for these editions were academic linguists, and the works selected for publications did not rate high on the popularity scale. In other words, the paths of establishment of the literary canon and of publication of editions of the highest quality began to diverge.

This tendency became much more pronounced in Soviet-occupied Lithuania after the war. The generation of philologists who graduated from universities before the war prepared more than 20 authoritative editions of old texts between 1945 and 1970. Yet the majority of these were collections of facsimiles or diplomatic transcripts, and thus were non-critical editions. Since they were specifically aimed at linguistic research, they had virtually no influence on literary reflection and were hardly linked with the canon. The few editions that placed greater weight on textual criticism were not works at the centre of the national literary canon, but rather marginal works.

In 1948, at the beginning of the Soviet occupation, when the Soviet institutions were still in the process of formation, a collection of the fables of the 19th century writer Simonas Stanevičius was published (Lebedys 1948). The publication may have been very modest in regard to printing quality, but contained a solid philological apparatus. It presented the version of the text in the authentic spelling and its transliteration side by side, along with textual variants and with an extensive discussion of the history of the text. However, the publication of the *Writings* of another 19th century writer, Žemaitė (Kalnius 1948), was stopped by the Soviet administration only a year later. The officials pointed out that the edition was too faithful (!) in rendering the authentic form of the texts and was therefore ideologically erroneous. First Secretary of the Lithuanian Communist Party Antanas Sniečkus even condemned the publication at the Communist Party Congress, insofar as it published the works of Žemaitė with all the "words from the feudal-ecclesiastical inheritance" (Sniečkus 1991, 192).

On the basis of the cases cited above, one might explain the sluggish development of textual scholarship as the result of Soviet colonisation policies. And yet, censorship and the direct restrictions on scholarly work were not the only hindrances that critical editions faced. Perhaps even more important was the belief held by the scholars of Lithuanian language and literature concerning their academic and national mission. From the very first days of the occupation, Soviet authorities started to reform the Lithuanian literary canon. Writers from the past were categorised according to Communist criteria into the "progressive" ones and the "enemies of the people", and the reception and dissemination of the latter was restricted. Living or recently deceased authors who collaborated with the occupying power were placed at the centre of the new canon. Lithuanian scholars, on the other hand, strove to safeguard the status of the writers previously considered as classics of the national literature through various ruses and compromises. They sought to ensure that these authors would be discussed in the schools and reprinted, albeit prefaced by ideological Marxist introductions.

And the first victim that the philologists themselves — unwittingly — sacrificed in their battle for the canon of national literature was ... textual scholarship. Why was that? The Soviet administration performed strict ideological selection of the texts for popular editions. For example, only thirteen short pieces survive from the writings of Antanas Strazdas, the author of the first book of lyrics in Lithuanian (Drazdawskas 1814). Nevertheless, one of those pieces – a religious hymn — cannot be found in any of the five editions of Strazdas aimed at the general public published in the Soviet-period.[3] In the case of any non-Soviet writer, the corpus of writings, a more exhaustive collection of texts, or texts with religious content could only be published under the cover of scholarly objectives and in the interests of narrow philological readership. For this purpose, the authorities permitted the establishment of the specialised series "Library of Lithuanian Philology" (*Lituanistinė biblioteka* 1966-2001). Most works that the editorial board included in the series were part of the national literary canon established before the Soviet occupation. The series was edited by researchers at academic institutions; quite a few of whom nurtured nationalist ambitions. Therefore, they considered it part of their mission to disseminate as widely as possible the works suspended by the Soviets and, thus, to rebuild, at least in part, the canon deformed by the Soviet invaders.

The goal of increasing the accessibility of these editions determined the editorial strategy. Authentic forms which contemporary readers would find hard to understand were reduced, the apparatus and commentaries were minimised, textual variants were presented in a very limited fashion,

---

[3] Antanas Strazdas (1951), *Dainos* [Songs], [8 out of 13 pieces]; (1952) *Raštai* [Writings], [11 out of 13 pieces]; (1957) *Raštai* [Writings], [11 out of 13 pieces]; (1963) *Poezija* [Poetry], [11 out of 13 pieces]; (1974) *Giesmė apie siratas* [Hymn about Orphans], [12 out of 13 pieces].

the more complex ways of presenting the history of the texts were discarded, etc. The result of this policy is that not even one of the 31 volumes of the specialised philological series is a critical edition in the proper sense of the word (see Figures 1 and 2). A similar rejection of aspirations for textual scholarship for the sake of wider dissemination was an almost universal phenomenon in the so-called academic editions. The authorities occasionally allowed the publication of a few past writers in multi-volume *writings*.[4] However, these writings were also primarily subordinated to the goal of popularisation, rather than philological and historical research, by their editors. Thus, the goal of defending and entrenching the canon of national literature became an objective obstacle in the development of textual scholarship, and hindered the renewal of editing methods. Moreover, one may note that the philologists themselves are still oblivious to this problem. This is because philologists, as well as the better part of nationally-minded intelligentsia, still regard the preparation of the editions of this kind as a positive patriotic activity, an act of cultural resistance to the Soviet occupation.

The Soviet invaders sought to inculcate the notion that new art and literature may acquire national, local forms, but must, nevertheless, have a Soviet content. The publications of the authors who belonged to the canon of national literature preserved the national content, i.e. the non-Soviet writings as such, but acquired a Soviet form (cf. Stojanović 1997, 155). This play of words is made possible by the insights of post-colonial theory which allows us to interpret the editorial model of the Soviet times as a hybrid of national content and Soviet form.

The Soviet empire, just as any other empire, sought to impose upon the periphery the acceptance of cultural superiority of the centre and of the dominating nation, in the present case — of Moscow and of the Russians. Placing the *writings* of Pushkin (1937-1959) and Maironis (1956, 1987-1992), who in Lithuanian literature performed a *rôle* similar to that of Pushkin in Russia side by side, it was obvious that Pushkin was the true classic, worthy of detailed research, while Maironis appears to be a local versifier, whose works are fitting only for a popular song-book. Maironis was delegated to this lower position in the philological hierarchy not only by the external restrictions, but also by the disposition of the patriotically-minded editors. This disposition proclaimed that one ought to defend the Lithuanian literature from Sovietisation by publishing its canon in the most popular form available. The reverse of this stance of

---

[4] E.g. Žemaitė (1956-1957), Biliūnas (1980-1981).

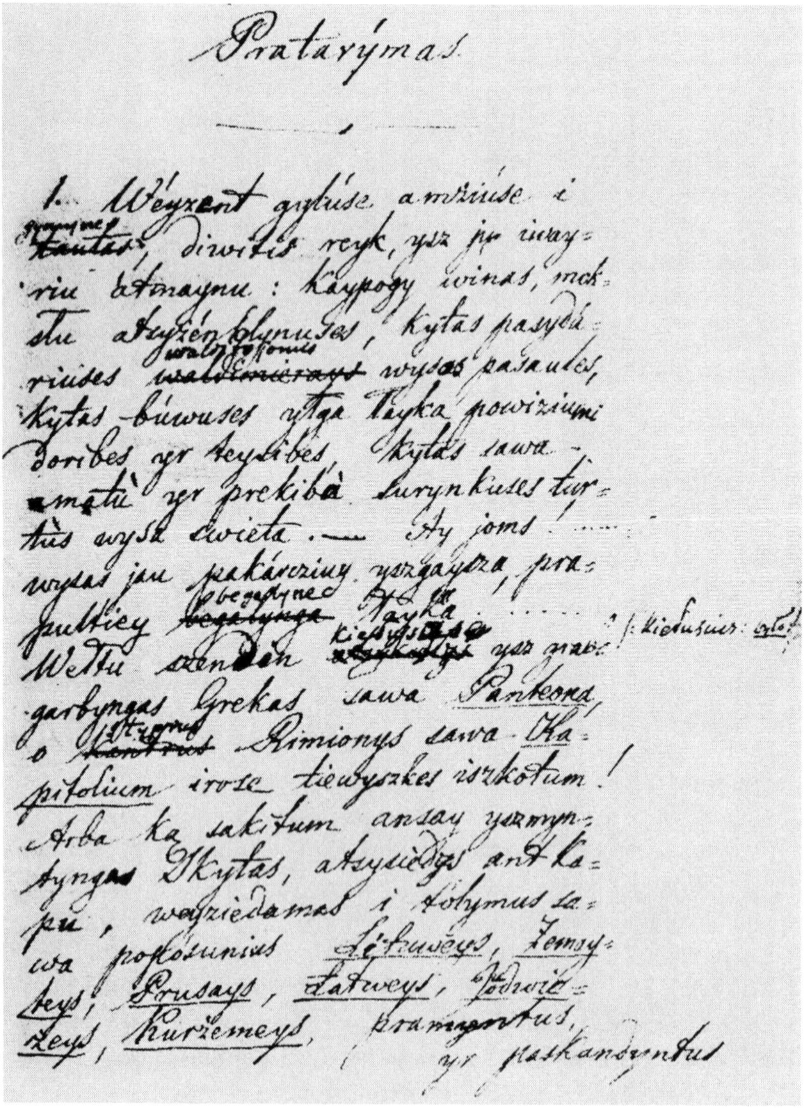

Figs. 1 and 2. Manuscript with corrections of "Darbai senųjų lietuvių ir žemaičių" [The works of antique Lithuanians and Samogitians] by Simonas Daukantas and the "plain" modernised text of the same paragraph without the apparatus in Daukantas' *Raštai* [Writings], Edited by Vytautus Merkys, (Vilnius: Vaga, 1976) vol. 1, 35, from series "Lituanistinė biblioteka" [Library of Lithuanian Philology].

PRATARYMAS

1. Veizint giliuose amžiuose į gimines, dyvytis reikia iš jų įvairių atmainų: kaipogi vienos mokslu atsiženklinusios, kitos pasidariusios valdytojomis viso pasaulio, kitos buvusios ilgą laiką povyziumi dorybės ir teisybės, kitos savo amatu ir prekyba surinkusios turtus viso svieto. Ai joms!.. visos jau pakarčiui išgaišo, prapultyj begalinio laiko!.. Veltui šiandien kėlusiuos iš grabo garbingas graikas savo Panteono, o stiprus rymionis savo Kapitolijaus irose tėviškės ieškotų! Arba ką sakytų ansai išmintingas skitas, atsisėdęs ant kapo, veizėdamas į tolimus savo poposūnius, lietuviais, žemaičiais, prūsais, latviais, jodviežiais, kuržemiais pramintus ir paskandintus galžudėse, apvergtus ir tarp gyvulių paskaitytus? Negut, pasigailęs jų, ištartų su paskuju apgynėju rymionų liuosybės tuos žodžius: „O dorybe! Tuščiu esi žodžiu šiame pasauly!"

Tokios atmainos giminių rūstintų kiekvieną protingą sutvėrimą, jei anos nė jokio ženklo buvimo savo nepaliktų. Bet, noris pačios giminės išgaišta, vienok jų raštai palieka, o anuose jų amžina garbė užrašyta, kurios nė kokia galybė šio pasaulio negali išnaikinti. Dėl to gi linksminas dar šiandien šviesus graikas, jog yra mokytoju pasaulio, o didžiuojas stiprus rymionis, jog parašė įstatymus visam svietui! Taigi, kad mokslas ir gudrybė giminės yra amžina ir visų didžiausia garbe, dėl ko gi lietuviai ir žemaičiai cultural defence was the fact that the Lithuanian scholars themselves, by rejecting elite publications of the canon, contributed to the cultural regime of proletarian egalitarianism, from which only the academic philology of Moscow diverged. In the words of one of the authorities in post-colonial theory, Homi K. Bhabha, the direct resistance to colonisation "paradoxically operates to reinstate the structures of authority which Empire was concerned to implement in the first place" (Boehme 2006, 355).

The editions that were closest to critical elite editions were the publications of source-texts in Old Slavonic, published in the Cyrillic alphabet by Lithuanian historians (e.g. Lazutka 1983-1991). This form of written communication was used in the Chancellery of the Grand Duchy of Lithuania from the 13th to the 17th centuries. Its monuments comprise works that belong to a narrow group of specific genres: chronicles, legal documents, and texts of the Orthodox Church. Their publication was based on the experience accumulated by the Russian scholars. The examples of textual criticism provided by Dmitryj Likhachev, as well as his theoretical work, as far as I can judge, were not inferior to the works of mid-20th century humanist scholars in the West (Likhachev 1962). Nevertheless, together with the undoubtedly positive influence, the impact of Likhachev's school of textual criticism was also a long-term colonising factor for Lithuania. The contrast of alphabets was the crucial factor here: Lithuanian scholars studied the research into texts written in the Cyrillic alphabet used in Russia, Cyrillic paleography was taught at the University, and even an original textbook of Cyrillic paleography was published in Vilnius (Pamerneckis 1992). However, Latin paleography was not taught – and it is not taught even now in any capital university.[5] There is likewise hardly any research in the field till very recently.[6] Yet it is in the Latin alphabet — in the Lithuanian, Latin, and Polish languages — that the absolute majority of works were written in the course of Lithuanian history. Only the Latin alphabet is used by the Catholic faith, the dominant religion of the land. Thus, Lithuanian textual scholarship found itself in the typical colonial situation. It was cut off from the traditional links to the European space of humanities and directed only towards a tiny part of the local inheritance — the part which in its genre and religious allegiance, as well as other cultural characteristics, was close to the centre of the Empire.

[5] Provincial Klaipėda University, famous for its good relations with German historians, established a course in Latin paleography in 1999.

[6] The first research work on the Latin paleography issued as a separate book was Rūta Čapaitė, *Gotikinis kursyvas Lietuvos didžiojo kunigaikščio Vytauto raštinėje* [The Gothic Italic in the Office of the Lithuanian Grand Duke Vytautas] (2007).

The cultural imprint of the Metropoly survives even after the restoration of independence. After the fall of the Iron Curtain, philologists were forced to learn the achievements of textual scholarship in the West practically from nil. The natural process by which scholarly tradition was transmitted and publications exchanged was interrupted. However, the rejuvenation of textual scholarship was impeded not only by these objective factors, but also by the subjective dispositions dictated by the attitude to the canon of national literature. The adherence to the publishing model established in the Soviet period survives to this day precisely due to the reform of the canon which has been going on very intensively since 1990. Once again school curricula were reviewed, the priorities of literary historians changed along with publishing policies. The short summary of those changes is as follows:

- Soviet works of literature are pushed out of the centre of literary values;
- older, especially religious, texts written in Lithuanian, Latin, and Polish acquire a higher status in the hierarchy;
- the authors of the 19th century and the first half of the 20th century censored by the Soviets return to the central position within the canon;
- the literary output of deportees, political prisoners, anti-Soviet resistance fighters, and the dissident underground is canonised;
- perhaps the greatest interest is devoted to the works written in the West, in the emigration following World War II sartistically the better part of them is considerably superior to the contemporary literature in occupied Lithuania.

All of this is a whole literary continent that was submerged during the Soviet period, and it was sought to uncover it as quickly as possible. Several academic institutions and individual philologists even aspired to publish scholarly *writings*, a series of voluminous *corpora*, and to perform a fundamental renewal of the stock of solid publications. Yet, the actual outcome of these intentions was determined by short publication deadlines, as well as by the conviction that the published books should perform not only the characteristic functions of critical editions, but also serve the goals of widest possible dissemination (e.g. Savickis 1990-1999, Vydūnas 1990-1994). But as this combination fundamentally conformed to the editorial strategy prevalent in the Soviet period, the strategy continued to be applied, and there was little progress in terms of textual scholarship. The publication and dissemination of the texts prohibited by the Soviets was a de-colonising act. Nevertheless, both the colonial, and post-colonial conditions are ambivalent, according to Homi K. Bhabha (2004, 121-130, 245-281). From the point of view of philological self-consciousness these publications only deepened and continued the effects of colonisation, because they entrenched – this time voluntarily, without the application of external violence – "textual creole"[7], the hybrid between Lithuanian literature and the Soviet type of edition. To paraphrase the famous metaphor of Frantz Fanon (1967, 11), the masks "epidermalized", and the publishing robe forced upon by unfavourable circumstances became part of the skin of national literature. It was precisely through this process of hybridisation that most authors were included into the reformed canon. One has to bear in mind that new editions of some of the works, owing to the scarcity of financial and human resources, will have to wait for at least several decades.

Another tendency has also survived in the post-colonial period. Several texts have received very competent scholarly editions, either critical, or facsimile, or both.[8] These are texts that are interesting to a comparatively narrow circle of linguists and religious, as well as general, historians. These editions mostly follow the German examples of publishing 16th to 18th century texts. No one knows when the experience in textual criticism gained in this manner will be applied to the classical – canonical – works of national literature.

Hence we may conclude that due to social and political circumstances, the canonical list of the classics of Lithuanian literature was reformed twice in the course of the 20th century. In both cases the most important rôle fell upon the editions, especially those of *collected writings*, which have been subordinated to the goal of popularisation. Instead of becoming a pre-condition for further development of textual scholarship, these editions turned out to be impediments to a critical and innovatory approach towards the methods of publication. On the contrary, the development of textual scholarship was determined by the publication of those works that failed to make it to the area of literary consumption. Viewed from this perspective, this postcolonial environment differs significantly from the Western context of humanities, insofar as in the latter it is literary theory and the editions of the works pertaining to the canon of world literature that drive forward discussions about textual scholarship.

---

[7] Cf. the concept of "theoretical creole", in Young (2001, 69).

[8] E. g. Simonas Daukantas, *Istorija Justinaus* [History of Justinian], (ed.) Roma Bončkutė, (2006); *Colloquium habitum Vilnae...*ed. Gelumbeckaitė (2006).

Bibliography

Alminauskis, Kazys, ed. 1939. "Vytauto skundas" [The Complaint of Vytautas]. *Archivum Philologicum* 8: 182-224.
Ambrazevičius, Juozas, ed. 1940. Kristijonas Donelaitis, *Metai* [The Seasons]. Kaunas: Švietimo ministerija.
Bhabha, Homi K. 2004. *The Location of Culture*. London-New York: Routledge.
Biliūnas, Jonas. 1980-1981. *Raštai* [Writings]. Edited by Meilė Lukšienė. 3 vol. Vilnius: Vaga.
Biržiška, Mykolas, ed. 1918. *Duonelaičio gyvenimas ir raštai* [Donelaitis' Biography and Writings]. Vilnius: Lietuvos mokslo draugija.
———, ed. 1921. *Duonelaičio gyvenimas ir raštai* [Donelaitis' Biography and Writings]. Second edition. Kaunas: Švyturio bendrovė.
———, ed. 1927. *Rinktiniai mūsų senovės raštai* [Selected Writings of Our Past]. Kaunas: Švietimo ministerija.
———, ed. 1927a. *Duonelaičio gyvenimas ir raštai* [Donelaitis' Biography and Writings]. Third edition. Kaunas: Vairas.
Biržiška, Vaclovas, ed. 1931. "Kunigo Cyprijono Nezabitauskio-Zabičio laiškai kun. Gailevičiui" [The Letters of Reverend Cyprijonas Nezabitauskis-Zabitis to Reverend Gailevičius]. *Tauta ir žodis* 7: 315-316.
Bloom, Harold. 1995. *The Western Canon: The Books and School of the Ages*. New York: Riverhead Books.
Boehmer, Elleke. 2006. "Postcolonialism." In *Literary Theory and Criticism*, edited by Patricia Waugh. 340-61. Oxford-New York: Oxford UP.
Bončkutė, Roma, ed. 2006. Simonas Daukantas. *Istorija Justinaus* [History of Justinian]. Vilnius: LLTI.
Čapaitė, Rūta. 2007. *Gotikinis kursyvas Lietuvos didžiojo kunigaikščio Vytauto raštinėje* [The Gothic Italic in the Office of the Lithuanian Grand Duke Vytautas]. Vilnius: Versus aureus.
Drazdawskas, Untanas. 1814. *Giesmes swietiszkas ir szwintas* [Secular and Sacred Hymns]. Vilnius: Drukarnioy Kunigu Missionoriu.
Fanon, Frantz. 1967. *Black Skin, White Masks*. Translated by Charles Lam Markmann. New York, Grove Press.
Gelumbeckaitė, Jolanta et Narbutas, Sigitas, eds. 2006. *Colloquium habitum Vilnae...* [1585]. Vilnius: LLTI.
Gerullis, Georg, ed. 1923. [Martynas Mažvydas] Mosvid, *Die ältesten litauischen Sprachdenkmäler, bis zum Jahre 1570* [The Oldest Monuments of Lithuanian Language, Facsimile Edition]. Heidelberg: C. Winter.

Herrnstein Smith, Barbara. 1988. *Contingencies of Value: Alternative Perspectives for Critical Theory*. Cambridge, MA: Harvard UP.
Janulaitis, Augustinas, ed. 1922. "Simono Daukanto laiškai" [The Letters of Simonas Daukantas], *Mūsų senovė* 1: 695-791.
Kalnius, Alfonsas, ed. 1948[-1949]. Žemaitė, *Raštai* [Writings]. Kaunas: Valstybinė grožinės literatūros leidykla. 4 vol. (from prepared 8 vol.).
Lazutka, Stanislovas and Edvardas Gudavičius et al., eds. 1983-1991. *Pirmasis Lietuvos Statutas = Pervyj Litovskij Statut* [The First Lithuanian Statute]. 2(3) vol. Vilnius: Mintis.
Lebedys, Jurgis, ed. 1948. Simonas Stanevyčia, *Pasakėčios* [The Fables]. Kaunas: Valstybinė grožinės literatūros leidykla.
Likhachev, Dmitryj Sergeevich. 1962. *Tekstologija: Na materiale russkoj literatury X-XVII v. v.* [Textual Scholarship: On the base of 10th-17th c. Russian Literature]. Moskva-Leningrad: Izdatel'stvo Akademii nauk SSSR. Second edition: 1983. Leningrad: Nauka. Third edition: 2001. Sank-Peterburg: Aleteija.
Lituanistinė biblioteka. 1966-2001. 31 vol. Vilnius: Vaga.
Maironis. 1956. *Rinktiniai raštai* [Selected Writings]. Edited by Leonas Ginetis et al. 2 vol. Vilnius: Valstybinė grožinės literatūros leidykla.
———. 1987-1992. *Raštai* [Writings]. Edited by Irena Slavinskaitė. 3(4) vol. Vilnius: Vaga.
Nesselmann, G. H. F., ed. 1869. Chriſtian Donalitius, *Littauiſche Dichtungen* [Lithuanian Poems]. Königsberg: Hübner & Matz.
Pamerneckis, Stasys. 1992. *Lietuvos Didžiosios Kunigaikštystės kirilinių tekstų paleografija* [The Paleography of the Cyrilic Texts of the Grand Duchy of Lithuania]. Vilnius: VU.
Pushkin, Aleksandr Sergeevich. 1937-1959. *Polnoe sobranie sochinenij* [Complete Writings]. Edited by Sergei Bondi et al. 17 vol. Moskva-Leningrad: Izdatel'stvo Akademii nauk SSSR.
Savickis, Jurgis. 1990-1999. *Raštai* [Writings]. Edited by Janina Žėkaitė. 6 vol. Vilnius: Vaga.
Schleicher, Aug., ed. 1865. Christian Donaleitis, *Litauische Dichtungen* [Lithuanian Poems]. St. Petersburg: Buchdruckerei der Kaiserlichen Akademie der Wissenschaften.
[Šliūpas, Jonas.] 1890. Lietuvos mylėtojas, *Lietuviszkieje rasztai ir rasztininkai* [Lithuanian writings and writers]. Tilžė: O. von Mauderodės sp.
Sniečkus, Antanas. 1991. "Lietuvos komunistų partijos (bolševikų) VI suvažiavimo stenograma (1949 m. vasario 15-18): Iš A. Sniečkaus

pranešimo" [The 6th Congress of the Communist (Bolshevik) Party of Lithuania: Report by A. Sniečkus]. *Rašytojas pokario metais* [The Writer in the Postwar Period]. Vilnius: Vaga, 188-92.

Specht, Franz, ed. 1929. Konstantinas] Šyrwids, *Punktay sakimu* = *Punkty kazań* [The Clauses of the Sermons, Facsimile Edition]. Göttingen: Vandenhoeck & Ruprecht.

Stojanović, Svetozar. 1997. "Postcommunism, Democracy, Nationality, and Capitalist Economy." In *Justice and Democracy: Cross-cultural Perspectives*, edited by Ron Bontekoe and Marietta Stepaniants. 149-59. Honolulu: University of Hawaii Press.

Strazdas, Antanas. 1951. *Dainos* [Songs]. Vilnius: Valstybinė grožinės literatūros leidykla.

———. 1952. *Raštai* [Writings]. Vilnius: Valstybinė grožinės literatūros leidykla.

———. 1957. *Raštai* [Writings]. Vilnius: Valstybinė grožinės literatūros leidykla.

———. 1963. *Poezija* [Poetry]. Vilnius: Valstybinė grožinės literatūros leidykla.

———. 1974. *Giesmė apie siratas* [Hymn about Orphans]. Edited by Vytautas Vanagas. Vilnius: Vaga.

[Tumas, Juozas.] 1899. Tėvynės sargo redakcija, "Pakvietimas ant vysk. Valančiaus jubiliejaus" [A Call to Celebrate the Anniversary of Valančius]. *Tėvynės sargas* 10: 52-54.

van Vliet, H. T. M. 2006. "Changing Structure, Changing Meaning: Multiple Versions of Modern Poetry Collections as an Editorial Problem." *Variants* 5: 191-204.

Vydūnas-. 1990-1994. *Raštai* [Writings]. Edited by Vacys Bagdonavičius. 4 vol. Vilnius: Mintis.

Young, Robert J. C. 2001. *Postcolonialism: An Historical Introduction*. Oxford: Blackwell.

Žemaitė. 1956-57. *Raštai* [Writings]. Edited by Aleksandras Žirgulys.

Žirgulys, Aleksandras, ed. 1956-1957. Žemaitė, *Raštai* [Writings]. 6 vol. Vilnius: Valstybinė grožinės literatūros leidykla.

Canon and Classicity

Editing as Canonising in Swedish Romanticism

Paula Henrikson

The transmission of texts constitutes the memory of mankind; this is a much repeated truth. As textual editors we participate in an ancient tradition of passing on knowledge, which has developed more and more fine-tuned instruments for the representation of texts. The critical edition, as we know it today, is a product of Historicism and has historical consciousness as its prerequisite. An edition is motivated because a rift in the understanding has occurred, and it is this rift that the editor is called upon both to point out and to bridge (cf. Senger 1987, 1 and ff.)

The concept of classics is a contested one. Well known is Gadamer's claim half a century ago, that classics are actually classics only insofar as they have the power to transmit themselves. "The 'classical' is something raised above the vicissitudes of changing times and changing tastes", he states; it is "immediately accessible", "a consciousness of something enduring, of significance that cannot be lost and that is independent of all the circumstances of time" (Gadamer 1995, 288). He continues: "[T]he classical preserves itself precisely *because* it is significant in itself and interprets itself". And: "What we call 'classical' does not first require the overcoming of historical distance, for in its own constant mediation it overcomes this distance by itself" (Gadamer 1995, 289-90).

This passionate confidence in the classics now seems untimely, almost embarrassing. Today, no one recoils from the fact that even the classics — in the highest degree the classics — are dependent upon our active assistance in their transmission. A work never possesses the status of "classic" once and for all; this must constantly be obtained anew. Among Gadamer's most fervent adversaries on this point was Hans Robert Jauß, who emphasised that the historical function of a work of art is to be found in its *reception*. In order to fully understand the decisive importance of the history of reception for how a work is transmitted to us as a "classic", Gadamer must, according to Jauß, abandon his obsolete notion of "classics". We must, Jauß claims, reconstruct the value-systems of ancient epochs; we must trace the manifold historical emanations of the literary works, so that we may discover to what degree understanding is truly productive. The notion of classical timelessness is therefore part of what Jauß has labelled the *philological metaphysics* (1970, 183-89).

Viewed from the perspective of the history of reception, the attribute of "classical" accrues cumulatively: a work of art deserves to be called a classic only when generation upon generation has used it as a prism for their own times, have interpreted their own times through it. Editorial scholarship has historically been intimately linked to the concept of classics — even, as Wilhelm Voßkamp states, constitutively associated and identified with it ("konstitutiv verknüpft", "wird sogar mit ihr identifiziert"; Voßkamp 2001, 289). On the one hand, scholarly editing has been one of the most decisive vehicles for ascribing value to literature, and on the other, the canonising of the national literatures was a prerequisite for the national philologies to evolve. My aim in this article is to illuminate how the concept of classics was extended to include national literature in the realm of editorial scholarship.

* * *

The modern literatures began to structure themselves in terms of indigenous classics from the 16th century and onwards; Italy came first and France not much later. The national canons emerged in constant interplay with the canon of Classical Antiquity, which was first institutionalised by the grammarians in Alexandria. Ernst Robert Curtius has emphasised that the institutionalisation of literature originated from a pedagogical need: for the education in the grammar schools, a handy selection was necessary. The concept of *classics* is first found in Aulus Gellius (*Noctes Atticae*, c. 170 A.D.), where the term, borrowed from one of the Roman taxation classes, is used as a criterion of grammatical correctness: classical are those authors who should be considered exemplary, standard, or excellent. This use of the concept remained current up to about 1800, according to Curtius. At that point the dramatic shift occurred which made the ancient culture as a whole a "classical" heritage, exemplary in much more fundamental ways than through its linguistic correctness (1978, 253 and ff.)

About 1800 a revolution took place with respect to the connotations of the notion *classic*. On the one hand the revaluations of the new Winckelmannian humanism made the classical epoch as a whole exemplary for Western culture — this is what Curtius has in mind. On the other hand the ancient classics were challenged by a concept of national classicity, which was introduced during the 18th century and established by the Romantics, not least through the institution of modern editorial scholarship.

In this article I wish to illuminate this ambivalent period, where the Romantics through massive publication of national — in this case: Swedish

— memorials established the idea of a national literary canon, in interplay with the idea of an exemplary epoch of classical antiquity. I confine myself to the notion of classicity in editing, as applied to Swedish literature. Methodically as well as rhetorically we can trace the idea of national classics as both an alternative and a complement to the ancient classics. In what way did the editors consider their task to be one of establishing a canon of national classics? What is the relation between nationalism and classicity, as reflected in the editions? I hope to display characteristics of an editorial scholarship serving the nation, but not without certain interesting inconsistencies. In the course of the 19th century, a conflict between (national) normativity and (historical) relativity becomes more and more acute.

The decades around 1800 meant a radical change in historical consciousness, through which history was separated from the present and thereby considered alien, unfamiliar, and unknown. The rise of temporal consciousness was, according to Reinhart Koselleck, a consequence of the accelerating modernity, i.e. a result of the discrepancy which had evolved between the "space of experience" (*Erfahrungsraum*) and the "horizon of expectation" (*Erwartungshorizont*; Koselleck 1979). The past could no longer predict the future; history had lost the prognostic function it once had. In literature a parallel development is discernible: the poetry of past times was no longer regarded as an eternally present repertoire, in constant re-use by every new poet, but as a chronologically structured "history of literature", clearly separate from the originality and inventiveness of contemporary poetry, as it was understood in Romantic poetics. Hence we could argue that the corpus of old literature was transformed to "literary history" at that point, when it no longer could possess immediate, i. e. un-mediated, validity for present time. And thus the Romantic plea for originality in modern authorship is intimately connected to the need to mediate — edit — not only the classical but also the national and vernacular heritage, whether it consisted in historical chronicles, ballads or the writings of newly deceased contemporary authors.

An essential source for this process was the historisation of the cultural heritage, as it was expressed through the newly invented classical discipline, *Alterthumswissenschaft*. While the vivid interest in classical antiquity dates back to the Renaissance, the new discipline designated first and foremost an integration of the scattered (archaeological, philological, historical, aesthetical) interests in the classical epoch. This also reinforced the need of hermeneutical reflection, as expressed by Christian Gottlob

Heyne, Friedrich August Wolf and Friedrich Ast (Cf. Grafton 1983; Detlev Kopp 1987; Henrikson 2008). The wording of Heyne is famous: "Every ancient work of art should be considered and judged by the notions and in that spirit within which the old artist made it."[1] By this proto-historicist demand Heyne was paving the way for a relativistic and general view on cultural history, influenced by Herder. Language is the key to human culture: by studying the language in its historical evolution one gets to the heart of humanity, which is essentially historically situated.

The pioneering philological methodology of the *Alterthumswissenschaft* was thus based on a modern historical relativism. At the same time it was deeply rooted in a view on the classical epoch as something unique and normative (Horstmann 1978, 54; cf. Stierle 1979, 266). "The Greeks are for us not only a nation it is useful to know, but an ideal", was the wording of Wilhelm von Humboldt.[2] This inherent contradiction which was built into the modern classical discipline meant that the historical relativism — to understand everything as a product of its historical context — only was to be applied to the normative cultures of Greece and Rome. This was an obstacle to overcome for the modern, vernacular philologies on the rise. And it is obvious that this contradiction supported, or even forced, a renewed conception of the normative claim.

The widening of the concept of "classic", evident throughout the philological discussion of the early 19th century, meant that the philological methodology extended its scope. We can see this in Friedrich Schlegel, who — in his notes *On Philology* (*Zur Philologie*, c. 1797) — embraced a notion of classicity which was not primarily epochally or geographically defined. "Classical" is according to Schlegel that which is an expression of its own epoch but also exceeds this epoch and achieves an unlimited "interpretivity" for all times (cf. Michel 1982, 54; Leventhal 1994, 290 n. 103; Arndt 1997, 12). The classical scholar August Boeckh drew the consequences of a widened concept of philology when he wrote: "Is it not obvious, that anyone who works with Italian or English literature, or with the literature and language of any nation, to speak only of language and

---

[1] "Jedes alte Kunstwerk muß mit den Begriffen und in dem Geiste betrachtet und beurtheilt werden, mit welchen Begriffen und in welchem Geiste der alte Künstler es verfertigte" (Heyne 1778, 13).

[2] "Die Griechen sind uns nicht bloss ein nützlich zu kennendes Volk, sondern ein Ideal"; quoted from Horstmann (1978, 54). Cf. Wolf: "In diesen und andern Rücksichten ist dem Forscher der Geschichte der Menschheit unter allen Nationen keine so wichtig, ja man darf sagen, so heilig, als die griechische" (1807, 133 and ff.)

literature, has a philological ambition? What the philologist does with classical antiquity, that do all these on modernity [...]"³

Thus philology could no longer be limited to classical antiquity; its functions were considered just as important for the modern literatures in vernacular languages. Natural as this view seems today, it was revolutionary for the development of the vernacular philologies. One could trace back to it the outlines of an entire new profession, which over time developed its own institutional structures and methodologies. The historical model that the Romantic philologists adopted owed a lot to the discipline of *Alterthumswissenschaft*, but also exceeded its limits. This double bind-relation to the classical epoch is discernible all over the Romantic enterprise.

An immediate predecessor to the editorial efforts of the Swedish Romantics was the ballad revival in England and Germany. Works such as Thomas Percy's *Reliques of Ancient English Poetry* (1765), Thomas Warton's *History of English Poetry* (1774–81) and Johann Gottfried von Herder's *Volkslieder* (1778–79) all indicated that the classical models for literature were being challenged. In its historicising approach the rising interest in the ballad has a certain connection to the normative branches of classical and biblical criticism. In his introduction to the *Reliques*, Percy outlines a continuous poetic tradition from pagan to Christian times, an argument which parallels not only F. A. Wolf's ambition to trace oral traditions in the *Iliad* in his *Prolegomena ad Homerum* (1795), but also the efforts of biblical scholars such as J. G. Eichhorn to unveil the layers and thus the human motives and traditions hidden in the biblical text (cf. McGann 1985, 150 and ff.) To put classical, biblical and vernacular texts on the same analytical desk and to expose them to the same analytical tools meant to discharge the normative texts from their exclusive claims. The remaining imperative was to historicise — whether ballads, classics or the Bible itself. Seen in this context the rising interest in vernacular literature and the corresponding emancipation

---

³ "Denn ist es nicht empirisch klar, dass jeder, welcher sich z. B. mit der italienischen oder englischen Literatur beschäftigt, oder mit der Literatur und Sprache irgend eines andern Volkes, um jetzt nur von Sprache und Literatur zu reden, ein philologisches Bestreben hat? Was die Philologen am Antiken thun, das thun alle diese am Modernen, z. B. an Dante, Shakespeare oder irgend einem Gegenstande aus dem Mittelalter. Da alle Kritik und Auslegung factisch philologisch ist, und in diesen das formale Thun des Philologen, wie sich späterhin zeigen wird, ganz aufgeht, so kann die Philologie nicht auf das Alterthumsstudium beschränkt sein, weil jene Funktionen auch alles Moderne berühren" (Boeckh 1886, 5 and ff.) Cf. also Stierle (1979, 269 and ff.) On the emergence of German Studies in Germany and their link to classical philology, see for example Weimar (1989, 210–19).

from classical norms also depict the humans' "release from their self-imposed immaturity", as Kant labelled the aim of the Enlightenment.

No doubt, philological endeavours had been invested in Medieval literature even earlier — we can think of editions of Icelandic sagas, historical chronicles or Scandinavian provincial laws, only to mention a few Swedish examples. It is a crucial fact that the Renaissance not only enhanced an interest in the classical antiquity, but also, and even more, in what was considered Scandinavia's own classical period, i.e., the Middle Ages. This also meant that the Romantic editors and critics could lean upon Renaissance philologists — mainly the "father of Swedish Poetry", Georg Stiernhielm — in their efforts to revitalise a national literary tradition. What they tried to bring to this antiquarian tradition was the historicising approach, the idea of historical development and growth. The accusation against the Old School aimed at their supposed oblivion and ignorance of other literary traditions than the French classicism — were it Medieval, Greek or Renaissance poetry. Apart from the Scandinavian impetus, the ideas of the Romantic editors and critics in Sweden were mainly, not to say totally, inspired by German authors and critics.

Turning now to Swedish philology in the Romantic era, I will examine only a few instances from the vast material available with the aim to illuminate how the concept of classicity was applied to national literature in editing. One of the early instances in which we find a variant of the term being used to point out Swedish literature as "exemplary", "excellent" is found in 1795, in an appeal to the nation's finest authors to collect their works:

> One has long waited in vain for our Poets of the first Class, honouring the Swedish Genius and benefitting the Literature, to collect and edit their Works. As it happens there is no better way to stay and for the future reject the literary fancy, which in these years threatens to drive good taste away.[4]

The call comes from no less an authority than the poet, critic and member of the Swedish Academy Johan Henric Kellgren (1751–1795). It is found in his review of a Swedish author who had issued a revised version of his own collected works, an action Kellgren recommends as exemplary. This edition, put together by Kellgren's colleague Gustaf Fredrik Gyllenborg (1731–1808) but also including works by Gustaf Philip Creutz

---

[4] "Länge hade man förgäfwes wäntat, at wåre Skalder af första Classen skulle, til Heder för Swenska Snillet och båtnad för Witterheten, börja samla och utgifwa deras Arbeten. Til Äfwentyrs gifwes intet säkrare sätt at hämma och för framtiden afböja det wittra swärmeri, som i senare åren hotat uttränga den goda smaken" (Kellgren 1795).

(1731–1785), he actually names "a classical Book". As we can see this is not only a value judgment, but also a demand for literary discipline of style and good taste. This is also the reason why the editions ought to be strictly selective and polished, rather than historically accurate and complete. The intimate connection between careful selections, polishing corrections and a classical value is obvious in editions by editors belonging to what after 1809 would be designated "the Old School", as opposed to "the New School", i.e., the Romantics. This recommendation, axiomatic for the Old School, was abandoned by the Romantics, who considered it unhistorical, and engendering nothing but fake.

The notion of classicity is used in a few of the editions of the 18th century authors — and not least in a review of Kellgren's own collected works, printed shortly after his death but revised in exemplary ways by himself. The quarrel over the term is obvious from a literary debate in 1820, when the Academist Nils von Rosenstein (1752–1824) used it in his introduction to an edition of the female author Anna Maria Lenngren (1754–1817), who by virtue of her moderation and adherence to classical models was labelled a "classical author" (Lenngren 1819). This was considered a provocation among the members of the New School. In his review of the edition the critic Lorenzo Hammarsköld (1785–1827) reacted against Rosenstein's use of the term. Tracing its history back to the grammarians in Alexandria, Hammarsköld wished to reserve the concept of classicity for authors that had "produced and developed all resources in each genre in inner prosperity" and at the same time displayed verbal perfection.[5] Through this formulation, Hammarsköld tried to avoid a definition of the concept which involved the normative claim.

The concept of a "modern classicity" thus remained a contested issue. Even if it was no longer considered an obvious *contradictio in adjecto*, the concept was still subjected to discussions, doubts and reflection. A number of the Romantic editors were also classical scholars, and classical philology is the obvious context for their considerations of modern classicity. In 1826 the classical as well as modern philologist Per Adolf Sondén (1792–1837) wrote in his edition of Jacob Frese (1690–1729), "We highly esteem the work of the learned, as they uncover remnants of the classical age; should not then our own authors deserve an attention, which we do not

---

[5] "framtedt och utwecklat alla resourcer inom hwarje Skaldeslag i inre rikdom" (Hammarsköld 1820, 199).

deny the Roman poets, although not all of these were Virgilian?"[6] Sondén defends the Romantic editions of old literature, at times ridiculed by the Old School for being mediocre and not worthy of philological attention, by comparing them to remnants from classical antiquity. At the heart of a formulation like this lies a continuing re-negotiation of the relationship between a classical and a modern literary heritage. The chief theorist among the Swedish Romantics, P. D. A. Atterbom (1790–1855), in 1820 expressed his wish to expand the concept of classicity. His analysis departs from a general consideration of the mission of art, which is "in a beautiful form to express an infinite meaning". He continues:

> A piece of art, a poem, which through its genius in invention and form satisfies *this* demand — it might in other aspects be of any kind and extent — is in *its* type *perfect*, or what we call *classical* [...]. Hence, it is obvious that the concept of *classicity*, rightly considered, can by no means *exclusively* refer to the most excellent works in Greek and Roman literature [...].[7]

Esaias Tegnér (1782–1846), professor of Greek at Lund University and later on bishop in Växjö, also stated that the Greek and Roman culture no more had any exclusive claims on classicity. In his farewell lecture from his professorship he claimed:

> A language is classical not only through its inner formation, but also and particularly through its literature. But such a literature exists nowadays in several of the living languages. The body of ideas, which made up the culture of the Ancients, has with time passed into general thought; we live by the funds, which ancient times have accumulated.[8]

---

[6] "Vi högakta de Lärdas flit, som framletat den klassiska fornålderns lämningar; skulle då icke våra egna Författare ha rätt till en uppmärksamhet, den man icke vägrar åt Roms Skalder, ehuru dessa icke alla vore *Maroner*?". Sondén in Frese (1826), unpaginated preface.

[7] "Ett konstverk, ett poem, som genom det snillrika i uppfinning och utarbetning tillfredsställer denna fordran–det må föröfrigt vara af hvad art eller omfång som helst–är i sitt slag fulländadt, eller hvad man kallar klassiskt [...]. Häraf är jämväl klart, att begreppet klassiskhet, riktigt genomtänkt, för ingen del kan uteslutande tillhöra det förträffligaste i grekernas och romarnes litteratur" (Atterbom (870, 242).

[8] "Klassiskt är ett språk icke blott genom sin egen inre utbildning, utan äfven och i synnerhet genom sin litteratur. Men en sådan litteratur hafva numera flera af de lefvande språken. Den massa af idéer, som utgjorde de gamlas bildning, har småningom öfvergått i det allmänna tänkesättet, vi lefva af de fonder, som forntiden samlat" (Tegnér 1920 [1824], 111).

According to Atterbom and Tegnér, classicity is a quality which a culture can achieve as soon as it has reached a certain level. There are differences between their views; according to Atterbom, classicity is a normative notion of value, while for Tegnér it rather represents extensive, accumulated knowledge in all its complexity. But for both, it has become possible for modern culture to enter into a sphere which was once reserved for Antiquity.

In his lectures on *The History of Poetry* (held during the 1840s), Atterbom even states that to understand Modernity, it is also necessary to understand Antiquity:

> It is not only a matter of understanding Antiquity in and for itself, but also to a great extent of understanding through Antiquity the qualities of Modernity; which, even if it initially seems to totally differ from Antiquity, nonetheless, meticulously observed, in many aspects appears to presuppose its existence and conform to its norms.[9]

Romanticism in general and Atterbom in particular have sometimes been pointed out as anti-classicist, rejecting classical norms and appraising originality and individuality. The reality is more complex. Turning to Greece rather than Rome, the Romantic movement was deeply influenced by the forms of classicising which we associate with the aesthetic humanism as found in late 18th century Germany. The question is not *whether* the ancients are exemplary, but *in which way* — in fact one could say that the negotiations on the true way of classicising are indeed fundamental for understanding the Romantic conception of a literary and cultural tradition.

The modelling of national editorial scholarship on classical paradigms, to elaborate here on editorial scholarship, had consequences not only for the methodological considerations made by the editors but also for the ideological perspectives supported by the editions. Works from national literature were edited with classical antiquity as background, and the whole paradigm of a treasure of national literature was modelled on ancient classicity. I will give some examples of this from the editions put forth by Romantic editors in Sweden.

---

[9] "Frågan är således här ej endast derom, att lära sig förstå antiken, i och för sig sjelf, utan tillika om, att i ganska betydlig måtto just genom den lära sig förstå det bästa af sjelfva moderniteten; hvilket, äfven om det vid första påseendet [...] synes helt och hållet afvika från antikens art, dock, vid närmare skärskådning, befinnes i ganska mycket förutsätta dess existens och rätta sig efter dess norm" (Atterbom 1861, 17).

My first example is the edition of *Swedish folk songs* (*Swenska folk-wisor*), published in three volumes in 1814–1816. It was edited by two of the combative Romantics, Erik Gustaf Geijer (1783–1847), author and later on professor of history in Uppsala, and Arvid August Afzelius (1785–1871), philologist and cleric. As an edition of European ballads it was neither original nor early; the editors refer to Danish, German and English examples. When planning the Swedish ballad edition the editors had been in contact with the Danish philologist, Rasmus Nyerup. Still the edition was a challenge, not to say provocation, in the literary situation in Sweden. Geijer expands on the demanding role of the editors in this edition:

> They find themselves in the unique situation of being called upon to presenting as a national asset what to the largest part of our general reading public nowadays is either totally unknown or, if the one or the other recognizes sounds from their childhood, is likely to be looked upon with ignorance and ridicule.[10]

The notion of a "national asset" is central. To clarify the ballads' importance as national treasures Geijer gives an account of the historical development of Western poetry, from ancient to modern times. He argues that the ballads represent the Scandinavian Homer, "in its original spirit […] even deeper than the antique". But while literature in the Antiquity developed and improved, Scandinavian literature remained stagnant. During the 18th century the Scandinavians had tried to regain the superiority of the ancient literature by imitating "the advantages of an already perfected culture" and by getting "grafted onto a foreign stem". Geijer concludes: "The art of this imitation prevents us however to believe, that it was grounded in a clear recognition of the large and important precedence of the old poetry, which lies in its organic development into an independent totality."[11]

---

[10] Geijer (1814, I): "De finna sig nemligen i den egna belägenheten, att tro sig såsom en national-egendom böra anmäla någon ting, som, för den talrikaste hopen af vår läsande allmänhet nu för tiden, antingen är alldeles obekant, eller också, om en och annan här skulle igenkänna ljud från sin barndomsdagar, med likgiltighet och åtlöje torde beses."

[11] Geijer (1814, XI): "till sin ursprungliga anda […] djupare än den Antika"; "en redan fullkomnad bildnings fördelar"; "inympas på en främmande stam". — "Beskaffenheten af denna härmning förbjuder oss dock tro, att den var grundad på något klart erkännande af den gamla poesiens stora och väsentliga företräde, hvilket ligger i dess organiska utvickling till ett sjelfständigt helt."

The national literatures should therefore tread in the footsteps of the ancient authors rather than imitate their surface. This viewpoint is important if we consider the Romantic idea of national classics. The question is yet again not *whether* the ancients are exemplary, but *in which way* — the classical epoch turns from a timeless norm to a historically understood model for the organic development of literature. Literary history was thus endowed with a real historical dimension, and in this historical system the ballad holds a position analogous to that of Homer as the starting point for a national literature. We get a hint of this already on the edition's title page, with its image of what probably is intended to be seen as a Nordic bard, with the harp in his hand, but which also evokes associations to representations of the blind Homer with his lyre.

The simultaneous glorification of Greek and Roman cultures in total, on the one hand, and the establishment of national canons through editing, on the other, is thus no contradiction. Rather they illustrate two aspects of one single process, characterised primarily by the demand for historisation.

This is obvious if we return to the notes *On Philology* by Friedrich Schlegel, which is also the first known instance of the word historicism ("Historismus"). Schlegel uses the expression to characterise the program of Winckelmann, and his discovery of the "immeasurable difference" ("den unermeßlichen Unterschied") between the moderns and ancients, and the "totally unique nature of Antiquity" ("die ganz eigne Natur des Alterhums" [Schlegel 1981, 35]). The distance and difference in relation to the ancients is a prerequisite for Schlegel's reflections on a modern philology, which implies a deep admiration for the ancient as well as the modern heritage. Even in his most neoclassical writings, Schlegel emphasises that what should be imitated is not the outer characteristics, but the inner spirit of Antiquity (so in *Über das Studium der Griechischen Poesie*, 1795–1796). Still in 1815, in his history of ancient and modern literature, he claims that the Romantic spirit does not deviate from true Antiquity: "Not the Old and Ancient, but only the Anciently, wrongly among us represented, all that without inner love only mimics the outer form, is contrary to the Romantic."[12]

---

[12] "Nicht dem Alten und Antiken, sondern nur dem unter uns fälschlich wieder aufgestellten Antikischen, allem was ohne innere Liebe bloß die Form der Alten nachkünstelt, ist das Romantische entgegengesetzt." (Schlegel 1961, 286)

The opposition between Ancient and Modern, which is deployed in so many Romantic writings, thus represents a form of double bind relationship. The edition of *Swedish folk songs* is not presented to diminish the Ancient heritage, but to supplement it with a national counterpart. By making the origins of national literature accessible again, it would also become possible for the national literature to ripen. The ballads were not perfect, and not to be imitated by the modern author, but as a national heritage they were the necessary starting point for the truly national poetry of the future.

In this way the ballads would at the same time replace and confirm the classics as a starting point for the national literature. Evidence of the same ambition is found in the second Romantic edition of Scandinavian ballads, published as late as 1843. The editor, Adolph Iwar Arwidsson (1791–1858), here points out the folk tradition as a source of knowledge about the national history, not of the kings and the state, but the "real people." In this context he suggests that the dissertations at the universities, which were usually devoted to translations of Greek and Latin authors, should rather be used for publishing "sagas, memorials, historical traditions, customs, proverbs, riddles, ballads, plays, dialects" of the Swedish provinces. In this way, he argues, the dissertations could become an archive of national memorials, rather than a place for classical devotion.[13]

Romantic editing contributed to the reshaping, or even the new construction, of a literary history for the Swedish nation. This means also that connections were established between the editions published. In his edition of Swedish ballads Geijer outlines an entire history of European literature, relating among others Ariosto, Tasso, Cervantes and Shakespeare not only to the ballad but also to a theory of literary succession and growth. Only in this perspective could the real nature of Swedish literature be made clear. Geijer writes:

> Moreover, there is one man in whom all rays that diversely emanate from an as yet unshaped poetry gathers as in a focus into radiant clarity, and who therefore stands at the head of a new era. This is Stiernhielm. [——] With him the History of Swedish Literature begins.[14]

---

[13] "fornsägner, minnesmärken, historiska traditioner, folkbruk och seder, ordspråk, gåtor, folkvisor, lekar och provins-ord, m.m." (Arwidsson (1837, 2: VI).

[14] "För öfrigt fins det en enda man, hos hvilken alla de strålar af en ännu obildad poesi, som man under denna period träffar spridda, såsom i en brännpunkt sedermera synas samlat sig till

The edition of this 17th century author appeared four years later, with Lorenzo Hammarsköld as editor. In the introduction he describes how the edition was made possible through a "revolution in general opinion", which again had made fashionable what was "nationally serious" (Stiernhielm 1818, II). In his review of this edition, Sondén reaffirms that the objective was not to present new normative models, intended for imitation, but to shed light on "the developmental history" of the nation:

> It is already becoming quite commonly realised that the writings of our old Poets truly deserve a closer scrutiny; not in order to be presented as models, since an ideal sought only from without always leads to deception; but because they make up an important link in the developmental history of the nation, which is indispensable if we want to know ourselves and our time.[15]

The real aim with the editing of national classics was to make the contemporary national poetry flourish in Sweden. A problem was that it appeared not to do so, in spite of all these excellent editions of the national treasures. Even the Romantics themselves drew attention to an embarrassing absence of literary works which could confirm the new era. One among them wrote: "It is true: still, no national genius in a large and mighty creation has produced a work at which we dwell with rapture: still we expect of happier and warmer days the bloom of the newly planted flowers."[16]

This absence was also the mightiest weapon in the hands of the enemies, the Old School. One of them called the Romantics "persons, […] without the merit of one single skilful work", and goes on:

> But, so the answer goes, we have on several occasions explained, that we do not believe in a positive way, and that means *through excelling works*, to have done anything for the national literature.

---

ett klart sken, och som derföre äfven begynner en ny tid. Det är Stjernhelm. [– – –] Med honom begynner Svenska Skaldekonstens Historia" (Geijer 1814, L–LI).

[15] "Man börjar redan temligen allmänt inse, att wåra gamla Skalders skrifter werkligen äro wärda en närmare undersökning: ej för att framställas såsom mönster, emedan ett ideal, endast utifrån sökt, alltid leder till förwillelse; utan derföre, att de utgöra en wigtig länk i nationens bildningshistoria, utan hwilken det ej är möjligt att känna sig sjelf och sin tid" (Sondén 1818, 364).

[16] V. F. Palmblad, quoted in Vinge: "Det är sant: ännu har ingen genius i fosterländska poesien, i en stor och mäktig skapelse, framställt ett verk, hvarvid vi med hänryckning dröje: ännu vänta vi af lyckligare, varmare dagar mognaden af de nyplanterade växterna." (1978, 131).

> Excuse me, gentlemen, I remember that, but thus it is obvious that *you have not damaged anything of the Old*, and that you are not *able to destroy* it.[17]

In this situation the so far unknown Erik Johan Stagnelius, 29 years old, died (1793–1823), and left a rich collection of unpublished manuscripts behind. Few authors get their breakthroughs with posthumous editions, but this was the case with Stagnelius, whose *Collected works* were edited by Lorenzo Hammarsköld.

This edition was meant to change the fact that the Romantics certainly had made editions of important works, but not yet produced something really superior of their own. By retroactively including this young author in the Romantic project the New School could gain polemical advantages from his success. Mobilising his works was a way to show that the Romantic efforts were fruitful.

The edition therefore was an important manifestation of literary strategy. In the introduction the editor claims that all poems by Stagnelius announced the "large and mighty influence, which the opinions of the New School in Swedish literature have had on the development of the poetic talent of Stagnelius."[18] The rhetorical strategies are also obvious in the very beginning of the introduction. Here the editor states:

> With the same feeling, which must strike the researcher who travels on the holy ground of Greece or Italy, when he finds in the earth the remains of a masterpiece of Praxiteles, Phidias or Skopas […] — with that same feeling I now take on the dear and honourable commission which has been confided to me, to edit the writings of Stagnelius.[19]

---

[17] "personer, […] utan all egen förtjenst af något enda dugligt arbete" and 89 and ff.: "Men, svarar man, vi ha på flere ställen i våra skrifter låtit förstå, att vi icke tro oss hafva i *positiv* väg, det vill säga, *genom ypperlige arbeten*, uträttat något särdeles inom den fosterländska Litteraturen. Förlåten mig, mine Herrar, jag påminner mig det, men då är det också, enligt hvad jag i det föregående visat, alldeles afgjordt, att *I ingenting förstört af det Gamla*, och att *I ingenting kunna förstöra* […]" (Wallmark 1821, 76).

[18] "det stora och mägtiga inflytande, som de åsigter, hvilka af den så kallade Nya Scholan i Vitterheten bekännas, haft på utvecklingen af STAGNELII skaldiska talent " (Hammarsköld 1824, I: 24 and ff.)

[19] "Med samma känsla, som måste intaga den, på Greklands eller Italiens heliga jord, resande Forskaren, när han i gruset finner lemningarne efter ett Praxiteles' Phidias' eller Skopas' mästerstycke […], med samma känsla går nu undertecknad, att utföra det honom anförtrodda dyrbara och hedrande uppdrag, att utgifva *E. J. STAGNELLI* efterlemnade skrifter" (Hammarsköld 1824, I:1).

The real connection between ancient sculpture and the Swedish author is the fragmentary status of both, but through the comparison Stagnelius is also endowed with the status of a national classic.

The editorial scholarship of the Romantics thus was a part of their ambition to rewrite literary history and make literature a matter of national importance. In the short run this ambition was in vain. Their revaluations were ridiculed and at the same time their conservative attitudes became politically outdated by the liberal movements. But in the long run the Romantics became the obvious winners, not least because of their massive and determined editorial endeavour. In fact, the growing institution of editorial scholarship in the 19th and 20th centuries could to a large extent be understood as an implementation of Romantic ideas, where the aim of literature was the fostering of national citizens.

An example of this is the series of national classics. As professional scholarly editions of the jewels of national literature were printed in small numbers for a cultural elite, a number of large-scale series of national classics also aimed at broader audiences. With titles such as *Classical authors in Swedish literature* (1834–1838), *Excellent and classical works by Swedish authors* (1836–1839) and *A miniature library of Swedish classics* (1850–1852), these series, published by different publishers for different purposes, were supposed to include the core of Swedish literature, serving as the norm for an educated citizen and at the same time delimiting a "Swedish" cultural identity. In these series the notion of "classics" is confidently used in editions of Swedish literature, and these series also demonstrated the development of a national canon.

The very first author in these series of national classics was, of course, the "father of Swedish poetry", the 17th century author Georg Stiernhielm, who is presented as the threshold to Swedish literature. The title of his work suited the series as if it were made for it: *Musæ suethizantes, that is, goddesses of song, now for the first time learning to write and play in Swedish*. In 1668, the appeal to "the Swedish muses" codified Stiernhielm's ambition to write Swedish poetry in classical forms; now, it codified the Romantic notion of national classics. The Greek goddesses had emigrated at last and learnt how "to write and play in Swedish".

* * *

Romanticism was the starting point for a golden century of editorial scholarship. The expansion, professionalization and institutionalisation which shaped national scholarly editing during the 19th century was a consequence of an increasing value being associated with national literature and national reading. This is apparent also in the Swedish educational system, where Swedish language and literature successively replaced the classical languages during the 19th century as an instrument for fostering and growth.[20] A literary canon was established through literary overviews and anthologies, and in 1897 and 1898 the first proper school editions, exclusively intended for educational purposes, appeared.

This increasing value of national literature was in many aspects an effect of the temporalisation of literature. The Romantics initiated not only, and perhaps not even foremost, a literary movement, but a new way of understanding oneself in the light of history — and in this case of understanding literature in the light of literary history. Up to the 18th century, literature primarily had the function of an eternally present repertoire. The writer was practicing on a general commons, where he belonged to a team of eternally contemporary colleagues, and where the classical Greek and Roman authors served as eternal archetypes. There was, so to speak, no historical distance between the modern and the old poet; they shared one single framework of literary references and literary strategies.

The decades around 1800 meant a radical change, through which history was separated from the present and thereby considered alien, unfamiliar, and unknown. Old literature was foreign and distant, and to be unveiled it demanded hermeneutic skills, adjusted to the unique circumstances which applied to the individual work. Modern philology sprang from the modern nation's need of a collective national identity and a national heritage around which to gather, and the new appeal to historical relativism was first and foremost informed by these national claims. Still, there remained a conflict between relativism and nationalism, which is also a conflict between scientific scrupulousness and ideological commitment, between cosmopolitan networks and national bias.

In a prospective view, the rejection of classical antiquity as an eternal model did not mean that the normativity associated with the classical era was abolished from modern editorial scholarship — on the contrary. As Karlheinz Stierle has pointed out, normativity is in fact one of the most important inheritances which classical philology left to modern philology. He even claims: "Because of this normative component philology can never be only science or exploration of facts; it always also refers

---

[20] On pedagogical perspectives, cf. for instance Martinsson (1989) and Thavenius (1991, 52–65).

back to the possibility of participation."[21] Philology remains shaped by an opposition between "science" and "commitment", which is typical also for the two other disciplines which traditionally have had a hermeneutic foundation, i.e. theology and law. In these three disciplines it is imperative to secure a correct reception of texts which are in some way normative for a society. The aim of modern philology cannot and should not primarily be to objectively accumulate knowledge, but also to reflect on the aim, function and meaning of historical knowledge.[22]

Bibliography

Arndt, Andreas. 1997. "'Philosophie der Philologie'. Historisch-kritische Bemerkungen zur philosophischen Bestimmung von Editionen." *editio* 11: 1–19.

Atterbom, P. D. A. 1861. *Poesiens historia.* Vol. 2. Örebro: N.M. Lindh.

———. 1870. *Samlade skrifter i obunden stil.* Vol. 7:1 (Litterära karakteristiker). Örebro: Abr. Bohlin.

Arwidsson, Adolf Iwar, ed. 1837. *Svenska fornsånger. En samling af kämpavisor, folk-visor, lekar och dansar, samt barn- och vall-sånger.* Vol. 2. Stockholm: Norstedt.

Boeckh, August. 1886. *Encyklopädie und Methodologie der Philologischen Wissenschaften*, edited by Ernst Bratuschek, 2nd ed. Leipzig: Teubner.

Curtius, Ernst Robert. 1978. *Europäische Literatur und lateinisches Mittelalter.* 9th Edition. Bern & München: Francke.

Frese, Jacob. 1826. *Valda skrifter af Jacob Frese. Samlade och å nyo utgifna af P.A. Sondén.* Stockholm: Nordström.

Gadamer, Hans-Georg. 1995. *Truth and method.* Translated by Joel Weinsheimer and Donald Marshall. New York: Continuum.

Geijer, Erik Gustaf and A. A. Afzelius, eds. 1814. "Inledning." *Swenska folkwisor.* Vol. 1. Stockholm: Strinnholm och Häggström.

Grafton, Anthony. 1983. "Polyhistor into *Philolog*: Notes on the Transformation of German Classical Scholarship, 1780–1850." In *History of Universities*, Vol. 3, edited by Charles Schmitt, 159–92. Amersham: Avebury.

---

[21] "Aufgrund ihrer normativen komponente kann Philologie nie allein Wissenschaft, Erforschung der Fakten sein; sie ist immer zugleich auf die Ermöglichung von Partizipation zurückbezogen" (Stierle 1979, 261).

[22] Cf. Stierle (1979, 260 and ff., 287 and ff.)

Hammarsköld, Lorenzo. 1820. *Swensk Literatur Tidning* no. 13.

———, ed. 1824. "Företal." In Erik Johan Stagnelius, *Samlade skrifter*. Stockholm: Wiborg.

Henrikson, Paula. 2008. "Klassiskt och modernt. Hermeneutik, filologi och Alterthumswissenschaft omkring år 1800." *Samlaren*: 64–91.

Heyne, Christian Gottlob. 1778. *Lobschrift auf Winkelmann*. Leipzig: Weygand.

Horstmann, Axel. 1978. "Die 'Klassische Philologie' zwischen Humanismus und Historismus. Friedrich August Wolf und die Begründung der modernen Altertumswissenschaft." *Berichte zur Wissenschaftsgeschichte*, 1 (1/2): 51–70.

Jauß, Hans Robert. 1970. "Literaturgeschichte als Provokation der Literaturwissenschaft." In *Literaturgeschichte als Provokation* 144–207. Frankfurt am Main: Suhrkamp.

Kellgren, J. H. 1795. *Stockholms Posten*. Feb. 27–28.

Kopp, Detlev and Nikolaus Wegmann. 1987. "'Die deutsche Philologie, die Schule und die Klassische Philologie'. Zur Karriere einer Wissenschaft um 1800." *Deutsche Vierteljahrsschrift für Literaturwissenschaft und Geistesgeschichte*. 61: 123*–151*.

Kosellek, Reinhart. 1979. *Vergangene Zukunft. Zur Semantik geschichtlicher Zeiten*. Frankfurt am Main: Suhrkamp.

Lenngren, Anna Maria. 1819. *Skalde-försök*. Stockholm: Olof Grahn.

Leventhal, Robert S. 1994. *The Disciplines of Interpretation. Lessing, Herder, Schlegel and Hermeneutics in Germany 1750–1800*. Berlin & New York: de Gruyter.

McGann, Jerome. 1985. *The Beauty of Inflections. Literary Investigations in Historical Method and Theory*. Oxford: Clarendon.

Martinsson, Bengt-Göran. 1989. *Tradition och betydelse. Om selektion, legitimering och reproduktion av litterär betydelse i gymnasiets litteraturundervisning 1865–1968*. Linköping: Tema kommunikation, Univ.

Michel, Willy. 1982. *Ästhetische Hermeneutik und frühromantische Kritik. Friedrich Schlegels fragmentarische Entwürfe, Rezensionen, Charakteristiken und Kritiken (1795–1801)*. Göttingen: Vandenhoeck & Ruprecht.

Schlegel, Friedrich. 1961. *Geschichte der alten und neuen Literatur* (1815). *Kritische Friedrich-Schlegel-Ausgabe*. Edited by Ernst Behler. Erste Abteilung, vol. 6. Edited by Hans Eichner. München, Paderborn etc.: Schöningh.

——— 1981. "Zur Philologie." *Kritische Friedrich-Schlegel-Ausgabe*. Edited by Hans Eichner. München, Paderborn etc.: Schöningh.

Senger, Hans Gerhard. 1987. "Die historisch-kritische Edition historisch-kritisch betrachtet." In *Buchstabe und Geist. Zur Überlieferung und Edition philosophischer Texte*, edited by Walter Jaeschke et al., 1–20. Hamburg: Meiner.

Sondén, P. A. 1818. *Swensk Literatur-Tidning*, no. 24.

Stierle, Karlheinz. 1979. "Altertumswissenschaftliche Hermeneutik und die Entstehung der Neuphilologie." In *Philologie und Hermeneutik im 19. Jahrhundert. Zur Geschichte und Methodologie der Geisteswissenschaften*, edited by H. Flashar, K. Gründer & A. Horstmann, 266–288. Göttingen: Vandenhoeck & Ruprecht.

Stiernhielm, Georg. 1818. *Vitterhets-arbeten*. Edited by L. Hammarsköld. Stockholm: Hedmanska tryckeriet.

Tegnér, Esaias. 1920. "Vid offentliga Föreläsningarnas slut." *Samlade skrifter*, edited by Ewert Wrangel & Fredrik Böök, Vol. 4. Stockholm: Norstedt.

Thavenius, Jan. 1991. "Modersmålet–från redskap till bildningsmedel." *Svenskämnet i förvandling. Historiska perspektiv–aktuella utmaningar*. Lund: Studentlitteratur.

Vinge, Louise. 1978. *Morgonrodnadens stridsmän. Epokbildningen som motiv i svensk romantik 1807–1821*. Lund: Gleerup.

Voßkamp, Wilhelm. 2001. "Klassisch/Klassik/Klassicismus." In *Ästhetische Grundbegriffe. Historisches Wörterbuch in sieben Bänden*, edited by Karlheinz Barck, Vol. 3, 289–305. Stuttgart: Metzler.

Wallmark, P. A. 1821. *Försök att upplysa publiken om föremålet och beskaffenheten af den elfva-åriga Tvisten inom vår Litteratur. Ett bidrag till vår Vitterhets Historia för åren 1809–1820*. Stockholm: Ecksteinska boktryckeriet.

Weimar, Klaus. 1989. *Geschichte der deutschen Literaturwissenschaft bis zum Ende des 19. Jahrhunderts*. München: Fink.

Wolf, Friedrich August. 1807. *Darstellung der Alterthums-Wissenschaft*. Berlin: Realschulbuchhandlung.

On the Margin of the Canon

Editions, the "Whole" Text and the "Whole" Codex

Gabriel Viehhauser

I

In a recent compendium of literary classics for the modern part-time *Bildungsbürger* in 2002, entitled *Bücher — Alles was man lesen muss* (Zschirndt 2002; the title could be translated as *Books — all you have to read*) only one "book" belonging to the field of Middle High German literature is cited. Surprisingly, this sole "book" is not the earlier work commonly held up as the literary apotheosis of its age, the *Nibelungenlied*, which has apparently since lost its canonical innocence owing to the abuse it suffered in being used as a remedy for the German nationalistic inferiority complex. Nor is it the *Parzival*, Wolfram of Eschenbach's great Grail romance, this being possibly due to the fact that in 2002 the *Da Vinci Code* remained yet to be deciphered.

Thus, the one Middle High German "book" you really have to read is the third "big player" of German medieval literature, Gottfried of Strassburg's *Tristan*. Its canonical dignity obviously arises from its treatment of the love-theme. It seems that in modern times *minne* has finally overcome its ever-present competitors from the times of courtly culture, the concepts of *aventiure* and tests of knightly valour.

It is quite obvious that a description of the Middle High German canon in such categories of "books that you have to read" is doomed to fail, if only because it is based on an illegitimate transfer of a capitalistic or "modernistic" model of literary production that implies the equation of "work", "text" and "book" (as published and marketable object) and that is by no means adequate to the pre-modern and semi-oral conditions of text-production in the Middle Ages. A more literary than sociological example might suffice to illustrate this point: It is a well known *bon-mot* in the research on Wolfram of Eschenbach, that even the denomination of his work as a "book" would have been taken as an insult by its author.[1] Of

---

[1] See the verses 115,29-116,4 of Wolfram's *Parzival*: disiu âventiure / vert âne der buoche stiure / ê man si hete für ein buoch, / ich wære ê nacket âne tuoch, / sô ich in dem bade sæze, / ob ichs questen niht vergæze ["this adventure goes its way without books' guidance. Rather than have people think it a book, I would be naked without a towel, as if sitting in the bath — provided I didn't forget the bundle of twigs."] (the text is taken from Schirok 2003; the translation of Lachmann's text is derived from Edwards 2004).

course this statement appears to be just an ironical joke on the scholarliness of some of Wolfram's writing rivals, and researchers tend not to take Wolfram too seriously here,[2] but the example shows that the problems of Middle High German canonization start with terminology. The status of medieval texts — and "books" — differs clearly from the one of texts in the time after the invention of the printed book and the establishment of the modern book-market.

However, for the beginning of my paper I will put these methodological considerations aside and very pragmatically take the selection of Zschirndt's compendium as what it is: as a squeeze of the accounts on Middle High German texts that can be found in literary histories. It is clear that no literary history would ignore the three undoubted "classics" mentioned before. But it is doubtful that there are many more (epic) texts that will be similarly indisputable. So as we can see, there is some truth in the fact that the canon of Middle High German literature appears to be rather limited in the account of Zschirndt.[3] One might want to add Hartmann's influential Arthurian novels, the *Erec* and the *Iwein*, Wolfram's *Willehalm* or even the *Eneit* of Heinrich of Veldeke, but that would probably be the utter amount of epic texts whose canonicity is out of question. This canon is not only limited in amount, but also in time, because all the texts mentioned here were created in the classical period of Middle High German literature around 1200 when the *Staufer* reigned the Empire. The epic works of later times were usually considered as epigenous and of lesser value, especially by earlier scholarship, and, even today, one has to admit that many of them do seem a bit too stereotyped for modern taste.

Therefore, an average history of medieval German literature that aims to cover more than just a few works normally consists of a core of classical works and some additional texts (Haug 1987, 259). Where the core of the canon is rather stable, the margins of the canon are vague

---

[2] See the short summary of the discussion on this well debated passage in the commented edition of Eberhard Nellman (1994, 2:517-18).

[3] See also Haustein (2001). Haustein equally stresses the traditional limitation of the German medieval canon: "Der 'innere' Kanon der Literatur des 13. Jahrhunderts ist weitgehend mit dem des 19. und frühen 20. Jahrhunderts identisch. Er ist auf die überschaubare Zahl literarisch ambitionierter Werke konzentriert." ["The 'inner' canon of the 13th century is widely identical with the one of the 19th and the early 20th century. It is concentrated on an overseeable number of literary ambitious works."],141. This limitation is mainly based on the nationalistic-idealistic paradigm from the beginning of German philology in the 19th century, see ibidem; also Gumbrecht (1973), Roloff (2003), and Classen (1993). The development of the 'inner' canon of the 13th century is discussed in Henkel (2005).

and undetermined because there is presumably no consensus on which additional works belong to it.

II

Especially in medieval literature, which can normally only be traced in non-authorised copies, attempts to establish a canon of classical works depend highly on the establishment of canonical editions of these works. Therefore, it is not all too surprising that most of the classical works of the core of the canon were first edited by Karl Lachmann, the founding father of systematic textual criticism and the discipline of German philology. Lachmann edited the *Nibelungenlied*, the *Iwein*, the *Willehalm* and the *Parzival*; only Gottfried's *Tristan* was neglected by Lachmann, because it appeared morally too questionable for him.[4] Some of these editions are still authoritative today, which means that Lachmann established the canonical form for a majority of the most important texts of Middle High German literature.[5]

Amongst the peripheral aspects of this canonised form, ranks the fact that Lachmann tried to structure most of his edited texts in units of thirty verses because he believed that this segmentation was a formal principle that served as a basic guideline for the epic poets of the classical period (Lachmann 1836, 162-63). This formal principle can be seen in its most distinct form in *Parzival*, for instance in several name lists which contain exactly thirty lines.[6] As a consequence, even today, the text is counted in units of thirty lines.

The thirty-line units are not only present in Lachmann's edition, they are also reflected in the manuscript transmission because quite a few manuscripts structure their text with initials that are repeated every thirtieth line, as can be seen e.g. in the Sankt Gallen codex 857 (Figure 1).

---

[4] See Lachmann's letter to Jakob Grimm from the 11th December 1819: "Den weichlichen und unsittlichen Gottfried kann ich kaum lesen" ["I am hardly able to read the softish and immoral Gottfried"], published in Leitzmann (1927, 15).

[5] For an overview on Lachmann's editorial impact see Ganz (1968) and Meves (2000).

[6] Compare e.g. the verses 770,1-30, 772,1-30 and 791,1-30 and their analogous lay-out (each unit takes one side) in the latest adaption of Lachmann's edition by Schirok (2003). Schirok also offers a critical survey on Lachmann's thirty-lines theory (LXXXVI-LXXXVII).

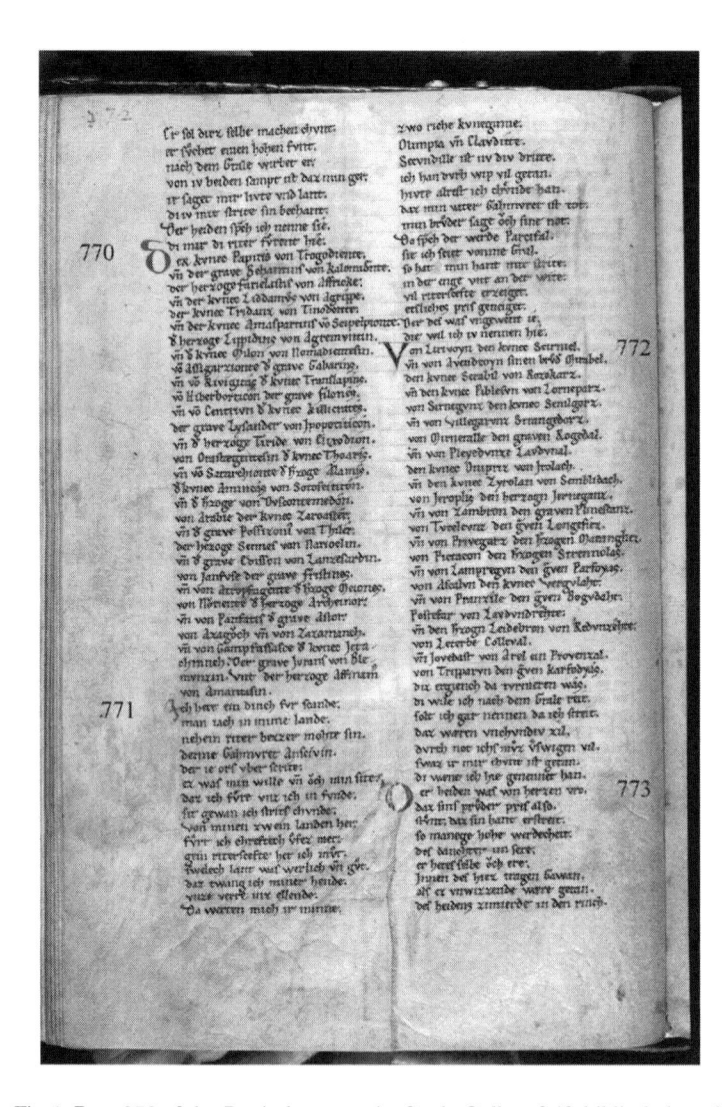

Fig. 1. Page 272 of the *Parzival*-manuscript Sankt Gallen, Stiftsbibliothek, cod. 857. The numbers 770-773 indicate the beginning of the thirty-line-units corresponding to Lachmann's edition.

Hence, there is some truth in Lachmann's finding. Unfortunately, the principle does not work for all parts of the text. Especially at the beginning, the text does not seem to be structured in these units at all. But still, the whole sum of verses can be evenly divided by thirty. Therefore, one might tend to believe that the thirty-line sequence is still a kind of hidden basis for text segmentation, even in those alternatively structured parts at the beginning.

But if we look closer at the text of the edition and its differences compared to the manuscript evidence, we will see that the fact that the verses add up to a multiple of thirty cannot be reached without some editorial tricks. As Lachmann already realised, the transmission of *Parzival* splits into at least two major groups: the version *D and the version *G. Owing to his method of textual criticism, Lachmann believed these versions to be two descendants of one original text, but he had to admit that very often it is impossible to decide which of these versions provides the "better" or more authentic text.[7] If we repeat the word count for both of these versions separately, we will find out that none of them transmit an exact multiple of thirty verses. In version *D for instance, there are twenty-two verses missing, which appear in *G.[8] It could be assumed that these verses were left out of a copy that was the basis for the *D version, but it is conspicuous that none of them are necessary to the plot and they look a bit superfluous.

Thus, just as those verses might have been omitted in *D, they might equally have been added in the *G-version. I would like to demonstrate this with an example: Verses 654,23-26 from Lachmann's edition report an emotional change in one of the main heroes in *Parzival*, the knight Gawan, in a two-fold manner:

> Gâwâns sorge gar verswant:
> niht wan freud er im herzen vant.
> Gâwân ûz sorge in fröude trat.
> den knappen erz verswîgen bat.
>
> ["Gawan's anxiety vanished entirely; He found nothing but joy in his heart. Gawan stepped out of anxiety into joy. He entreated the squire to keep it secret."]

This sounds a bit repetitive, and, in fact, if we look at versions *D and *G separately, we will see that neither individual version has this whole text, but only one of the pair of verses: *D has the first two lines, *G the second two lines. Only in a manuscript from the 14th century (Heidelberg, cpg.

---

[7] See the preface of Lachmann's edition, reprinted in Schirok (2003, XI-XXVI).

[8] The verses 17,1-2, 52,3-8, 101,3-4, 103,3-4, 140,1-2, 172,5-6, 185,17-18, 203,23-24 and 654,25-26 of Lachmann's edition. For a discussion of these verses see Bonath (1970/71, 1: 124-26). The missing verses of *G are listed ibidem, 2:107-08.

364), which might have drawn from both groups, do we find the "whole" text as it appears in Lachmann's edition. This is no great surprise since this manuscript appears to have a mixed text of both versions elsewhere too (Bonath 1970/71, 2:180-87). It is somewhat paradoxical that Lachmann, who strived to reconstruct the original text, in this case follows such a late manuscript that actually has to be considered not very reliable from the point of view of his own school of textual criticism, in appearing to be a contaminated version, obviously drawn from two different sources.

Thus, if we look at the manuscript evidence, it appears to be more likely that these two pairs of verses were alternative phrasings of both groups. As can be seen from this example, the problem boils down to the question whether it is legitimate to compile the texts of two different versions, such as *D and *G to form a complete reconstructed text. As Joachim Bumke (1996) suggested in a recent influential study on the transmission of the so-called *Nibelungenklage*, a text which is basically an adjunct to the famous *Nibelungenlied*, it might be more appropriate in the interest of categorising Middle High German literature to move away from the idea that there was only one original text at the base of the transmission and rather proceed from different versions of the text.

It is very significant that such versions can be found in the transmission of almost any Middle High German epic. Although it is unclear whether this division into early versions results from the specific medieval conditions for the production of literature or whether it is a methodological problem and that we cannot penetrate deeper into the history of the transmission,[9] it will inevitably have consequences for incorporating a specific text-form into the classical corpus. Rather than to establish one canonised text that integrates all different versions, it would be better to consider various versions that could offer a different scope to the text — the latter we have seen in the case of the *Parzival*-transmission.

But nevertheless, if we claim to take into account the differences between those versions, this does not mean that their similarities should be overlooked. Of course, the versions of a text match in many ways. Thus, as in the history of the Middle High German literature, there is a stable canonical core of the text that is surrounded by a rather indeterminate margin, which can differ in the specific versions.

---

[9] See the critical discussion of Bumke's concept in Hausmann (2001).

In fact, our studies at the Berne *Parzival*-project[10] showed that the broader textual deviations do often occur at places which mark transitions of different passages. Hence, one could say that textual variance often sparks off at the margins of rather stable episodes and provides different frames for the events of the plot.

I will give an example of this phenomenon. In our research at the *Parzival*-project, we found out that it is likely that more early versions of the text existed than simply the two that Lachmann suggested (Schöller 2009, Viehhauser 2009). These further versions, called *m and *T, are transmitted only rudimentarily, so that they can only be reconstructed for parts of the text. A passage where version *m shows a very distinct variance can be found at the beginning of the 553rd thirty-line unit, which marks a noticeable break in the story. The subordinate hero of *Parzival*, the knight Gawan, is about to meet his most important adventure, the liberation of the bewitched castle *Schastel marveile*.

	Lachmann	version *m
553,1	*Grôz müede im zôch diu ougen zuo:*	*Gros mŭde im zoch die ougen zu̇*
	sus slief er unze des morgens fruo.	*Sus slief er vntz des morgens fru̇*
		Der nu̇ welle der verneme
		Ob ym sin mu̇t gesceme
		Hie slichet ein aufentur her
		Des bin ich gawanes wer
		Die brieffet man zu̇ sollicher not
		Die niht glihet wan der tot
		Sy pfliget angestlicher sit
		Doch fert do pris vnd ere mitt
		Wem alda gelinget
		Dar nach sy frȯde bringet
		Nu̇ min her gawan gepflag
		Gu̇ter ru̇we vncz an den tag
553,3	*do rewachete der wîgant.*	*Do erworhtte der wigant*

In the conventional text the narrator only depicts how Gawan goes to sleep the evening before and awakes in the morning. (Translation: "Great weariness dragged his eyelids down. Thus he slept till early morning. Then the warrior awoke"). In version *m the narrator is more talkative, he announces dangerous adventures and prepares the audience for the following story (Translation: "Great weariness dragged his eyelids down.

---

[10] The project aims at a new electronic edition of the text that is based on a solid exploration of its transmission-history, see Stolz (2002; 2003).

Thus he slept till early morning. Who now is willing can hear the following story if he is brave enough: An adventure is sneaking up here now, which — and therefore I am Gawan's warrantor — equals to nothing but death itself. It brings along fear, but also prize and honour. For, to whoever passes it, it will bring joy. So after Sir Gawan had rested till the break of day, he awoke").

The verses of *m do not change the course or the outcome of the adventure, but they provide a different setting for the episode. Lachmann, who was only interested in a presumed original, regarded them as a non-authorised addition to the canonical *Parzival*-text and therefore banned them in the apparatus, where they have been hardly ever noticed since. However, our research showed that there can be found quite a few more of these transitional passages in the text of version *m, which can not be disregarded as isolated idiosyncrasies of some confused scribes, but reveal a distinct intention to form the text (Viehhauser 2009, 174-236). Of course, the text of *m does not seem to be aesthetically superior compared to the conventional text, at least if we judge it from a modern point of view, and there is absolutely no reason to privilege this version over the other forms of the text. But my point is not to propose that those lines should be in the one canonised text; rather I would like to suggest that we should consider more than one canonised text and provide the reader with an edition that makes it possible to view the different versions in their entirety.

III

Before I present the editorial solution to this problem that we found at the Berne Parzival-project, I want to go just one or two steps further in rethinking the concept of the margins of the canon. When I discussed the transitional "plus"-verses of version *m, I left out a detail that appears in most of the manuscripts of the group (Figure 2).

After the first two conventional lines that are shared by all different versions (553,1-2), a heading can be found which announces the following adventure of the castle *Schastel marveile* and even a drawing that depicts a motif from the episode. It is not certain, whether this heading was added at the same level as the additional verses, but it is quite clear that the heading has the same function, namely to mark the transition to the next episode more clearly.

Fig. 2. Page 359r of the *Parzival*-manuscript Vienna, ONB, cod. vind. 2914.

According to Gerard Genette, headings belong to the *paratext*, textual elements that surround the actual text (Genette 1987). They accompany the text at its margins. But as can be seen here by this functional similarity, the boundaries between text and *paratext* are often blurred and not clearly defined. This is even more evident in the case of rhymed headings, as in the following example.

Gabriel Viehhauser On the Margin of the Canon

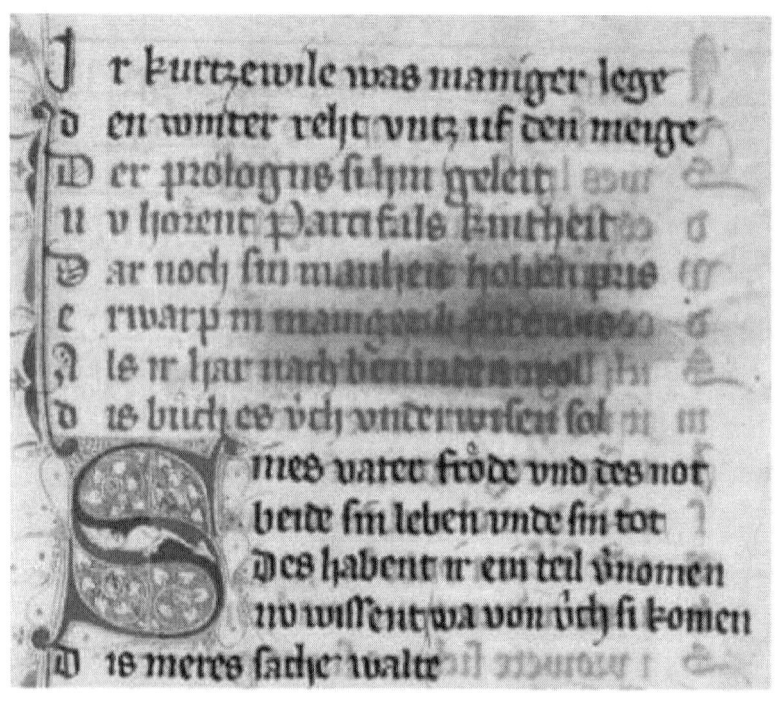

Fig. 3. Page 20r of the *Parzival*-manuscript Karlsruhe, Badische Landesbibliothek, Codex Donaueschingen 97

Figure 3 shows a part of a page from a 14th century manuscript from Strassburg, sometimes called the *Rappoltsteiner Parzival*, because it was commissioned by Ulrich of Rappoltstein, an Alsatian nobleman (Wittmann-Klemm 1977, Bumke 1997, Scholz 1987). The heading refers to a so-called *prologus*, which is basically an individual insertion into the *Parzival*-text that was added by this specific manuscript, and marks the transition between this prologue and the story of Parzival's childhood. [Translation: "The prologue has ended; now listen to the story of Parzival's childhood, who gained high prize because of his bravery, as the book will show you."] If the heading had not been written in red, it would have been impossible to discern these lines from the main text; they would have appeared as a "normal" transitional passage.

Apart from the prologue, the Rappoltstein manuscript offers further genuine additions that are very extensive. For instance, there is a broad translation of several continuations of the French *Perceval*-text which is inserted right inside the conventional text. This piece of text was given the name *der nüwe Parzifal* ["the new Parzival"] and canonised as a work of its own in literary histories. It can normally be found in the group of the post-classical, "epigenous" epics, and thus belongs to the additional, more marginal texts of the Middle High German canon.

Since there is no clear separation between the conventional "old" *Parzival* and the new one in the manuscript (Figure 4), because the different verses are only held apart by headings but are not detached otherwise (e.g. with a page-break), we can see once again how the boundaries between canonised texts and their marginal additions are blurred. The canonised text of *Parzival* is extended by an additional piece of text that could be regarded as an independent work with its own canonical dignity, though the texts are almost indistinguishable in the manuscript that transmits them.

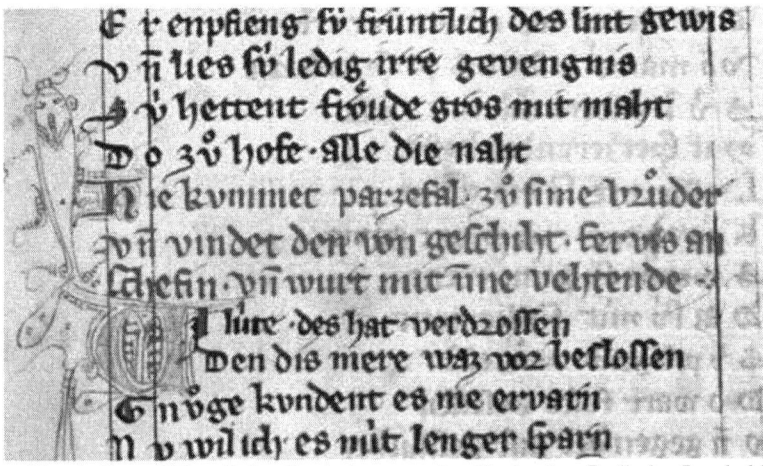

Fig. 4. Page 302r of the *Parzival*-manuscript Karlsruhe, Badische Landesbibliothek, Codex Donaueschingen 97. The lines before the heading are the last verses of the "new" *Parzival*. The heading, which only announces a new episode, but does not refer to the change of the texts at all, is immediately followed by the conventional *Parzival*-text.

As many other antecedent or sequel texts of classical Middle High German show — there are, for instance, continuations or prequels of the *Nibelungenlied*, the *Tristan*, the *Erec* and the *Willehalm* — this clash of canonised and uncanonised texts is not at all uncommon in medieval literature and its transmission. The "whole" codex has often more to offer than the "whole" text that can be read in a canonised edition. More theoretically speaking, medieval codices quite frequently provide divergent boundaries between texts and their trans-texts. They define different scopes of inter- and infra-textuality than the ones found in literary histories. It might have appeared a categorical leap at first to discuss two concepts of canonisation at the same time, the canonisation of classical authors as encountered in literary histories on the one hand and the canonisation of a specific text-form in editions on the other, but it is likely not as imprecise as it may seem to link these two nuances of the term, especially in the field of medieval literature. After its "material turn" in the past decades,[11] German medieval philology tends to put the reliability of concepts such as "authorship" and "authentic work" more and more into question and rather defines the status of texts through the (material) aspects of their transmission.[12] It might be due to pragmatic reasons that so far literary histories have borne the consequences of these new insights even less than editions,[13] but the awareness of the history of transmission should certainly be a guideline for both of these forms in their selection and canonisation of texts.

IV

The shown diversity of the transmission and the precarious status of medieval texts confront the editor with a difficult task. Thus, to conclude, I would like to give a very brief outlook on a possible solution for an edition of *Parzival* that tries to provide more than one canonised text, but also restricts the material in some ways so that it remains presentable and manageable. As a result of our research within the *Parzival*-project on the transmission-history of the text, which, as I mentioned before, suggested that there existed at least four early versions, but also showed the difficulties of their reconstruction due to their rudimentary transmission, we decided to establish a variable editorial model that presents three to four base-texts of these early versions, depending on their visibility in the transmission (see Appendix I). The differences between the versions are marked in bold. Each version has its own apparatus; the apparatus itself is split into variants concerning the structure of the text (like initials or headings) and relevant semantic and linguistic variants.

---

[11] Concise surveys on recent paradigm shifts can be found in Bumke (1996, 3-88) and Baisch (2006, 1-98).

[12] Even if most scholars would not go as far as Bernard Cerquiglini, who totally dissolves the consistency of medieval texts into the variants of transmission; compare his famous quotation "l'écriture médiévale ne produit pas des variantes, elle est variance." (Cerquiglini 1989).

[13] Though this has been claimed repeatedly: see Ruh (1985), and Bein (2001).

The edition exists in two media formats: one for electronic display on the computer and one for print.[14] This media replication can be achieved very easily by using the application neutral XML-code for our data. Of course, the electronic edition has some advantages regarding the variability of the presentation. The verses of the base-text are linked with the corresponding lines of the apparatus[15] and there is even the possibility to activate a transcription and a facsimile of the individual manuscripts.[16] Thus, there is always an option to retrieve an overview on the complete transmission.

This overview cannot be achieved technically in the print version, therefore we are more limited and forced to select from the plurality of the manuscript material. The only texts that can be provided in their whole extent are the base-texts of the versions, whereas the individual variations of the single manuscripts have to be listed in the apparatus. This means that where Lachmann privileged one text over the rest of the transmission, we privilege three to four texts. Thus, we establish a new canonisation, which, however, is justified by the fact that most of the variants that have wider semantic consequences appear to go back to the early versions. In comparison, the changes in the single manuscripts — except for special cases like the *Rappoltsteiner Parzival* — are rather casual. This might be due to the "hardening" of the texts in the later transmission, when they were no longer so influenced by the semi-oral conditions that were common at the time of their creation.[17] Therefore this peculiarity of medieval transmission allowed us to establish a well arranged presentational form for our edition that is representative and that nevertheless maintains the margins of the canon.

---

[14] Examples of the electronic version can be found online at <http://www.parzival.unibe.ch/editionen.html> [28 September 2010].

[15] Each verse is provided with a specific line-number, which corresponds to Lachmann's counting (e.g. 738.01). Structuring variants are linked through the numeration of the thirty-line-unit, semantic variants through the numeration of the verse. For example, in the verse 738.01 of version *m, the blue colour of the numeration 01 indicates that there is a semantic variant in the verse in some of the manuscripts of the group. A mouse-click on the numeration will lead to the corresponding line in apparatus 2.

[16] By clicking on the short-form-letter of the manuscript in the apparatus or in the navigation-bar at the top of the page.

[17] On this process of the "hardening" of the texts in the 13th century see Bumke (1996, 80-84).

Appendix: Print edition of *Parzival* 738,1-30

*D

738 **M**în kunst mir des niht witze gît,
daz ich **gesage** disen strît
bescheidenlîch, als er ergienc.
ieweders ouge blic enpfienc,
5 daz er den andern komen sach.
sweders herze **dar umbe** vreuden jach,
dâ stuont ein **trûren** nâhe bî.
die lûtern truopheite vrî,
ieweder des andern herze truoc;
10 ir vremde was heinlîch genuoc.
Nûne mag ich **disen heiden**
von dem getouften niht gescheiden,
si**ne wellen** haz erzeigen.
daz solt in vreude neigen,
15 die sint erkant vür guotiu wîp.
ieweder durch vriundinne lîp
sîn verch gein **der herte** bôt.
gelücke **scheidez** âne **tôt**.
Den lewen sîn muoter tôt gebirt,
20 von sînes vater galme er **lebendec** wirt.
dise **zwêne wâren ûz** krache **erborn**,
Von maneger tjost **nâch** prîse erkorn.
Si kunden ouch mit tjoste,
mit sper **zerender** koste.
25 **Leischierende** si die zoume
kurzten unt tâten goume,
swenne si **punierten**,
daz si **niht** failierten.
si pflâgens **unvergezzen**.
30 dâ wart vaste gesezzen

D

---
6 sweders] swederz D **17** herte] herten D

*m

mîn kunst mir des niht *witz*e gît,
daz ich **gesage** disen strît
bescheidenlîch, als er ergienc.
ietweders ougen blic enpfienc,
5 daz er den andern komen sach.
ietweders herz **dar umbe** vröude jach,
dâ stuont ein **trûren** nâhe bî.
swie vrömede ietwederm sî,
daz er des andern herz truoc,
10 ir vremde was heimlîch **doch** genuoc.
Nû mac ich **niht gescheiden**
den getouften von dem heiden,
si **wellent** haz erzeigen.
daz solt in vröude neigen,
15 die sint erkant vür guoten wîp,
wan ietweder durch vriundin lîp
sîn verch gegen **der hurte** bôt.
g*l*ück **scheidet daz** âne **nôt**.
den lewen sîn muoter *tôt* gebirt,
20 von sînes vater galm er **lebendic** wirt.
dise **ûz** krach **sint erborn**,
von maneger just **nâch** prîs erkorn.
si kunden ouch mit juste,
mit sper **zierende** koste.
25 **l**eisierende si die zoume
kurz*t*en und tâten goume,
wan si **punierten**,
daz si **nihi**t failierten.
si pflâgens **unvermezzen**.
30 dâ wart vaste gesezzen

---
m n o V V'

---
11 *Großinitiale* n *Initiale* V *Überschrift:* Also parcifal vnd der heiden mit einander stritten m (n)

1 *Die Verse 737.15–738.4 fehlen* V' · witze] mýnne m **4** *Die Verse 738.4–5 fehlen* o **5** daz er] Jr ietlich V' **6** Jr keiner ouch da nit ensprach V' · ietweders] Sweders V **7** *Die Verse 738.7–12 fehlen* V' · dâ] Do m n o V **8** swie vrömede] Die fröde m (n o) · sî] by vnd sÿ m **9** herz] herczen o · **11** *Die Verse 738.11–739.3 fehlen* o · mac] enmag V · gescheiden] bescheiden n **13** Sie beide ir sper do neigeten Vnd einander do erzeigeten Eine starke iust die was gros Daz man an in beiden sie kos V' **14** *Die Verse 738.14–739.6 fehlen* V' **15** vür guoten] vor gûten m n fúr gúte V **16** wan] Wenne n Wande V · ietweder] ieweder V **17** hurte] herte V **18** glück] Slug m · scheidet daz] scheide es V · nôt] [*]: lebende V · wirt] wúrt V **22** nâch] vs n [*]: vs V **23** kunden] kvndent V **24** sper zierende] sperzierender n sperzerender V **25** leisierende] [Lassier*]: Lassierten V **26** kurzten] Kurtzen m n **27** wan] Wenne n Swenne V · punierten] pumierten n **28** niht] *om*. m **29** unvermezzen] vnuergessen V **30** dâ] Do m n V

*G

Mîn kunst mir des niht witze gît,
daz ich sage disen strît
bescheidenlîch, als er ergienc.
ietweders ougen blic enpfienc,
5 daz er den andern komen sach.
sweders herze vröude jach,
dâ stuont ein trôst nâhen bî.
die lûtern tumpheit vrî,
ietweder des andern herze truoc;
10 ir vremde was heinlich genuoc.
nûne mac ich disen heiden
von dem getouften niht gescheiden,
sine wellen haz erzeigen,
daz solt in vröude neigen.
15 die sint erkant vür guotiu wîp.
ietweder durch vriundinne lîp
sîn verch gein der herte bôt.
gelücke scheide si ân den tôt.
den lewen sîn muoter tôt gebirt,
20 von sînes vater galme er lebende wirt.
dise wâren ûz krache erborn,
von maniger tjost ûz brîse erkorn.
si kunden ouch mit tjoste.
mit sper zerender koste
25 leisierten si die zoume,
kurzten si unde tâten goume,
swenne si punierten,
daz si iht failierten.
si pflâgen unvergezzen,
30 dâ wart vaste gesezzen

G I L M Z Pr24

1 *Initiale* L Z Pr24 3 *Initiale* I 19 *Initiale* I

1 des] *om.* Z 2 sage] gesage L M Z Pr24 3 bescheidenlîch] Beschemliche L · ergienc] gienc M 4 ietweders] Jetweder L. Jclicher M · ougen] ovge L Z Pr24 · blic] bliche I L (Z) 6 sweders] Beders L. Widers M Jetweders Z · vröude] darvnmme vroide M (Z) 7 trôst] truren M (Z) 8 die] der e I · tumpheit] trvpheit Z 9 ietweder] Jetwederre L Pr24 Jclichir M 10 heinlich] eyn heymmetich M 11 mac] mage Pr24 · disen heiden] niht gescheiden L 12 niht gescheiden] disen heiden L. 14 solt] sol I · neigen] geben neigen L. 15 die] Si M 16 ietweder] Jetwederre L Z Pr24 Jclichir M 17 herte] herre I 18 scheide] schiet L · den tôt] not I 20 sînes] siner I des L · lebende] lebendic I Z (Pr24) lebin M 21 dise] Dise zcwene M (Z) · krache] hoher art I · erborn] Geborn I (M) 22 ûz] zû I 23 sper] spern I L · zerender] ze ender G 25 leisierten] Zcu yserten M Lesiernde Z 26 kurzten si] kurztans I kvrtzten Z 27 swenne] Wenne L (M) 28 iht] niht L (M) Z Pr24 29 si pflâgen] des phlagen si I

*T

Mîn kunst mir des niht witze gît,
daz ich gesage disen strît
bescheidenlîche, als er ergienc.
ietweder sîte, si ougen blicke enpfienc,
5 daz er den andern komen sach.
ietweders herze darumbe vreude jach,
dâ stuont ein trûren nâhe bî.
der lûtern tumpheit vrî,
ietweder des andern herze truoc;
10 ir vremede was heimelîche genuoc.
nûne mac ich disen heiden
von dem getouften niht gescheiden,
si enwellen haz erzeigen.
daz solde in vreuden neigen.
15 die sint erkant vür guotiu wîp.
ietweder durch vriundinne lîp
sîn verch gein dem herzen bôt.
gelücke scheide si âne den tôt.
den lewen sîn muoter tôt gebirt,
20 von sînes vater galm er lebendic wirt.
dise zwêne wâren zuo krache geborn,
von maneger jost ûz prîse erkorn.
si kunden ouch mit joste.
mit spere zerender koste
25 leisiereten si die zoume,
kurzeten si und tâten goume,
wanne si gepungiereten,
daz si niht fallieren.
si pflâgen unvergezzen,
30 dâ wart vaste gesezzen

U W Q R

1 *Initiale* W R

1 Mîn] Mine U 3 er ergienc] der ginck Q 4 ietweders augenblick entpfieng W (Q R) · ietweder] Jequeder U 6 ietweders] Weder daz U Weders Q Deweders R · jach] des iach R 7 *Vers 738.7 fehlt* U · dâ] Do W Q · ein] en R 8 der] Die Q R · lûtern] luttrem R 9 ietweder] Jequeder U Jetwedrer R · herze truoc] herzen by im trûg R 10 heimelîche] haimlich W (Q R) 11 nûne] Nene Q · mac] enmag R 13 enwellen] wöllen W (Q R) · haz] [b*z]: haz U 14 daz] Die W · solde] sett R · vreuden] fröde W (Q R) 15 sint] sein W seint Q · vür] durch Q 16 ietweder] Jequeder U 17 verch] werck Q [*]: Roch R · dem herzen] der herte W Q R 18 scheide si] schaide ich W sy schoide R 20 vater] varers Q · galm] galm vnd geschey R · lebendic] lebend W 21 zwêne] zwen R · zuo] auß W vser R · geborn] erborn W gancz erborn R 22 maneger jost] mengen strit R 23 *Versfolge 738.24–23* U · jost] tiosten Q ir tiosts R 24 spere zerender] sperzernder W (Q R) · koste] kosten Q 25 leisiereten] Lersiereten U Leifirten Q Lisierten R · zoume] zeime U 26 tâten] tatens W 27 wanne] Wan Q · gepungiereten] pungierten W (Q R) 30 dâ] Daz U Do W Q

Bibliography

Baisch, Martin. 2006. *Textkritik als Problem der Kulturwissenschaft. Tristan-Lektüren*, 1-98. Berlin and New York: de Gruyter.
Bein, Thomas. 2001. "Zum Umgang mit handschriftlichen Autorzuweisungen: Bilanz und Vorschläge für eine literaturhistoriographische Handhabe." In *Entstehung und Typen mittelalterlicher Lyrikhandschriften. Akten des Grazer Symposiums 13. – 17. Oktober 1999*, edited by Anton Schwob and András Vizkelety, 15-36. Bern et. al.: Peter Lang.
Bonath, Gesa. 1970/71. *Untersuchungen zur Überlieferung des Parzival Wolframs von Eschenbach*. Lübeck and Hamburg: Matthiesen.
Bumke, Joachim. 1996. "Die vier Fassungen der 'Nibelungenklage.' *Untersuchungen zur Überlieferungsgeschichte und Textkritik der höfischen Epik im 13. Jahrhundert*. Berlin and New York: de Gruyter.
— 1997. "Autor und Werk. Beobachtungen und Überlegungen zur höfischen Epik (ausgehend von der Donaueschinger Parzivalhandschrift G$^\delta$)." In *Philologie als Textwissenschaft. Alte und neue Horizonte*, edited by Helmut Tervooren and Horst Wenzel, 87-114. Berlin: Erich Schmidt.
Cerquiglini, Bernard. 1989. *Éloge de la variante. Histoire critique de la philologie*. Paris: Ed. du Seuil.
Classen, Albrecht. 1993. "Kanon und Kanon-Transgression. Betrachtungen zur mittelhochdeutschen Dichtung. Zugleich ein Einleitung." In *Canon and Canon Transgression in Medieval German Literature*, edited by Albrecht Classen, 1-36. Göppingen: Kümmerle.
Edwards, Cyril, trans. 2004. *Wolfram von Eschenbach. Parzival, Translated by Cyril Edwards, With Titurel and the Love-Lyrics*. Cambridge: D.S. Brewer.
Ganz, Peter F. 1968. "Lachmann as an Editor of Middle High German Texts." In *Probleme mittelalterlicher Überlieferung und Textkritik. Oxforder Colloquium 1966*, edited by Peter F. Ganz and Werner Schröder, 12-30. Berlin: Erich Schmidt.
Genette, Gérard. 1987. *Seuils*. Paris: Ed. du Seuil.
Gumbrecht, Hans-Ulrich. 1973. "'Mittelhochdeutsche Klassik'. Über falsche und berechtigte Aktualität mittelalterlicher Literatur." *Zeitschrift für Literaturwissenschaft und Linguistik* 11: 97-116.
Haug, Walter. 1987. "Klassikerkataloge und Kanonisierungseffekte. Am Beispiel des mittelalterlich-hochhöfischen Literaturkanons." In *Kanon und Zensur. Beiträge zur Archäologie der literarischen Kommunikation*

II, edited by Aleida Assmann and Jan Assmann, 259-270. München: Wilhelm Fink.

Hausmann, Albrecht. 2001. "Mittelalterliche Überlieferung als Interpretationsaufgabe. 'Laudines Kniefall' und das Problem des 'ganzen Textes.'" In *Text und Kultur. Mittelalterliche Literatur 1150-1450*, edited by Ursula Peters, 72-95. Stuttgart and Weimar: Metzler.

Haustein, Jens. 2001. "Kunst- oder Kulturwissenschaft? Zum Kanonproblem der germanistischen Mediävistik." Gerhard R. Kaiser and Stefan Matuschek (eds.), *Begründungen und Funktionen des Kanons. Beiträge aus der Literatur- und Kunstwissenschaft, Philosophie und Theologie*, 139-154. Heidelberg: Winter.

Henkel, Nikolaus. 2005. "Wann werden die Klassiker klassisch? Überlegungen zur Wirkungsweise und zum Geltungsbereich literarisch-ästhetischer Innovation im deutschen Hochmittelalter." In *Tradition, Innovation, Invention. Fortschrittsverweigerung und Fortschrittsbewusstsein im Mittelalter*, edited by Hans-Joachim Schmidt, 441-67. Berlin and New York: de Gruyter.

Lachmann, Karl. 1836. *Zu den Nibelungen und zur Klage*. Berlin: Reimer.

Leitzmann, Albert, ed. 1927. *Briefwechsel der Brüder Jacob und Wilhelm Grimm mit Karl Lachmann*. Jena: Frommannsche Buchhandlung.

Nellmann, Eberhard, ed. 1994. *Wolfram von Eschenbach Parzival. Nach der Ausgabe Karl Lachmanns revidiert und kommentiert von Eberhard Nellmann. Übertragen von Dieter Kühn*. Frankfurt a. M.: Dt. Klassiker-Verlag.

Meves, Uwe. 2000. "Karl Lachmann (1793-1851)." In *Wissenschaftsgeschichte der Germanistik in Porträts*, edited by Christoph König, Hans-Harald Müller and Werner Röcke, 20-32. Berlin and New York: de Gruyter.

Roloff, Hans-Gert. 2003. "Kanon-Modelle im Bereich der Mittleren Deutschen Literatur (1400-1750) und ihre Konsequenzen." In *Zeitenwende - die Germanistik auf dem Weg vom 20. ins 21. Jahrhundert: Akten des X. Internationalen Germanistenkongresses Wien 2000 Vol. 8: Kanon und Kanonisierung als Probleme der Literaturgeschichtsschreibung*, edited by Peter Wiesinger, 79-86. Bern et. al.: Peter Lang.

Ruh, Kurt. 1985. "Überlieferungsgeschichte mittelalterlicher Texte als methodischer Ansatz zu einer erweiterten Konzeption von Literaturgeschichte." In *Überlieferungsgeschichtliche Prosaforschung. Beiträge der Würzburger Forschergruppe zur Methode und Auswertung*, edited by Kurt Ruh, 262-272. Tübingen: Niemeyer.

Schirok, Bernd, ed. 2003. *Wolfram von Eschenbach Parzival. Studienausgabe 2. Auflage. Mittelhochdeutscher Text nach der sechsten Ausgabe von Karl*

Lachmann. *Übersetzung von Peter Knecht. Mit Einführungen zum Text der Lachmannschen Ausgabe und in Probleme der 'Parzival'-Interpretation von Bernd Schirok.* Berlin and New York: de Gruyter.

Scholz, Manfred G. 1987. *Zum Verhältnis von Mäzen, Autor und Publikum im 14. und 15. Jahrhundert. 'Wilhelm von Österreich' – 'Rappoltsteiner Parzifal' – Michel Beheim.* Darmstadt: Wissenschaftliche Buchgesellschaft.

Schöller, Robert. 2009. *Die Fassung *T des 'Parzival' Wolframs von Eschenbach. Untersuchungen zur Überlieferung und zum Textprofil.* Berlin and New York: de Gruyter.

Stolz, Michael. 2002. "Wolframs 'Parzival' als unfester Text. Möglichkeiten einer überlieferungsgeschichtlichen Ausgabe im Spannungsfeld traditioneller Textkritik und elektronischer Darstellung." In *Wolfram von Eschenbach - Bilanzen und Perspektiven. Eichstätter Kolloquium 2000*, edited by Wolfgang Haubrichs, Eckart C. Lutz and Klaus Ridder, 294-321. Berlin: Erich Schmidt.

— 2003. "New Philology and New Phylogeny. Aspects of a Critical Electronic Edition of Wolfram's Parzival." *Literary and Linguistic Computing* 18: 139-150.

Viehhauser, Gabriel. 2009. *Die 'Parzival'-Überlieferung am Ausgang des Manuskriptzeitalters. Handschriften der Lauberwerkstatt und der Straßburger Druck.* Berlin and New York: de Gruyter.

Wittmann-Klemm, Dorothee. 1977. *Studien zum 'Rappoltsteiner Parzifal.'* Göppingen: Kümmerle.

Zschirndt, Christiane. 2002. *Alles, was man lesen muss. Mit einem Vorwort von Dietrich Schwanitz.* Frankfurt a. M: Eichborn.

Medieval Canonicity and Rewriting

A Case Study of the Sigune-figure in Wolfram's *Parzival*

Michael Stolz

As the title indicates, the present article deals with a special aspect of the concept of canon — the one of canonicity and rewriting. In the first section these two terms will be explained; in the second section they will be illustrated regarding the example of the Sigune-figure in Wolfram's *Parzival*.

The concept of canonicity was developed in bible studies; it derives from the question of which books should represent authoritative writings of God's revelation and which should be excluded from the canon as being apocryphal (Bahnsen 1990; Künneth 1988, 562-70). In the field of Old French studies Karl Uitti used this concept to describe literary processes in the age before printing (1994, 133-52). As Uitti puts it, "medieval canoncity [...] includes *both*, the notion of 'authorship' *and* a variable textuality reflecting scribal 'creativity' and refashioning" (1994, 142). In this context, canonicity comprises two levels: an author's text *and* its transformation in the hands of a scribe who introduces alterations and sometimes even new interpretations to the text.

Uitti and his colleagues in French studies call this process rewriting or "réécriture" (Poirion 1981, 109-18). To explain what is meant by medieval rewriting Daniel Poirion coined the term "manuscriture" that denotes an activity of the hand (*manus*) belonging to the body of a person who on his or her part has the status of an author — an author who with his or her authority (*auctoritas*) is responsible for the text and guarantees its authentic status.[1]

Of course, we might not attribute this quality willingly to every medieval scribe.[2] There are a great number of so-called "simple" or "stupid" scribes, who just copy texts, even without understanding them. On the other hand, there are individuals who have left texts that document a

---

[1] "L'écriture médiévale est une 'manuscriture'. C'est une activité, une production qui reste attachée à la main qui écrit, et, par le bras, à l'épaule d'un *auctor*. Cet auteur (non pas l'*acteur* de la littérature orale) est celui qui garantit de son *auctoritas* et qui prend en charge, le texte" (Poirion 1981, 117).

[2] Medieval scribes are dealt in more detail by Rudolf A. Hofmeister (1973); Paul Gerhard Schmidt (1994); Martin J. Schubert (2002).

real act of refashioning.³ These scribes give the impression that texts are handed over from one author to another, even by referring to the authority (*auctoritas*) of the poet whose text they have altered. Scribes of this standing are not just copyists; they may claim to be continuators, compilers or even authors on their own.

The medieval practice of rewriting, in the sense of "réécriture" or "manuscriture", is the reason why the concept of authorship, overlapped by modern ideas of originality and ownership, seems inadequate to describe the process of text production in pre-modern times. Instead, the term "canonicity", suggested by Uitti, takes into account the variable and fluid character of medieval textuality.

One famous representative of medieval canonicity is the scribe Guiot who is named in the equally famous manuscript Bibliothèque Nationale, fr. 794, fol. 105r, written in the second quarter of the 13th century, that assembles texts composed by Chrétien de Troyes and some other authors (ms. A, containing also Wace's *Roman de Brut*).⁴ In fact, Guiot proves to have adapted Chrétien's epic poems such as *Yvain* or *Perceval* by downgrading the amazing aspects and by introducing a more rationalist note to the texts.⁵

In the German middle ages, we find a comparable case in the Codex germanicus monacensis 19 (Cgm 19) from around 1250 that is preserved in the Bavarian State Library in Munich.⁶ This manuscript gathers texts composed by Wolfram von Eschenbach: his *Parzival* and *Titurel*, and some of his dawn-songs. As far as the *Parzival* is concerned, the text transmitted in Cgm 19 can be shown to be a carefully abridged version — an example shall be given later on.

---

³   More recently, scribal activities of this kind are considered in the context of "retextualisattion" and "transferences", i.e. medieval manners of reproducing such as retelling, translating, and the shift from text to image (Bumke 2005; Hausmann 2001, 2005).

⁴   Cf. Keith Busby (1993, 2:28-31) and Lori Walters, who refers to Guiot as follows: "copiste, continuateur, compilateur et auteur à différents moments de sa carrière. […] le même personnage exerce la double fonction de copiste du travail d'autrui et d'auteur à son propre compte" (1985, 316-17).

⁵   Cf. Walters: "[L]es modifications de Guiot vont dans le sens de la rationalisation par une tendance à la suppression des effets du merveilleux" (1985, 314), after Poirion (Poirion 1981). Cf. also Uitti and Greco, with slightly different observations: "he downplays Chrétien's playfulness and humor" (1994, 141).

⁶   Cf. Peter Jörg Becker (1977, 82-85); Martin Baisch (2006, 109-32); Michael Stolz (2008).

In his *Parzival*, composed in the early 13th century, Wolfram refers to Chrétien de Troyes as his source; but he also mentions a mysterious authority named Kyot that has never been able to be identified. Some scholars believe that Kyot might refer to the French name Guiot, and that there might even be a relation to the namesake scribe who wrote the manuscript Bibliothèque Nationale, fr. 794.[7] It is tempting to suppose that Wolfram's double reference to the pair Chrétien and Kyot might reflect the phenomenon of medieval canonicity in Uitti's sense, i.e. the fact that Wolfram dealt with a source that actually was Chrétien's *Parzival* reworked by a scribe in terms of what Poirion calls "réécriture" or even "manuscriture".[8]

In the following, we shall consider acts of rewriting concerning a figure that appears in both Chrétien's *Perceval* and Wolfram's *Parzival*. This is the female cousin of the protagonist, a young lady who is nameless in Chrétien's epic, and who is called Sigune by Wolfram von Eschenbach. In fact, the syllables *Si-gu-ne* form an anagram of the French word *cousine*. In both texts, the girl is mourning her lover who has been killed in a chivalrous combat when introduced into the story. Chrétien puts the scene below an oak tree, whereas Wolfram evokes the idea that Sigune is placed on the branches of a lime tree.[9]

This position detached from the ground has inspired medieval illuminators. One of the illustrations is to be found in a manuscript that contains the *Jüngerer Titurel* (or: *Second Titurel*), a German poem of the end of the 13th century that transforms the unhappy story of Sigune and her lover into an exhaustive encyclopaedic narrative (Munich, Bavarian State Library, Cgm 8470, Austria, Tyrol ?, 2nd quarter of the 15th century, = ms. W, fol. 182v).[10] In the left withered part of the lime tree, we see the lamenting Sigune; in the right blooming part her lover, called Schianatulander, is lying in a coffin. Below this tree, Parzival who has returned from the Grail castle without having saved the king Anfortas by asking the redeeming question speaks to his cousin Sigune.

[7] Cf. the extensive research summary by Joachim Bumke (2004, 244-47).

[8] The idea that Wolfram might have used a manuscript such as Bibliothèque nationale, fr. 794 as his source of Chrétien's *Perceval* is suggested by Eberhard Nellmann (1996, 327-44). Cf. also Jürgen Wolf (2002, 331).

[9] Cf. Verse 3431 by Chrétien de Troyes (1993, 146): "Une pucele soz .i. chaisne"; and verse 249,14-15 by Wolfram von Eschenbach (1994, 1:414): "vor im ûf einer linden saz/ ein magt." See also Nellmann's commentary in his edition (1996, 2:589-90); Susanna Backes (1999, 8-9 and 164-66); and Michael Stolz (2010b).

[10] Cf. Figure 1 and Becker (1977, 130-32); Uta Drecoll (2000, 387); Ulrich Montag and Karin Schneider (2003, 60-63).

Fig. 1. Albrecht, *Jüngerer Titurel*, ms. W (Munich, Bavarian State Library, Cgm 8470, Austria, Tyrol ?, 2nd quarter of the 15th century), fol. 182v – © Bavarian State Library, Munich.

The fact that in the tradition set up by Wolfram Sigune is sitting in the lime tree seems to be caused by a simple confusion of letters — that of *z* and *r* occurring in the Old French prepositions *soz* and *sor*, meaning "below" and "over". In French manuscripts written shortly after 1200 — this is the period when Wolfram wrote his *Parzival* — the letters *z* and *r* are very similar, as the *z* often lacks the tail that helps to distinguish it from the letter *r*.

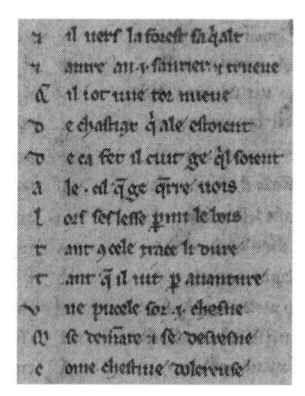

Fig. 2. Chrétien de Troyes, *Perceval*, ms. A (Paris, Bibliothèque Nationale, fr. 794, 2nd quarter of the 13th century), fol. 373vc (detail) – © Bibliothèque Nationale de France, Paris.

For instance, in manuscript Bibliothèque Nationale, fr. 794, fol. 373vc, the similarity of the letters *r* and *z* in final position after the vowel *o* is obvious in the words *tor* ("tower") and *soz* ("over").[11] There is even a manuscript in which the preposition *soz* ("under") is replaced by *sour* ("over"). This variant occurs in manuscript P, written in the fourth quarter of the 13th century: Bibliothèque de l'Université de Mons-Hainaut, cod. 331/206, p. 52b.[12]

Fig. 3. Chrétien de Troyes, *Perceval*, ms. P (Bibliothèque de l'Université de Mons-Hainaut, cod. 331/206, 4th quarter of the 13th century), p. 52b (detail) – © Bibliothèque de l'Université de Mons-Hainaut.

This palaeographic phenomenon suggests that, in one way or another, Wolfram had access to a copy of the French text that represented the young girl sitting *on* a tree. We can imagine that Wolfram or a person reading out the text for him misinterpreted the preposition *soz* as *sor*; but it is also possible that Wolfram already found the reading *sor un chaisne* in the French text that he had at his disposal.

In Wolfram's *Parzival* the passage concerned reads:

> vor im ûf einer linden saz
>
> ein magt, der fuogte ir triwe nôt.
>
> ein gebalsemt ritter tôt
>
> lent ir zwischenn armen (249,14–17).

> (Ahead of him, up in a lime-tree, sat
>
> a maiden whose loyalty caused her distress.
>
> An embalmed knight, dead,
>
> leaned between her arms.)[13]

---

[11]   Cf. Figure 2 containing the two words in the third and tenth line: "Que il i ot une tor nueue — Vne pucele soz .j. chesne," corresponding to the verses 3424 and 3431 (Chrétien 1993, 146).

[12]   Cf. Figure 3, fourth line: "Vne puciele sour .j. kaisne;" (Chrétien 1993, 146), for the manuscript see also Busby (1993, 2:54-56).

[13]   For the Middle High German text see Wolfram von Eschenbach (1994, 1:414); the English translation follows Cyril Edwards (Wolfram 2004, 79). The scene is discussed by Werner

Neglecting the change of letters on which the scene is based, scholars have offered all sorts of interpretations to explain the strange scene. Some have referred to the gesture of *pietà*, i.e. the Virgin Mary holding the dead body of Christ in her arms.[14] Others have looked for the evidence that saints sitting in trees were adored in pre-modern times,[15] others again mentioned the fairy topic of a saving tree (Schwietering 1923, 142) or they related the scene to the tree of life (after *Genesis* 2,9)[16] to be found in medieval iconography. There is also an explanation that refers to the motif of the turtledove sitting on a withered branch after its partner has died (Groos 1968) — and this episode actually occurs in the revised scene that is presented in the text of the *Jüngerer Titurel*.

All these explanations attest that the scene showing Sigune sitting in a lime tree — produced by a simple change of letters — is refashioned not just in medieval literature, but also in modern scholarship. It seems that the scene has provoked a permanent process of rewriting that continues up to the present day.

In the following, it will be shown how the scene was handled in the manuscript transmission of Wolfram's text. In fact, we shall encounter here what Daniel Poirion calls the "manuscriture" of medieval texts.

As far as the phrase *ûf einer linden* is concerned, the text is stable in the ancient tradition of the 13th century. However, there are obvious changes in younger manuscripts. The witnesses concerned belong to the Alemannic region in the south-western parts of the German speaking countries; most of them come from Alsace, a region close to the French language border (*Parzival*-Project *Editionstexte* v. 249,1 and ff.)

Some of these witnesses maintain the position of Sigune sitting in the lime tree, representing the scene not just in words, but also by means of illustrations. This is generally the case in manuscripts produced around 1450 in the workshop conducted by Diebold Lauber in the town of Haguenau. The miniatures serving as title images show Parzival and Sigune, the latter either alone or holding the dead lover in her arms.[17]

Wolf (1965, 3-17); Ute Schwab (1989, 110-42); Claudia Brinker-von der Heyde (1996, 324-31).

[14] Cf. Julius Schwietering (1923, 113-14); Karl Bertau (1983, 259-85); and the research summaries in Brinker-von der Heyde (1996, 325-26); Backes (1999, 161-62).

[15] Cf. Julius Schwietering (1920, 141-42).

[16] Cf. Horst Wenzel (1996, 229-30).

[17] Cf. ms m: Wien, Österreichische Nationalbibliothek, cod. 2914, fol. 160r; ms n: Heidelberg, Universitätsbibliothek, Cpg 339, fol. 185v; ms. o: Dresden, Sächsische Landesbibliothek,

Other manuscripts, however, replace the preposition *ûf* ("on") by *under* ("below"), and thus return to the original version of the French text. This is the case in two witnesses, written shortly after the middle of the 15th century, the one coming from Alsace (ms. L), the other from the Swiss area (ms. R).[18] This alteration might have been provoked by the fact that Chrétien's text was still known in these regions. This also pertains to a manuscript that includes in its version of *Parzival* the German translations of some Old French continuations of the Grail story left unfinished by Chrétien. The witness V, written in Strasbourg during the thirties of the 14th century, reads *ûf einer linden*, but this reading turns out to be the result of a later correction.[19] Perhaps the reading *ûf einer linden* has actually replaced the version *under einer linden* related to Chrétien's French text. One should note in this concern that a scribe systematically revised manuscript V by using a second exemplar.[20]

These examples demonstrate the extent to which Wolfram's text underwent acts of rewriting in its "manuscriture" — its written tradition. In their way, the scribes contributed to refashioning the scene of Sigune and the lime tree.

In another passage of the text, Sigune reproaches Parzival for not having saved the Grail king. With angry words, the "grief-laden maiden" complains having under her eyes her cousin who has failed to ask the redeeming question. She names the marvels that Parzival had seen when he approached the Grail.

> 'ôwê daz iuch mîn ouge siht',
> sprach diu jâmerbæriu magt,
> 'sît ir vrâgens sît verzagt!
> ir sâhet doch sölch wunder grôz

---

cod. M 66, fol. 175r (Wolfram 1985, 23, 70 and 127); further details in: Becker (1977, 79-82). For the sigils cf. Heinzle (1993, 62) and the *Parzival*-Project.

[18] Cf. ms. L: Hamburg, Staats- und Universitätsbibliothek, cod. germ. 6, pag. 114b; ms. R: Bern, Burgerbibliothek, cod. AA 91, fol. 49rb ; further details in: Becker (1977, 92-94 and 96-97).

[19] Cf. ms. V: Karlsruhe, Badische Landesbibliothek, cod. Donaueschingen 97, fol. 41ra ; for further details see Becker (1977, 87-91). The large translated parts of Old French continuations of the Grail story can be found in Karl Schorbach's edition (Parzifal von Claus Wisse und Phillipp Colin 1888).

[20] Cf. for this manuscript, also called the *Rappoltsteiner Parzival*, Wittmann-Klemm (1977); Oltrogge and Schubert (2002); Viehhauser (2009).

> (daz iuch vrâgens dô verdrôz!),
> aldâ ir wârt dem grâle bî:
> manege frouwen valsches vrî,
> die werden Garschiloyen
> und Repans de schoyen,
> und snîdnde silbr und bluotec sper. [...]' (255,2-11)[21]

> (' 'Alas that my eyes see you,'
> said the grief-laden maiden,
> 'since you were too daunted to ask the question!
> But you saw such great marvels there —
> to think that you should have refrained from asking then!
> There you were in the presence of the Grail –
> many ladies free of falsity,
> noble Garschiloye,
> and Repanse de Schoye,
> and cutting silver and bloody spear. [...]' ') (Wolfram 2004, 81)[22]

In this passage, the above-mentioned Cgm 19, preserved in the Bavarian State Library (cf. p. 76), shows signs of rewriting at the early stage of the textual tradition. The text transmitted in this witness (i.e. ms. G in *Parzival* scholarship) lacks the couplet mentioning the two Grail ladies Garschiloye and Repanse de Schoye. Consequently, the manuscript reads that Parzival has seen *manege fröwen valsches fri sniden silber und blötch sper*, that he has seen "many ladies free of falsity who cut something using silver blades" and that he has seen "the bloody spear" (fol. 20vc, end).[23] In this case, the verses seem to allude to a meal evoked by some verses in the context of the Grail ceremony (234,16-24).

Here we encounter one of the numerous abridgements that occur in this manuscript. The shortened version of *Parzival* presented in Codex 19 actually goes back closely to Wolfram's lifetime (cf. Baisch, 2006, 123-31; Stolz 2008, 55-57). It has been written in a professional workshop that is to be situated in the courtly milieu of the emperor Conrad IV, a member of

---

[21] See Wolfram (1994, 1:424)

[22] The scene is discussed in Nellmann's commentary (Wolfram 1994, 2: 594-95), also in his article "Produktive Missverständnisse. Wolfram als Übersetzer Chrétiens" (1994, 143-44).

[23] For details see the electronic edition of the passage at www.parzival.unibe.ch and the digital facsimile: *Münchener Wolfram-Handschrift* (Bayerische Staatsbibliothek Cgm 19), 2008, edited by the *Parzival*-Project.

the Staufen dynasty (Stolz 2008, 35-36). But this manuscript is also famous for another peculiarity.

Besides the text of *Parzival* it transmits the fragmentary poem entitled *Titurel* in which Wolfram reports the story of Sigune and her lover Schianatulander in a more detailed way. The author himself has therefore refashioned a subject matter upon which he had already touched in his main poem *Parzival*. With his strophic *Titurel* Wolfram von Eschenbach turned out to be involved himself in rewriting his own text. And this process of rewriting continues in the *Jüngerer Titurel*, composed by a poet called Albrecht, who with his colossal work tried to accomplish Wolfram's fragmentary text (Neukirchen 2006; Volfing 2007).

On its last four pages, manuscript G presents, as one might say, the most comprehensive form of Wolfram's unfinished *Titurel* (71r-74r). Two other fragments (the mss. H and M) transmit even more incomplete versions. The only other traces of Wolfram's *Titurel* we have are certain strophes integrated in the text of the *Jüngerer Titurel* composed by Albrecht.[24]

An exemplary passage may show the degree of refashioning that is to be found in this restricted tradition. Again, graphical differences play a part in this circumstance. The verses belong to a dialogue between Sigune and Schianatulander who in their beginning adolescence fall in love with each other.

In manuscript G, the strophe 58 appears as follows:

> "Minne — ist daz ein êre? maht dû minne mir tiuten?
> ist daz ein site? kumet mir minne, wie sol ich minne getriuten? [...]"
> (Wolfram 2006, 227)
>
> ("Love — is that something honourable? Can you interpret Love to me?
> Is it a custom? If Love comes to me, how am I to cherish Love? [...]")

With these words Sigune addresses Schianatulander. — In contrast, the version of *Titurel* transmitted in the famous book of Ambras, written by the tollkeeper Hans Ried in the first decades of the 16th century under the

---

[24] The mss. G, H (Wien, Österreichische Nationalbibliothek, Cod. Ser. nova 2663, written by Hans Ried near Bozen, 1504-1516/17, "book of Ambras") and M (Munich, University Library, 8° Cod. ms. 154 [= Cim. 80^b], ca. 1300) as well as the strophes contained in the *Jüngerer Titurel* are considered in the edition of Wolfram's *Titurel* translated and commented by Joachim Bumke and Joachim Heinzle (2006). Cf. also the edition based solely on mss. G, H, M, translated and commented by Helmut Brackert and Stephan Fuchs-Jolie (Wolfram 2002), a shortened students' edition appeared 2003.

patronage of the Austrian emperor Maximilian I, the couplet appears in a different form. The manuscript (ms. H) reads:

> "Ist minne ein si oder ein er? maht dû mir minne bediuten?
> und ist minne ein si, kumt mir minne, wie sol *ich* si triuten? [...]" (Wolfram 2006, 227.)

In this context, the abstract values of honour and custom have changed in categories related to the grammatical gender of love: "Love — is that a she or a he (is it of feminine or masculine quality)? Can you interpret Love to me? — And if Love is of female quality and she comes to me, how am I to cherish Love? [...]"[25]

Again, the variance is based on the difference of a few letters: In the German words, the *êre* ("honour") changes with the personal pronoun *er*, the *site* ("custom") with the personal pronoun *si*. It would be vain to ask which version is the origin of the other. We cannot exclude that the Ambras codex, dating from the early 16th century, transmits an older version that precedes the one contained in manuscript G; but we can equally entertain the contrary notion. The history of the difficulties the passage has caused to scholars would be long to retrace, all the more, as these efforts have not lead to a satisfying result. We have to content ourselves with the truth that we are dealing with two versions that both have their particular signification.[26]

What is interesting in this context is the fact that Albrecht included the strophe in the *Jüngerer Titurel*, and that the numerous manuscripts transmitting this poem present the version in which Signue questions the gender of love: is it of feminine or masculine quality?[27] The insolubility of this question is reflected in the imponderables of textual criticism dealing with this passage. It seems that the canonicity the Signue figure gained in German literature *and* criticism provoked a process of rewriting that doesn't come to an end.

At this point, we might finally ask the question, whether there are cases in which medieval "réécriture" or "manuscriture" can be seen at work. — Indeed there are, as attests the *Parzival* manuscript V', written by the

---

[25] This version might relate to the changing gender of the Old Provençal and Old French words for "love" (*amor/amors*); see the commentary in Wolfram von Eschenbach (2002, 276-77). The English translation is adapted from Edwards' translation (Wolfram 2004).

[26] Cf. Bumke (1973, 179 and 184).

[27] Cf. Wolfram (2006, 226).

middle of the 14th century, that is a supposed duplicate of manuscript V mentioned above.[28]

Within the *Parzival* tradition, this manuscript features an extreme variance: Like V, V' integrates the translations of Old French *Conte du Graal* continuations into the text. This leads to additions against the whole remaining textual tradition of the poem. To give an example, in the text of both manuscripts (and only there) King Arthur accompanies the protagonist while the latter proposes the "question of compassion" during his final visit at the Grail-castle. This exceptional version of the narrative causes numerous textual interventions introduced by the redactors. Now, in spite of these additions, V' shows numerous shortenings against V which are carefully rearranged at the switch points. And sometimes we can even look over the shoulders of the scribe, watching the corrections he has left, when he altered his own written text. Unfortunately, V' conveys only the German translation of the continuations added to *Conte du Graal* as well as the last two books of *Parzival*. All the other parts of the epic were either never treated in this manuscript or were included in a separate volume that is lost now.

We shall now concentrate on a scene contained in the last book of the verse novel, in which Sigune, after her painful affliction, finally dies and is buried beside Schianatulander (Stolz 2010a, 287-91). The passage concerned describes the very significant moment, when Parzival discovers his cousin Sigune who has passed away praying beside Schianatulander's grave in her hermitage. Thereupon Parzival orders the stone coffin lid to be lifted, so that Sigune can be laid to her dead lover. Now Schianatulander's unharmed body becomes visible:

> Schîanatulander schein
> unrefûlt schône balsemvar.
> man leit si nâhe zuo zim dar,
> diu magtuomlîche minne im gap
> dô si lebte, und sluogen zuo daz grap[29]. (804,28 – 805,2)

("Schionatulander appeared
unrotten, handsome, balm-coloured.

---

[28] Rome, Biblioteca Casanatense, cod. 1409; further details can be found in Becker (1977, 89 n. 8). Cf. also Matthias Miller and Karin Zimmermann (2007, 69-71). For the fact that V' is a duplicate of V cf. Michael Stolz (2010a, 286-87).

[29] See Wolfram (1994, 2:370).

> They laid her in there next to him,
>
> she who had given maidenly love to him when she lived,
>
> and closed the grave." (after Wolfram 2004, 257)

In manuscript V these verses appear as follows (the caption below the text will be discussed later):

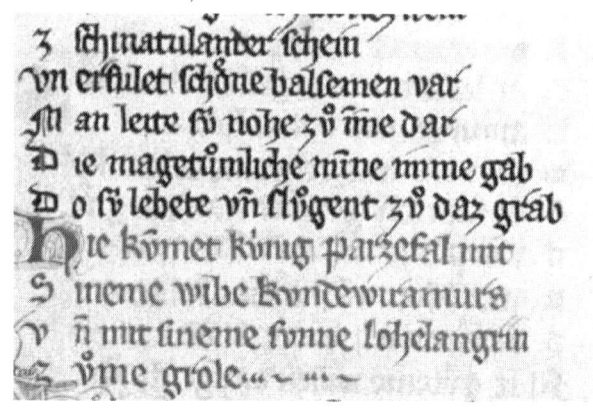

Fig. 4. Wolfram von Eschenbach, *Parzival*, ms. V (Karlsruhe, Baden State Library, cod. Donaueschingen 97), fol. 313va (detail) – © Baden State Library, Karlsruhe.

When Sigune is laid by Schianatulander, his corpse shows no traces of decay. He "appears unrotten, handsome, balm-coloured" or, as manuscript V puts it, slightly modifying the main tradition, he looks *vnerfulet scho°ne balsemen var*. Manuscript V', however, has the following text in this passage:

> Er smacket wol er schein
>
> Vnerfulet wol balsem var
>
> Man leite sie naher zu ime dar
>
> Die magetumliche minne >sy< ime gap
>
> Do sie lebete man sluc zu daz grap

In verse 804,29, the adverb is changed from *scho°ne* ("beautiful", "handsome") to *wol* ("well", namely "well balm-coloured"). The same adverb appears in V' also in the preceding verse where the scribe has significantly altered the wording of V. Instead of the subject-predicate sequence of V (*Zschinatulander schein*, i.e.: "Schianatulander appeared"), followed by the predicative adjectives *vnerfulet scho°ne balsemen var*, V' offers the wording: *Er smacket wol er schein/ Vnerfulet wol balsem var* ("He smelt deliciously, he appeared – or even gleamed – unrotten and perfectly balm-coloured").

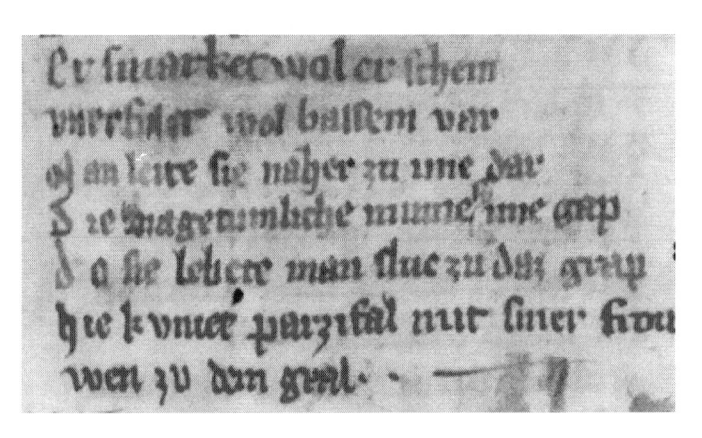

Fig. 5. Wolfram von Eschenbach, *Parzival*, ms. V' (Rome, Biblioteca Casanatense, cod. 1409), fol. 178ra (detail) – © Biblioteca Casanatense, Roma.

What happened here? – The scribe of V' obviously didn't know what to do with the name *Zschinatulander* abruptly mentioned in this passage. The name appears in Wolfram's *Parzival* in yet three other places, situated, however, in the far distant passages of the books III and IX (138,21; 435,19; 440,18 – here in each case verse-filling).[30] The change carried out by the scribe in the present verse can possibly be evidence for the fact that he didn't know the other *Parzival* books and had never copied them.

If one looks at the letter sequence of both verses in mss. V and V' more closely, the following can be observed: V places here – and only here – the letter *Z* at the beginning of the name: the name appears in the form *Zschinatulander*. The scribe of V', however, might have interpreted the initiatory and slightly departed *Z* as an abbreviation for *er*; in any case, he began his verse by the corresponding personal pronoun *er* ("he"). Out of the name itself he made the verb-adverb construction *smacket wol* ("he smelt well" or "he smelt deliciously"). If one compares both letter sequences exactly, one has the impression that the scribe misread the letter chain *schinat* of V as *schmac* (reading *-in-* as *m*, and *t* as *c*), out of which he seems to have gained his verb *smacket* ("smelt"). He could have interpreted the letter chain *-nd-* in the two final syllables of the name *Zschinatu-lander* as a *w-o-l* ligature, what led to the adverb *wol* ("well"). The scribe would have inserted this adverb

---

[30] Manuscript V has the following writings at these places: *Schinoten de lalander* (138,21; fol. 24rb, after correction of a second scribe): *Schinahtulander* (435,19; fol. 69va); Schinatulander (440,18; fol. 70rb, after correction of a second scribe). Other than in 804,28 (fol. 313va), the name appears at these places without the initiatory affricate *Z*.

twice, once in the present, and then in the following verse – and both times against his exemplar V and the whole documentable *Parzival* tradition.

Quite obviously the scribe was unsure of his reading. This can be testified by the fact that almost the whole verse, with the exception of the verb *schein*, was written over an erasure. Other textual manipulations also occur in the surrounding of the line. Against the supposed exemplar V and the whole textual tradition the personal pronoun *sy* ("she") is added in verse 805,1. In this way, the relative pronoun *diu* (which manuscripts of the later Middle Ages often render as *die*) is changed into the definite article *die* belonging to the following syntagm *magtuomlîche minne*; the verse is now independent from the previous and means "(the) maidenly love she gave to him". This modification might be caused by a misunderstanding of the following verse 805,2, whose first part (*dô si lebte*, "when she lived") usually would belong to the previous sentence, meaning: Sigune, during all her lifetime, gave her maidenly love to Schianatulander. The version of V', however, replaces the copula *und* with the personal pronoun *man* (what also occurs in manuscript G) and, by inserting the pronoun *sy* in verse 805,1, seems even to bind the two parts of verse 805,2 together, reading: "when she was still alive, they closed the grave". As (in contrast to manuscript G) V' is lacking any punctual sign between *lebete* and *man*, its text might suggest that Sigune is still not dead, when she is buried

Later on, in verse 805,10 Kyot, the above-mentioned authority that is still puzzling the interpreters of *Parzival*, appears with his Provençal surname: *op der Provenzâl die wârheit las* ("if the Provençal read the truth"). The scribe of V' complemented this reference by the personal pronoun *ich* and wrote: *Ob der prouenzal die worheit >ich< laz* ("if I have read the truth concerning the Provençals"). Finally, there are the captions introducing the following passage that both V and V' have introduced against the other *Parzival* tradition after verse 805,2. V has a more complete version reading *Hie kvmmet kvnig Parzefal mit Sineme wibe kvndewiramurs Vnd mit sineme svnne Lohelangrin Zvᵒme grole*, whereas V' condenses this text as: *Hie kvmet parzifal mit siner frouwen zv dem gral*. In the latter, the names of Parzival's wife *Condwiramurs* and their son *Lohelangrin* (normally *Loherangrin*) mentioned by V are left out.

This obvious tendency of V' towards deletion of names coincides with the work of the scribe at verse 804,28 to which *Schianatulander*'s name fell victim. Another striking fact is that a foreign dry-point gloss, which is unfortunately not visible in the picture, documents that the glossator intended exactly this very name to be written (or perhaps to be restored). In the original manuscript V' the letter sequence *atulander* is still readable on the left side of the verse in question.

The scribe of V' ignored this name, but what emerged under his hands is an imaginary projection with almost olfactory qualities: "He smelt deliciously", as the text says. Yet, the fragrance that exudes from the corpse of Sigune's lover can be associated with the discourse of the chivalric epic poetry of the early 13th century. Wolfram's second epic poem, titled *Willehalm*, may be recalled here. In this text, dealing with combats of Christians and Arabs in southern France, the author states that a beguiling odour would stream out of the corpses of excellent knights, killed in battle on either side (Wolfram 1991).[31] In the course of the copying process the scribe of V' seems to have erased or even annihilated Schianatulander's name and evokes instead his balmy corpse.

The example demonstrates to what extent the rewriting of a text may alter its sense. Manuscript V' is a rare witness that makes scribal work visible. The scribe obviously tried to read his exemplar, to understand, and to interpret the writing and the text he found in his copy. And we can even discern the changes and corrections he inserted during this process. With his attempt to read the text and to write what he thought and imagined he might have seen, he produced a new text. In this concern, the work of the creatively active scribe in manuscript V' is much more palpable than the one of his colleagues in other *Parzival* witnesses that we have encountered in the beginning of this article. Criteria of modern textuality such as "authorship", "genealogy of writing" or even "writing scenes"[32] might not be sufficient to describe these processes of textual production that are always bound to a source the scribe had to deal with. Perhaps in the future, with the help of large textual material, as it is currently gathered in the manuscript transcriptions carried out by the *Parzival*-Project, scribal changes can be analysed in a more systematic way that considers replacements, reorganisations, additions and omissions on different levels such as letters, words, phrases, verses, verse groups and even larger textual segments. These peculiarities of a pre-modern vernacular writing culture are

---

[31] The fragrance of aloe is mentioned in the context of the death of the Christian Vivianz (69,12-15), sugar at the occasion of the death of the heathen Tesereiz (88, 2-11).

[32] Cf. in this context the most useful volumes by Martin Stingelin (2004); Davide Giuriato (2005; 2006).

still to be explored in greater detail, and the notions of "medieval canonicity" and "rewriting" coined by scholars in the field of Old French may well help to tackle phenomena worth studying in the history of both authorship and textual culture. As could be shown, the Sigune-scenes in Wolfram's *Parzival* are "canonical" (in the conventional sense of the term), as they always require a certain configuration of characters (Parzival, Sigune and Schianatulander) and a certain setting (as the lime tree or, at a later stage, the couple's grave), but other details such as positions of certain narrative elements or their forms of appearance may well differ between the witnesses. This is also the reason why the status of "canonical authorship" – the traces that the author Wolfram von Eschenbach has left – are still to be discerned behind what goes on in the fluid writing of the different manuscripts. And in this concern, Karl Uitti is completely right with his statement that "medieval canonicity" is of a special kind: it "includes *both*, the notion of 'authorship' *and* a variable textuality reflecting scribal 'creativity' and refashioning".

Bibliography

Backes, Susanna. 1999. *Von Munsalvaesche zum Artushof. Stellenkommentar zum fünften Buch von Wolframs "Parzival."* Herne: Verlag für Wissenschaft und Kunst.

Bahnsen, Greg. 1990. The Concept and Importance of Canonicity. *Antithesis* (1,5), <http://www.reformed.org/webfiles/antithesis/index.html> [accessed 15 October 2010].

Baisch, Martin. 2006. *Textkritik als Problem der Kulturwissenschaft: Tristan-Lektüren*. Berlin and New York: de Gruyter.

Becker, Peter Jörg. 1977. *Handschriften und Frühdrucke mittelhochdeutscher Epen: Eneide, Tristrant, Tristan, Erec, Iwein, Parzival, Willehalm, Jüngerer Titurel, Nibelungenlied und ihre Reproduktion und Rezeption im späteren Mittelalter und in der frühen Neuzeit*. Wiesbaden: Reichert.

Bertau, Karl. 1983. "Regina lactans. Versuch über den dichterischen Ursprung der Pietà bei Wolfram von Eschenbach." In *Wolfram von Eschenbach: Neun Versuche über Subjektivität und Ursprünglichkeit in der Geschichte*, edited by K. Bertau. Munich: C.H. Beck.

Brinker-von der Heyde, Claudia. 1996. *Geliebte Mütter – mütterliche Geliebte; Rolleninszenierung in höfischen Romanen*. Bonn: Bouvier.

Bumke, Joachim. 1973. "Titurelüberlieferung und Titurelforschung: Vorüberlegungen zu einer neuen Ausgabe von Wolframs Titurelfragmenten." *Zeitschrift für deutsches Altertum und deutsche Literatur* 102:147-188.

———. 2004. *Wolfram von Eschenbach*. 8th ed. Stuttgart and Weimar: J.B. Metzler.

———, et al., ed. 2005. *Retextualisierung in der mittelalterlichen Literatur.* Berlin: E. Schmidt, 2005.

Busby, Keith. 1993. *Les Manuscrits de Chrétien de Troyes: The Manuscripts of Chrétien de Troyes.* 2 vols. Amsterdam and Atlanta: Rodopi.

Chrétien de Troyes. 1993. *Le roman de Perceval.* Edited by K. Busby. Tübingen: Max Niemeyer.

Drecoll, Uta. 2000. *Tod in der Liebe – Liebe im Tod : Untersuchungen zu Wolframs 'Titurel' und Gottfrieds 'Tristan' in Wort und Bild.* Frankfurt: Lang.

Giurato, Davide et al., ed. 2005. *Schreibkugel ist ein Ding gleich mir: von Eisen: Schreibszenen im Zeitalter der Typoskripte.* Munich: Fink. .

———, ed. 2006. *System ohne General: Schreibszenen im digitalen Zeitalter.* Munich: Fink.

Groos, Arthur B. 1968. "Sigune auf der Linde and the Turtledove in Parzival." *Journal of English and Germanic Philology* 67:631-646.

Hausmann, Albrecht. 2001. "Mittelalterliche Überlieferung als Interpretationsaufgabe: 'Laudines Kniefall' und das Problem des 'ganzen Textes.'" In *Text und Kultur: Mittelalterliche Literatur 1150–1450,* edited by U. Peters. Stuttgart, Weimar: Metzler.

———. 2005 "Übertragungen: Vorüberlegungen zu einer Kulturgeschichte des Reproduzierens." In *Übertragungen. Formen und Konzepte von Reproduktion in Mittelalter und Früher Neuzeit,* edited by B. Bussmann. Berlin, New York: de Gruyter.

Heinzle, Joachim. 1993. *Klassiker-Edition heute.* In *Methoden und Probleme der Edition mittelalterlicher deutscher Texte,* edited by R. Bergmann and K. Gärtner. Tübingen: Max Niemeyer.

Hofmeister, Rudolf A. 1973. "In Defense of Medieval Scribes." *Colloquia Germanica* 7: 289-300.

Künneth, Walter. 1988. "Kanon." *Theologische Realenzyklopädie* 17:562-570.

Miller, Matthias, and Karin Zimmermann. 2007. *Die Codices Palatini germanici in der Universitätsbibliothek Heidelberg.* Wiesbaden: Harrassowitz.

Montag, Ulrich, and Karin Schneider. 2003. *Deutsche Literatur des Mittelalters. Handschriften aus dem Bestand der Bayerischen Staatsbibliothek München*

mit Heinrich Wittenwilers Ring als kostbarer Neuerwerbung. Munich: Bayerische Staatsbibliothek.
Münchener Wolfram-Handschrift (Bayerische Staatsbibliothek Cgm 19). 2008. Edited by the *Parzival*-Project.
Nellmann, Eberhard. 1996. "Produktive Missverständnisse: Wolfram als Übersetzer Chrétiens." *Wolfram-Studien* 14:134-48.
———. 1996. "Zu Wolframs Bildung und zum Literaturkonzept des Parzival." *Poetica* 28: 327-44.
Neukirchen, Thomas. 2006. *Die ganze 'aventiure' und ihre 'lere': Der Jüngere Titurel' Albrechts als Kritik und Vervollkommnung des 'Parzival' Wolframs von Eschenbach.* Heidelberg: Winter.
Oltrogge, Doris, and Martin J. Schubert. 2002. "Von der Reflektographie zur Literaturwissenschaft: Varianzen im Rappoltsteiner Parzifal." *Wolfram-Studien* 17: 347-76.
Parzifal von Claus Wisse und Philipp Colin (1331-1336). Eine Ergänzung der Dichtung Wolframs von Eschenbach. 1888. Edited by K. Schorbach. Straßburg and London: n. p.
Parzival-Project. Available from www.parzival.unibe.ch. [Accessed 15 October 2010]
Poirion, Daniel. 1981. "Écriture et Ré-écriture au Moyen Âge." *Littérature* 41: 109-118.
Schmidt, Paul Gerhard. 1994. "Probleme der Schreiber – der Schreiber als Problem." *Sitzungsberichte der wissenschaftlichen Gesellschaft an der Johann Wolfgang Goethe-Universität Frankfurt am Main* 31, 5: 175-86.
Schubert, Martin J., ed. 2002. *Der Schreiber im Mittelalter.* Berlin: Akademie Verlag.
Schwab, Ute. 1989. *Zwei Frauen vor dem Tode.* Brussels: Verhandelingen van de Koninklijke Academie voor Wetenschappen. Klasse der Letteren année 51, n. 132.
Schwietering, Julius. 1920. "Sigune auf der Linde." *Zeitschrift für deutsches Altertum und deutsche Litteratur* 57: 140-43.
———. 1923. "Mittelalterliche Dichtung und bildende Kunst." *Zeitschrift für deutsches Altertum und deutsche Litteratur* 60:113-127.
Stingelin, M., ed. 2004. *Mir ekelt vor diesem tintenklecksenden Säkulum: Schreibszenen im Zeitalter der Manuskripte.* Munich: Fink.
Stolz, Michael. 2008. "Die Münchener Wolfram-Handschrift Cgm 19: Profile einer volkssprachigen 'Autorhandschrift' des 13. Jahrhunderts." In *Introduction booklet to the digital facsimile: Münchener*

Wolfram-Handschrift (Bayerische Staatsbibliothek Cgm 19), edited by *Parzival*-Project. Simbach/Inn: Müller & Schindler, 2008).

———. 2010a. "'Copying processes:' Genetische und philologische Perspektiven." In *Materialität in der Editionswissenschaft*, edited by M. J. Schubert. Tübingen: Niemeyer.

———. 2010b. "Cousine sous le chêne – Sigune sur le tilleul. Réflexions sur la réécriture médiévale." In *Mélanges Claude Lecouteux*, edited by F. Bayard. Paris: Presses universitaires de France.

Uitti, Karl D., and Gina Greco. 1994. "Computerization, Canonicity and the Old French Scribe: The Twelfth and Thirteenth Centuries" *Text: Transactions of the Society for Textual Scholarship* 6:133-152.

Viehhauser, Gabriel. 2009. *Die Parzival-Überlieferung am Ausgang des Manuskriptzeitalters: Handschriften der Lauberwerkstatt und der Straßburger Druck*. Berlin and New York: de Gruyter.

Volfing, Annette. 2007. *Medieval Literacy and Textuality in Middle High German. Reading and Writing in Albrecht's 'Jüngerer Titurel'*. New York and Houndmills/Basingstoke: Palgrave Macmillan.

Walters, Lori. 1985. "Le rôle du scribe dans l'organisation des manuscrits des romans de Chrétien de Troyes." *Romania* 106: 303-325.

Wenzel, Horst. 1996. "Herzeloyde und Sigune. Mutter und Geliebte: Zur Ikonographie der Liebe im Überschneidungsfeld von Text und Bild." In *Eros – Macht – Askese: Geschlechterspannungen als Dialogstruktur in Kunst und Literatur*, edited by H. Sciurie and H.-J. Bachorski. Trier: Wissenschaftlicher Verlag.

Wittmann-Klemm, Dorothee. 1977. *Studien zum Rappoltsteiner Parzifal*. Göppingen: Kümmerle

Wolf, Jürgen. 2002. "Wolfram und das mittelalterliche Buch: Beobachtungen zur literatur- und buchgeschichtlichen Relevanz eines großen Autornamens". *Wolfram-Studien* 17:322-46.

Wolf, Werner. 1965. "Sigune auf der Linde: Vortrag, gehalten in der Sitzung der Societas Scientiarum Fennica am 14. Februar 1964." *Societas Scientiarum Fennica. Årsbok – Vuosikirja* 42 B (4).

Wolfram von Eschenbach. 1985. *Parzival: Die Bilder der illustrierten Handschriften*. Edited by B. Schirok. Göppingen: Kümmerle.

———. 1991. *Willehalm. Translation and commented edition after the manuscript St. Gallen, Stiftbibliothek, cod. 857*. Edited by J. Heinzle. Frankfurt am Main: Deutscher Klassiker Verlag.

———. 1994. *Parzival. Edited and commented by E. Nellmann*. Frankfurt am Main: Deutscher Klassiker Verlag.

———. 2002. *Titurel.* Edited, translated and commented by H. Brackert and St. Fuchs-Jolie. Berlin and New York: de Gruyter.

———. 2004. *Parzival.* Translated by C. Edwards, with Titurel and the Love-Lyrics, and with an essay on the Munich Parzival illustrations by J. Walworth. Cambridge: D.S. Brewer.

———. 2006. *Titurel. Mit der gesamten Parallel-überlieferung des 'Jüngeren Titurel.'* Edited, translated and commented by J. Bumke and J. Heinzle. Tübingen: Niemeyer.

The Beißnerian Mode, the Zellerian Mode, and the Canonical Way of Modern Editing

Upheavals and Deviations in German Editorial Methodology — and its Historiography

Rüdiger Nutt-Kofoth

Since editorial treatment of texts by modern authors began in the 19th century, one question has increasingly come to the fore: How should the variants of textual genesis, which in contrast to the transmission of ancient or medieval texts can often be found in large numbers, and even the whole process of textual development, encompassing the first notes, the following drafts, the fair copies and the printed books, be presented within an edition? In more recent times, there have been several surveys of the academic history concerning German scholarly editing and its treatment of textual genesis with modern German authors (cf. Plachta 2006, 27-45; Plachta 2001, 375-98; Nutt-Kofoth 2005a, 97-110; Nutt-Kofoth 2005b, IX-XXIX; Nutt-Kofoth 2005c). The stages of methodical development seem to be quite clear.

Reinhold Backmann's theoretical reflections of 1924 are generally regarded as a starting point. In a reversal of traditional editorial concepts, Backmann ascribed to the apparatus an "independent value compared with the printed text" and even a "larger amount of significance than the latter". The decisive issue was Backmann's demand that "*textual development*" should be considered the "most important aspect" of editorial conception (Backmann 1924, 638).[1] However, Backmann's article, which was hardly read in the beginning, could make no practicable suggestion about how his ideas could be translated into an editorial technique. It was only Friedrich Beißner who found a solution. He developed a presentation in stair-step form of separated parts of textual genesis related to the edited text and first tested it on manuscripts by Christoph Martin Wieland in 1937/38. From 1943 onwards, he then created the model of this presentation of textual genesis in his Stuttgart Hölderlin edition (Beißner 1938; Nutt-Kofoth 2005b, 142-46; Hölderlin 1943-85). In the 1950s, Hans Zeller developed a different model for the C.F. Meyer edition, namely the

---

[1] "selbständigen Wert gegenüber dem Textabdruck"; "ein Übergewicht an Bedeutung über den letzteren"; "die *Entwicklung* als obersten Gesichtspunkt". Reprinted by Nutt-Kofoth (2005b, 125).

synoptic apparatus which could render textual genesis independently of the edited text. It was first presented in 1958 (Meyer 1958-1996; Zeller 1958 [reprinted Nutt-Kofoth 2005b, 194-214]). Yet the striking difference between Beißner's and Zeller's models was that Zeller's recording system included the most precise possible description of the manuscript record, which Beißner had intentionally done without. While Beißner stressed the interpretative dimension of all editorial activities by using Manfred Windfuhr's dictum "editing is interpretation", Zeller aimed to differentiate between record-related and interpretation-related elements within an edition and to make them visible in this way (Beißner 1964b, 23 ["Edition ist Interpretation"]; Windfuhr 1957, 440 ["*Edition ist Interpretation*"; reprinted Nutt-Kofoth 2005b, 191]; Zeller 1971, 1995).

The implications of Beißner's and Zeller's models have repeatedly been pointed out in detail, so there is no need to do it once again here (cf. Hoffmann and Zils 2005; Nutt-Kofoth 2005d; Waleczek 1994, 131-245). For the time being, it is only important to say that Zeller not only presented his model as a rival concept, but that Beißner immediately viewed Zeller's model as a rival concept too. In the introduction to his article of 1958 Zeller himself described "the history of German editorial technique in the 20th century […] as a chain of reactions" (1958, 356)[2] and thus implicitly announced that the model he was to introduce afterwards was superior to Beißner's. Beißner, in turn, vehemently crusaded against Zeller's model and tried to show "the dangers of the Zellerian example" (1964b, 23: "die Gefährlichkeit des Zellerschen Vorbilds"). This formulation can be understood as an attempt to keep supremacy in matters of editorial procedure since Beißner had virtually managed to canonize his model in the preceding years. In 1953 Hans Pyritz called Beißner's Hölderlin edition a "great scholarly feat" and judged the editorial results to be "the limits of what could be achieved" (1953, 104 and 85: "eine gelehrte Großtat"; "die Grenze des überhaupt Erreichbaren").

Looking back on the history of modern German scholarly editing in 1989, Zeller not only mentioned Pyritz's words as a contemporary example "of a general admiration" for Beißner's achievement, but also remarked that he himself had shared this admiration at first: "I was in complete agreement with the people by whose order I worked when I, like many others too, thought that the questions concerning the apparatus

---

[2] "die Geschichte der germanistischen Editionstechnik im 20. Jahrhundert […] als eine Kette von Reaktionen.." Reprinted by Nutt-Kofoth (2005b, 194).

for the Meyer edition had been solved by Beißner" (1989, 5).[3] But already in the 1950s Zeller had realized that Beißner's system did not meet the requirements of a complete presentation of textual genesis, mainly because the system contained too many "paradigms of variants without recognizable syntagmatic constructions" (1986, 48). As a consequence, Zeller had developed his synoptic mode of presentation to render this aspect more precisely too. In this sense, Zeller viewed in 1989 the early and initially unreserved admiration for Beißner's procedure, which had unprecedentedly and apparently completely made textual genesis visible for the first time, as a "fruitful error which drove his successors to come closer to the required standard." Zeller, who spoke at that time opening the conference of the Association of German Scholarly Editing in Berlin, then modestly kept in the background when, on describing Beißner's achievement in detail, he hinted at the significance of his own work in just one sentence: "A further development created the synoptic apparatus recording several contemporary text witnesses in a score-like manner and thus increasing the meaningfulness of the apparatus and facilitating its use respectively" (1989, 5-7).[4]

As already mentioned, all this has been described on several occasions and in much greater detail. Thus, there would be no need for repetition if Zeller's most recent publication on academic history did not reveal a shift of emphasis concerning these matters. In his contribution of 2003 Zeller writes: "The models of modern genetic editing saw themselves as countermoves to Beißner's model" (2003, 143).[5] This programmatic sentence can be found at the beginning of Zeller's article entitled "The Development of Textual Genetic Editing in the 20th Century" ("Die Entwicklung der textgenetischen Edition im 20. Jahrhundert"), which appeared in the anthology "History of Editorial Procedures from Antiquity to the Present Day: a Survey" ("Geschichte der Editionsverfahren vom Altertum bis zur Gegenwart im Überblick"). The fact that by means of the title Zeller focuses solely on "textual genetic editing" in the 20th century rather than

[3] "einer allgemeinen Bewunderung"; "Ich selbst [...] befand mich in bester Übereinstimmung mit meinen Auftraggebern, wenn ich wie andere die Apparatfragen für die Meyer-Ausgabe durch Beißner für gelöst hielt."; see also Meyer (1958-1996, 5:2, 403).

[4] 5-6: "fruchtbarer Irrtum, der seine Nachfolger dazu trieb, mehr von diesem Anspruch einzulösen"; 7: "Eine andere Weiterentwicklung gelangte zum synoptischen Apparat, der mehrere einander textnahe Zeugen partiturmäßig verzeichnet und damit die Aussagekraft des Apparats weiter steigert bzw. seine Benützung erleichtert."

[5] "Die Modelle der modernen genetischen Edition haben sich als Gegenzug zu Beißners Modell verstanden."

on the general development of editing in that period narrows down the "task" given by the organizer of the underlying series of lectures, namely to "render the development of editorial procedures after the Second World War" (2003, 143),[6] even though Zeller refers to the 20th century as a whole. Zeller's historical presentation thus gives the impression that the concept called "textual genetic editing" was the only and methodically decisive development in German scholarly editing in the 20th century.

This perspective, which looks reductionist considering the complex history of scholarly editing, becomes rather tricky inasmuch as Zeller firmly says in the following: "Although modern genetic editing developed in reaction to the Stuttgart Hölderlin edition […], it was by no means a development of it, neither technically nor conceptually in particular" (2003, 152).[7] At first you rub your eyes with astonishment and look back on Zeller's historical assessment of 1989 in which he explicitly described the synoptic apparatus as a "development" (1989, 7: "Weiterentwicklung") of Beißner's reflections and referred to his Meyer edition in an accompanying footnote. Beißner's "successors" mentioned by Zeller in 1989 were clearly not just successors in terms of chronology. Zeller characterized them as those who thought that Beißner's form of presentation did not reach the standard demanded by himself, but who were nevertheless driven to "come closer to this standard" (1989, 6; cf. previous sentence: "It was believed that Beißner's representation of the manuscript reached the standard it demanded and was thus able to render the textual development of the poem in each verse, from stage to stage up to the final version.") required by Beißner.[8] Thus, in 1989 Zeller could talk about the "historic significance of this deed" (1989, 5: "historischen Bedeutung dieser Tat"), namely Beißner's apparatus model in the Stuttgart Hölderlin edition.

At first glance, Zeller's contribution of 2003 seems to contain just a little deviation from the common view of the history of the academic discipline, but a closer look shows that it turns out to be a shift with far-reaching consequences. Similar to the direct confrontation between

---

[6] "Auftrag, die Entwicklung der Editionsverfahren nach dem Zweiten Weltkrieg darzustellen."

[7] "Die moderne genetische Edition entwickelte sich zwar in Reaktion auf die Stuttgarter Hölderlin-Ausgabe [...], sie war jedoch keineswegs deren Weiterentwicklung, weder in technischer noch vor allem in ideeller Hinsicht."

[8] "Nachfolger"; "mehr von diesem Anspruch einzulösen". "Man glaubte, Beißners Handschriften-Wiedergabe löse den Anspruch ein, den sie erhob, die Textentwicklung des Gedichts in jedem Vers von Stufe zu Stufe bis zur letzten Fassung darzustellen."

Beißner and Zeller in the late 1950s and early 1960s, this appears once again to be a question of academic supremacy. Yet the consequences go a lot further than that. In the 1950s and 1960s there were only two examples on which the effects of the textual genetic models could be tested, namely the two editions of the protagonists, Beißner's Stuttgart Hölderlin edition and Zeller's C.F. Meyer edition. Half a century later, however, there are a large number of editions which follow either the tradition of Beißner's apparatus in stair-step form or that of Zeller's synoptic apparatus. Those editions based on Beißner's technique have tried to remove in different ways the shortcomings of the Beißnerian procedure, especially the insufficient presentation of manuscript records (mainly with regard to indication of deletions, repetitions of words, alternative variants). Among these are, for example, the Düsseldorf Heine edition (1973-1997), the Frankfurt Brentano edition (1975–), the Droste-Hülshoff edition (1978-2000) and the critical Kafka edition (Fischer publishing house, 1982–). On the other hand, the model of the synoptic apparatus has been adopted, for example, by the Salzburg Trakl edition (1969), the Frankfurt Hölderlin edition (1975–2008), the Bonn Celan edition (1990–), the Heym edition (1993), the Innsbruck Trakl edition (1995–) and the Marburg Büchner edition (2000–). Despite the different conceptions of all the editions just mentioned it must be stressed that the presentation of textual genesis occupies a central position in each of them.

Due to the most recent shift of the starting point for textual genetic editions from the Stuttgart Hölderlin edition to the Meyer edition in Zeller's article of 2003, it is not only the Stuttgart Hölderlin edition that now appears to be a non-textual genetic edition. This verdict must, of necessity, also apply to the above-mentioned editions based on the Beißnerian system, that is the Heine, Brentano, Droste-Hülshoff and critical Kafka editions, even though they have greatly improved Beißner's system by a whole series of additions and measures of precision. Zeller does not explicitly state the separation of this type of edition anywhere in his contribution, but *ex negativo* this becomes all the more obvious inasmuch as these editions are not included in the context of the term "genetic editing".

Many of the more recent "genetic editions" in Zeller's understanding are characterized by the fact that they no longer offer a so-called edited text, that is to say a separate presentation of a text version as a reading text, as the first part of the edition. They only provide a reading text version subsequent to the genetic presentation at the back or in the second part of the edition, as is the case with the Frankfurt Hölderlin edition and the Marburg Büchner edition, or they completely do without it like the Heym edition or the Innsbruck Trakl edition. In this sense, these editions mainly or exclusively stress the dynamic character of the text, the process character of textual development and thus follow Gunter Martens' 1971 concept of textual dynamics (1971). All these editions could make particularly good use of the synoptic apparatus when independently rendering textual genesis, because this apparatus needs no reference text for variant recording. Therefore, it was not really necessary for these editions to have a reading text in the sense of an edited text, not even for reasons of editorial technique. Yet the Meyer edition in particular shows that the rear position of a representative version serving as a reading text or even the omission of such an edited text do not establish the textual genetic character of an edition, because the Meyer edition, which Zeller himself declared to be the initial model of textual genetic editing, contains within the poetry section, which Zeller is responsible for, a representative reading text version of the poems called "text" in volume 1 (1963), while the accompanying volumes 2 to 5 (1964-1997) are each described as "apparatus". Volumes 6 and 7 of the poetry section containing independent text collections and bundles of papers are also separately presented as "text and apparatus" as late as 1988 and 1991 respectively.[9] The question of how to deal with an edited text, a representative reading text version, in an edition thus reveals a larger or smaller amount of emphasis placed on textual dynamics, the process character of the text, but it does not constitute the overall textual genetic or non-textual genetic character of an edition.

What may be the reason for the aforesaid shift of historical perspective in Zeller's retrospective article of 2003 as compared with his contribution of 1989? A look at the context in which Zeller sets off "modern genetic editing" against Beißner in 2003 shows that Zeller refers to an idea put forward by Klaus Hurlebusch in 1998 (Zeller 2003, 152). Hurlebusch wrote: "In German editorial philology and beyond the opinion still prevails that Friedrich Beißner is the father of modern, that is of exhaustive textual genetic presentation of draft manuscripts. I [Klaus Hurlebusch] think this assessment cannot be justified historically." Hurlebusch's perspective, however, is no longer purely editorial considering that he views an author's manuscripts not only as "text sources", but also as "unique

---

[9] This formulation can be found on the title pages in the Meyer edition (1958-1996), vol. 6) *Bilder und Balladen, Zwanzig Balladen, Romanzen und Bilder. Text und Apparat*, ed. by Hans Zeller (Bern: Benteli, 1988); vol. 7, *Die Gedichte aus dem Nachlaß. Text und Apparat.*

writings" (Hurlebusch 1998, 26-27).[10] As Hurlebusch is interested in a "hermeneutics of textual genetic writing" (1998, subtitle), textual genetic presentation is not an objective for him, but a means of inducing people to read the manuscript itself (1998, 49).[11] That is why he can consistently demand the following: "The preparation of textual genetic authorial manuscripts should no longer remain solely in the hands of editorial philologists" (1998, 49).[12]

From this position outside strict editorial philology one can refer back to Zeller's first presentation of his model of a synoptic apparatus in 1958. At that time he explained the necessity of indicating the position of variants in the manuscript, which is a characteristic feature of his model. The indicated positions "not only" enabled the user "to control" the editor, but they also "made it possible for the reader to get an idea of the manuscript. It is my [Zeller's] desire at least to retranslate the printed representation into the manuscript." By indicating the positions of the variants within the genetic presentation "one can imagine what the manuscript looks like or reconstruct it on paper" (1958, 362).[13] Since Zeller here takes up Backmann's demand of 1924 for the *"recoverability of the manuscripts* for the apparatus user" (Backmann 1924, 653 *"Wiederherstellbarkeit der Manuskripte durch den Benutzer des Apparates"* see also 641 and Zeller 1958, 358), it becomes obvious in what way Hurlebusch can describe the objective of "manuscript reading" as a phenomenon repeatedly accompanying scholarly editing's search for an adequate presentation of textual genesis throughout the 20th century.[14] But Hurlebusch himself made it quite clear

---

[10] "Nach wie vor überwiegt innerhalb und außerhalb der germanistischen Editionsphilologie die Meinung, Friedrich Beißner sei der Vater der modernen, d.h. der erschöpfenden textgenetischen Wiedergabe von Entwurfshandschriften. Diese Wertung ist, wie ich glaube, historisch nicht zur rechtfertigen."; 27: "Textquellen", "Schriften sui generis."

[11] "Das *Ziel* der textgenetischen Darstellung sollte die Lektüre und Interpretation der textgenetischen Handschriften selbst sein und das *Erläuterungsmittel* hierzu ihre Transkription," which can be translated as "The *objective* of textual genetic presentation should be to read and interpret the textual genetic manuscripts themselves, and the transcription of the latter should be the *means of explanation* to this end."

[12] "Die Erschließung textgenetischer Autographen sollte nicht länger nur in den Händen der Editionsphilologen bleiben."

[13] "nicht bloß zur Kontrolle"; "sich der Leser von der H[and]s[chrift] ein Bild machen kann. Mir wenigstens ist ein Bedürfnis, die gedruckte Wiedergabe in die H[and]s[chrift] zurückzuübersetzen."; "kann man sich die H[and]s[chrift] vorstellen oder sie auf dem Papier rekonstruieren."

[14] As early as 1964, however, Zeller returned to the narrower boundaries of editorial philology in the first apparatus volume of the Meyer edition (Meyer 1958-1996, vol. 2). In this volume

that this objective goes beyond the limits of strict editorial philology (1998, 50).

According to Beißner, the editorial task of presenting textual genesis consisted solely in "writing down a clear and readable chronological order extracted from the spatial muddle." (1964a, 78: "ein aus dem räumlichen Durcheinander herausgewickeltes zeitliches Nacheinander [...] übersichtlich und lesbar aufschreiben"; reprinted in Nutt-Kofoth 2005b, 252-72). For Beißner the manuscript's spatial character was the working basis for reconstructing the chronological dimension of textual genesis. For this reason, only the time axis appeared in the edition. From his point of view, which focused on the manuscript and the author's specific writing process, Hurlebusch regarded Beißner's decision to do without the spatial dimension in the edition as an "act of abandonment" as early as 1986 (1986, 19-20; 1988, 111-13).

However, Zeller's procedure of marking the positions of variants through indices within the synoptic presentation has not become generally accepted in scholarly editing. Editions paying attention to the spatial dimension too went over to using photography as the medium which could effortlessly replace the best possible description with concrete clarity. Since 1975 the Frankfurt Hölderlin edition has served as the model of the large-scale use of manuscript facsimiles in editions, and the Innsbruck Trakl edition as well as the Marburg Büchner edition have followed suit. All these editions employ facsimiles primarily to check the editor's work at the subsequent editorial stages in the sense of an archival working basis. The case is different with the historical-critical Kafka edition (Stroemfeld publishing house, 1995–) which parallels Hurlebusch's demands of 1998 in that it considers the facsimile to be the objective of its editorial concept. The accompanying transcription with individual genetic hints chiefly serves the purpose of conveying the manuscript text in a readable manner. Thus, the transcription refers back to the manuscript. Quite consistently, the editorial concept is completed with that. A real reconstruction of textual genesis is no longer intended by the historical-critical Kafka edition. Its editor Roland Reuß wrote accordingly in 1999: "Diplomatic transcriptions containing a subtly differentiated chronological presentation are adequate

---

he wanted to render the "graphic dimension of the manuscript" ["graphischen Gegebenheiten der Hs"] only as a means of "justifying and controlling [editorial] interpretation" ["Begründung und Kontrolle der Interpretation"] (Meyer 1958-1996, 110) Zeller then calls the manuscript the "semiotic basis" ("Zeichengrundlage") of "text constitution" ("Textkonstitution") (1971, 80). Cf. Hurlebusch (1998, 25).

editorial means of rendering even the most complicated constellations in a manuscript. [...] Textual genetics can safely be left to the people reading and interpreting the text"(1999, 24-25).[15]

Thus, scholarly editing can definitely cater for the interest in manuscripts considered to be material objects of writing and documents of an author's writing acts, as Hurlebusch showed. It thereby approaches the procedures of French genetic criticism ("critique génétique") and expands the boundaries of the academic discipline in a highly profitable way. Yet Hurlebusch based his argumentation on the editorial recovery of the manuscript's spatial dimension. From this point of view, one can indeed criticize Beißner's procedure of completely excluding the spatial dimension from the edition. But at the core this does not concern the chronological dimension, that is textual genesis itself.

Consequently, the fact that Zeller refers to Hurlebusch of all people when most recently excluding Beißner from the ancestral line of *textual genetic* editing seems to be due to a misunderstanding which might be inherent in Hurlebusch's argumentation itself. With Hurlebusch aiming at the material character of the manuscript, Zeller could undoubtedly feel encouraged to take up both his former idea of "reconstructing the manuscript" by means of the apparatus and Backmann's similar demand of 1924. The consequence of making this interest more absolute, however, can be seen if the representation of the material record outweighs the interest in textual genesis, as seems to be the case with the historical-critical Kafka edition (Stroemfeld publishing house). Therefore, it should rather be said that this line of tradition alone does not necessarily lead to textual genesis and certainly not to "textual genetic editing". Editions can try to mirror the dimensions of material, space and time as largely as possible. Beißner's procedure, which is restricted to the dimension of time within the apparatus, nevertheless corresponds with the core of the term "textual genesis". The fact that Beißner's model was still insufficient and imprecise in many ways has clearly been shown by the ongoing discussion in scholarly editing. The development of alternative models also belongs to the history of the academic discipline. But to exclude the model of the Stuttgart Hölderlin edition from the canon of "modern genetic editing" and, as the inversion of the argument can only be, to regard all editions following

---

[15] "Diplomatische Umschriften, die eine chronologisch differenzierte Darstellung in sich bergen, sind das adäquate editionstechnische Mittel, wie auch immer komplizierte Handschriftenkonstellationen wiederzugeben. [...] Die Textgenetik [...] kann man dann getrost den Lesern und Interpreten des Textes überlassen."

and improving Beißner's procedure in many respects as "pre-modern editions" would be inappropriate.

If various text dimensions, such as material, topography, process character or the stasis expressed in individual versions, could be represented within the edition, textual genesis would be a very important editorial aspect, but only *one* among others. Therefore, there is no reason for associating "modern" editing merely with this single aspect. In this respect, the discussion about primogeniture with regard to "modern genetic editing" appears to be somewhat historical itself.

Translated from the German by Dieter Neiteler

Bibliography

Backmann, Reinhold. 1924. "Die Gestaltung des Apparates in den kritischen Ausgaben neuerer deutscher Dichter. (Mit besonderer Berücksichtigung der großen Grillparzer-Ausgabe der Stadt Wien)." *Euphorion* 25:629-662.

Beißner, Friedrich. 1964a. "Editionsmethoden der neueren deutschen Philologie." *Zeitschrift für deutsche Philologie* 83 (Tagung der deutschen Hochschulgermanisten vom 27. bis 31. Oktober 1963 in Bonn):72-95.

———. 1964b. "Lesbare Varianten. Die Entstehung einiger Verse in Heines 'Atta Troll.'" In *Festschrift Josef Quint anläßlich seines 65. Geburtstages überreicht*, edited by H. Moser, R. Schützeichel and K. Stackmann. Bonn: Emil Semmel. 15-23.

———, ed. 1938. *Neue Wieland-Handschriften*. Abhandlungen der Preußischen Akademie der Wissenschaften. 1937. Vol. 13, Phil.-hist. Klasse. Berlin: Verlag der Akademie der Wissenschaften.

Hoffmann, Dierk O., and Harald Zils. 2005. "Hölderlin-Editionen." In Nutt-Kofoth and Plachta 2005c, 199-245.

Hölderlin, Friedrich. 1943-1985. *Sämtliche Werke. Große Stuttgarter Ausgabe*. 8 vols. in 15. Edited by F. Beißner [and A. Beck]. Stuttgart: J.G. Cottasche Buchhandlung Nachfolger / W. Kohlhammer.

Hurlebusch, Klaus. 1986. "Deutungen literarischer Arbeitsweise." *Zeitschrift für deutsche Philologie* 105 (*Editionsprobleme der Literaturwissenschaft*):4-42.

———. 1988. "Conceptualisations for Procedures of Authorship." *Studies in Bibliography* 41:100-135.

———. 1998. "Den Autor besser verstehen: aus seiner Arbeitsweise. Prolegomenon zu einer Hermeneutik textgenetischen Schreibens."

In *Textgenetische Edition*, edited by H. Zeller and G. Martens. Beihefte zu *editio*. Vol. 10. Tübingen: Niemeyer.

Martens, Gunter. 1971. "Textdynamik und Edition. Überlegungen zur Bedeutung und Darstellung variierender Textstufen." *Texte und Varianten. Probleme ihrer Edition und Interpretation*, edited by G. Martens and H. Zeller. München: C.H. Beck'sche Verlagsbuchhandlung. 165-201.

Meyer, Conrad Ferdinand. 1958-1996. *Sämtliche Werke. Historisch-kritische Ausgabe*. Edited by H. Zeller and A. Zäch. 15 vols, Bern: Benteli.

Nutt-Kofoth, Rüdiger. 2005a. "Textgenese. Überlegungen zu Funktion und Perspektive eines editorischen Aufgabengebiets." *Jahrbuch für Internationale Germanistik* 37,1: 97-122

——— ed. 2005b. *Dokumente zur Geschichte der neugermanistischen Edition*. Bausteine zur Geschichte der Edition. Vol. 1. Tübingen: Niemeyer.

——— and Bodo Plachta, ed. 2005c. *Editionen zu deutschsprachigen Autoren als Spiegel der Editionsgeschichte*. Bausteine zur Geschichte der Edition. Vol. 2. Tübingen: Niemeyer.

———. 2005d. "Meyer-Editionen." In Nutt-Kofoth and Plachta 2005c, 361-387.

Plachta, Bodo. 2001. "Germanistische Editionswissenschaft im Kontext ihrer Geschichte." *Anglia* 119: 375–398.

——— 2006. *Editionswissenschaft. Eine Einführung in Methode und Praxis der Edition neuerer Texte*. 2., ergänzte und aktualisierte Aufl. First edition 1997. Stuttgart: Reclam.

Pyritz, Hans. 1953. "Zum Fortgang der Stuttgarter Hölderlin-Ausgabe." *Hölderlin-Jahrbuch*: 80-105.

Reuß, Roland. 1999. "Schicksal der Handschrift, Schicksal der Druckschrift. Notizen zur 'Textgenese.'" *Text. Kritische Beiträge* 5. *Textgenese* 1:1-25.

Waleczek, Lioba. 1994. *"Doch Vergangenes ist, wie Künftiges heilig ...". Zur Editionsproblematik der Stuttgarter und Frankfurter Hölderlin-Ausgabe*. Baden-Baden: Battert.

Windfuhr, Manfred. 1957. "Die neugermanistische Edition. Zu den Grundsätzen kritischer Gesamtausgaben." *Deutsche Vierteljahrsschrift für Literaturwissenschaft und Geistesgeschichte* 31:425-442.

Zeller, Hans. 1958. "Zur gegenwärtigen Aufgabe der Editionstechnik. Ein Versuch, komplizierte Handschriften darzustellen." *Euphorion* 52:356-77.

———. 1971. "Befund und Deutung. Interpretation und Dokumentation als Ziel und Methode der Edition." In *Texte und Varianten. Probleme ihrer Edition und Interpretation*, edited by G. Martens and H. Zeller. München: C.H. Beck'sche Verlagsbuchhandlung. 45-89.

———. 1986. "Die Typen des germanistischen Varianten-Apparats und ein Vorschlag zu einem Apparat für Prosa." *Zeitschrift für deutsche Philologie* 105 (*Editionsprobleme der Literaturwissenschaft*):42-69.

———. 1989. "Fünfzig Jahre neugermanistischer Edition. Zur Geschichte und künftigen Aufgaben der Textologie." *editio* 3:1-17.

———. 1995. "Record and Interpretation: Analysis and Documentation as Goal and Method of Editing." In *Contemporary German Editorial Theory*, edited by H. W. Gabler, G. Bornstein and G. B. Pierce. Ann Arbor: The University of Michigan Press. 17-58.

———. 2003. "Die Entwicklung der textgenetischen Edition im 20. Jahrhundert." In *Geschichte der Editionsverfahren vom Altertum bis zur Gegenwart im Überblick*, edited by H.-G. Roloff. Berliner Beiträge zur Editionswissenschaft. Vol. 5. Berlin: Weidler. 143-207.

The Canon Beyond Academia

Alternative Sources of Canonicity in Twentieth-Century Literature in English

Jesús Varela Zapata[1]

There is no doubt that when dealing with the literary canon we are close to Antonio Gramsci's notion of cultural hierarchy or hegemony when he talks about the existence of a normative or dominant culture that is modelled, among other factors, by the education system, newspapers, artistic and popular writers, all of them involved in the process of canon formation (Forgacs 1988). This is a debate that started in Britain in the mid-19th century, when English and American universities began to teach vernacular literature, at a time when Oxford and Cambridge scholars discovered the rhetoric and aesthetic values of an emerging genre, the novel, so far confined to "dissenting" or Scottish institutions (Crawford 1998).

By the end of the 19th century, the "Cambridge English Project" pioneered by Matthew Arnold was actively promoting the teaching of literature in English across all levels of education and society. This fact probably had an effect in the rise of publications concerned about canonicity; among the earliest examples we can mention figures such as John Lubbock, who joined a trendy Victorian habit of drafting lists of literary masterpieces by encouraging readers, influential intellectuals and personalities to respond to his list of best writing, a selection of one hundred books that starts with the Bible and ends with Scott's novels (Lubbock 1886). Later on, in the wake of this movement, F.R. Leavis would promote his idea of the canon in two seminal works: *Revaluation* (1936) and *The Great Tradition* (1948). Somehow, Leavis is a key figure for those who think that in matters of canonicity professors and critics are bound to influence large groups of readers and, what is even more important, they are bestowing on works a seal of approval that will be instrumental in their renown. Along this line, figures such as Frank Kermode (Kermode 1985) and Richard Ohmman (Ohmann 1975) uphold that scholars, with the intervention of filters such as academic journals, constitute the ultimate echelon of canon formation. However, there are voices that do not subscribe to this point of view; critics such as Dean Kolbas (Kolbas 2001) state that the role of scholars and traditional education in canon formation has been exaggerated and,

---

[1] This research article has been funded by the R&D Department of Galicia PGIDIT.

similarly, some members of the Frankfurt School consider that the judgement of works of art is a sociological and historical process that is affected by various institutions or, to use Marxist terms, different fields of cultural production.

This is the reason why we will pay attention in this article to non-academic sources of canon formation, such as different kinds of surveys undertaken mainly by the media, publishers or booksellers. We have already mentioned the upsurge of literary surveys of, so called, "best books" in Victorian Britain; in America we can mention similar polls carried out by newspapers and journals such as *Vanity Fair, Bookman and Literary Digest* (all three published in 1923); and *Book Week* (1965). This kind of surveys have continued and we can say that, by the end of the 20th century, they have become fashionable, as can be seen in the projects undertaken by Random House: their readers' poll to choose their favourite 20th century novel was a successful project launched in 1988, drawing the attention and votes of over 200,000 people; at the same time, a parallel list was prepared by Random House's publishing board. Also in America, *Time* published in 2005 a selection of best novels in print since the magazine's appearance in 1923; this was compiled by critics Lev Grossman and Richard Lacayo.

In Britain, Waterstones, a bookstore chain, with assistance from Channel 4, launched its own survey in 1997 to find out what the public considered to be the hundred greatest books of the twentieth century, with some 25,000 people taking part in the poll. The BBC Big Read Project was a much more important event, carried out between March and December 2003, with support from other institutions such as the Reading Agency, the National Literacy Trust and Booktrust; BBC2 broadcast a series of programmes where writers and other celebrities chose their favourite books, members of the public were then asked to vote for their best-loved novel and eventually over 140,000 people took part.[2]

Finally, we can mention the survey conducted by the Norwegian Book Club, in association with the Nobel Institute, by asking 100 writers worldwide to choose the ten most influential books from any culture. The list of those who were invited to give their opinion seems in itself a representation of the canon they were trying to elicit; for example, in the case of the English language we can name among them Salman Rushdie, Nadine Gordimer, V.S. Naipaul, Paul Auster, A.S. Byatt, Ben Okri, Fay Weldon, Wole Soyinka and Norman Mailer.

---

[2] A report on the project is available at the BBC webpage, describing the process and its follow-up. http://www.bbc.co.uk/arts/bigread/ [20 June 2009]

The analysis of all these lists provides us with preliminary results about coincidences, as well as with an opportunity to assess the especial attention paid to contemporary literature in surveys of this kind:

SURVEYS (YEAR OF PUBLICATION)
1. Waterstones (1997)
2. Ramdom House (1988- Reader's Survey
3. Random House (1988)- Board Survey.
4. BBC Big Read (2003)
5. Norwegian Book Club(2002)
6. Time (2005).

WRITERS	LISTED IN SURVEYS
JOYCE	1,2,3,4,5-*
NABOKOV	1,2,3,4,5, 6
ORWELL	1,2,3,4,5, 6
BURGESS	1,2,3,4,-, 6
CONRAD	1,2, -,4,5, *
FITZGERALD	1,2,3,4,- , 6
FOWLES	1,2,3,4,-, 6
GOLDING	1,2,3,4,-, 6
KEROUAC	1,2,3,4,-, 6
SALINGER	1,2,3,4,-, 6
TOLKIEN	1,2,3,4,-, 6
WOOLF	1,2, -,4,5, 6
D.H. LAWRENCE	1,- ,3,4,5, -
D.ADAMS	1,2,3, -,-, -
GRAVES	1,2, -, 4,-, 6
HARPER LEE	1,2,3, -,-, 6
S.KING	1,2, 3, -,-, -
T.MORRISON	1,2, -,-,5, 6
VONNEGUT	1,2,- ,4,-, 6
ATWOOD	1,2, -, -,-, 6

Fig. 1. Best book surveys.

Thus, it makes sense to ponder on the possibility of attaching a label of canonicity to the writers mentioned above with mentions in several lists. Some absences can be attributed to restrictions in the selection of the corpus; i.e., *Time* only incorporates writers who published after 1923; this excludes Joyce and Conrad since the bulk of their work was done before that date. Furthermore, we can compare these results to the selection made in *The Western Canon* by Harold Bloom. This American scholar has done an impressive coverage of classical and modern literary tradition that is arguably one of the most emblematic contributions to the canon debate of the last decades; although Bloom places figures such as Shakespeare, Dante and Cervantes at the zenith of the literary altar, his final appendix provides also lists of many contemporary and present-day authors (Bloom 1995 [1994]). If we compare the table above with Bloom's selection we will find a striking coincidence, the only absences being Fowles, Kerouac, Tolkien, Lee and King; all the other fifteen names are listed in *The Western Canon*.

	BLOOM	SURVEYS
JOYCE	√	√
NABOKOV	√	√
ORWELL	√	√
BURGESS	√	√
CONRAD	√	√
FITZGERALD	√	√
FOWLES		√
GOLDING	√	√
KEROUAC		√
SALINGER	√	√
TOLKIEN		√
WOOLF	√	√
D.ADAMS	√	√
LAWRENCE	√	√
GRAVES	√	√
HARPER LEE		√
S.KING		√
T.MORRISON	√	√
VONNEGUT	√	√
ATWOOD	√	√

Fig. 2. Best book surveys and Bloom's list.

One more element that is also of paramount importance in any discussion on canon formation is the phenomenon of literary prizes, which has gained momentum in the English speaking countries, especially during the second half of the 20th century; in this respect, Jason Cowley wrote in *The Observer*:

> ours is truly the age of awards. Prizes are becoming the ultimate measure of cultural success and value. One prize inevitably spawns another, in imitation or reaction, as the perceived male dominance of the Booker spawned the Orange Prize for women's fiction. There are now so many, in so many different fields, that it can be difficult to find a professional artist, writer or journalist who has not been shortlisted for a prize. (Cowley 2009)

David Lodge also refers to the proliferation of prizes, making them one more element of competitiveness in the cultural realm:

> There is a sense in which all literary novels published in the same year or season compete with each other - for readers, for sales (not quite the same thing, though the two are of course connected), for critical approval, and

> (a fairly new phenomenon, this) for prizes. The proliferation in the last few decades of literary prizes like the Booker, with their published shortlists and (more recently) longlists, has intensified and institutionalised the element of competition in the writing and publishing of fiction. (Lodge 2006)

In America one of the earliest great literary awards is the Pulitzer Prize for the Novel, later renamed as the Pulitzer for Fiction. A review of the awards list will show that the key figures in contemporary writing are included. On the other hand, the National Book Award has been given since 1950, acknowledging the career of prominent American writers from William Faulkner to Annie Proulx.

Australian critics such as Brian Kiernan (1997) and Xavier Pons (1993) have linked the foundation of a high number of literary awards in their country to a political intention to foster patriotic feelings. Among the most important in Australia we can mention the Miles Franklin, the Australia/Vogel and those instituted by the government of several federated States, such as Victoria and Queensland. In 2007, shortly after swearing in, the Labour government announced the new Prime Minister's Literary Prize that was awarded for the first time in 2008, in the non-fiction and fiction categories. The most relevant prizes in Canada are the Giller, the Scott Griffin (for poetry) and the Governor General's Literary Award, the most prestigious and long-standing, which has been awarded for a record fifth time (in the English-speaking section) to Michael Ondaatje.

In Britain a number of prizes were inaugurated in the 1990's, among them the David Cohen, in 1993, acknowledging lifelong literary careers, such as those of V.S. Naipaul, Harold Pinter, Muriel Spark and Doris Lessing. The T.S. Eliot prize for poetry, inaugurated in the same year by Eliot's widow, is given to the best collection of new poetry published in the UK and Ireland; it has been received, among others, by Ted Hughes, Les Murray and Carol Ann Duffy. The Orange Prize for Fiction is bestowed on women from any country writing in English, and has been awarded to figures such as Margaret Atwood, Shirley Hazzard, Andrea Levy and Zadie Smith. The Whitbread, now renamed as the Costa Book Awards, has also become increasingly influential over the years. It is noteworthy mentioning that Andrea Levy, for *Small Island,* and Zadie Smith, for *White Teeth,* have received recently both the Orange and the Whitbread. The Commonwealth Writers Prize was set up in 1987, with nominees from four regional divisions (Canada and Caribbean; South-East Asia and South Pacific; Africa; and Eurasia); it has been given by the Queen in an annual ceremony to writers from all continents such as Peter Carey (twice awarded), J.M. Coetzee, Murray Bail, Vikram Seth, Caryl Phillips and Janet Frame.

Special mention must be made of the Booker Prize, since this is arguably the most relevant British award. There is no doubt that the list of recipients comes close to the idea of a contemporary canon in English, including figures such as V.S. Naipaul (1971) and Nadine Gordimer (1974). Salman Rushdie has been especially prominent in the history of the Booker; he was overall winner in 1981 and made it into the shortlist in 1995; furthermore, in 1993 he received a special prize for *Midnight's Children*, to commemorate the 25th anniversary of the prize. Equally worth mentioning is the case of Margaret Atwood who was not only an overall winner, but has also been shortlisted in three different years within a single decade.

In 2005 a new prize, the Man Booker International, was launched. The first winner was Albanian Ismail Kadaré; English-speaking writers were well represented in the shortlist: Atwood, Bellow, Lessing, McEwan, Roth, Muriel Spark, Updike. The second and third awards (2007 and 2009) were won by Anglophones, Nigerian Chinua Achebe, and Canadian Alice Munro. Once more, other English-speaking writers featured prominently in the shortlist, and some names had already been nominated in the previous edition, such as Atwood, Lessing, McEwan and Roth. Other contenders were well-known names in literary contests: Banville, Carey, DeLillo, Ondaatje, Rushdie and Naipaul. Also international in scope, the Dublin Impac Award is advertised as the world's largest literary prize for a single work of fiction published in English, including translated works. It has been bestowed since 1996 on writers from several nationalities; among English-speaking authors, we can name Irish Colm Toíbin, Canadian Alistair McLeod, Australian David Malouf and Afro-American Michael Thomas.

We should note that, if we consider the literary prizes mentioned above as a source of canon formation, especially relating present-day literature from Britain and the Commowealth, we have found a pattern of names that are especially prominent and become recurrent in these awards lists. However, a number of intellectuals have frowned upon the conversion of literary prizes into a show-business affair. Thus, Martin Amis states that the Booker "demystifies and declasses the writer. Writers become something you can bet on" (2000) Amis's negative perception coincides with the view expressed by critics such as Gilbert Phelps, who has similarly compared the circumstances surrounding literary awards to the football pools, concluding that this results in serious literature being neglected (Phelps

1992). Therefore, it should not come as a surprise that some writers have asked their editors not to enter their works for the Booker contest; notably among them, we can mention Graham Greene, John Fowles, Doris Lessing, Muriel Spark and Margaret Drabble ("Judging Britain's Booker Prize." 1997). Similarly, David Lodge has expressed his view that the Booker had been a languishing event until a series of changes served to revamp it. Among the causes of the upsurge in attention, he mentions the fact that the publication of shortlists has increased public awareness and, as mentioned above, even betting; the televised live coverage of the banquet when the winner is announced has added new degrees of emotion and some mischievous complacency at the writers' nervous tension (Lodge 2007). Robert McCrum (2007) shares this opinion:

> Ten years ago, after a series of dreadful shortlists, the Booker management galvanised itself. The upshot was a very welcome sponsorship deal with the Man Group, an obscure but loaded hedge fund. At first, it was all rock'n'roll. Man's young Turks called the shots and Booker's wheezy gerontocracy shuffled into compliance. Prize night was transformed and new television coverage deals were struck.

All this has resulted in some critics deriding cultural production especially oriented towards commercial goals. They regret that authors and readers of any literary artefact (or in Jakobson's terminology the senders and receivers of the message or act of communication) have become, respectively, mere producers and consumers of culture. Cees J. van Rees refers to what he considers sub-standard works: "the cultural value of these 'commercial' products is negligible [...] the less so when compared with works resulting from the field of restricted production" (1985). In turn, Pascale Casanova explains that large publishing houses are now demanding higher profits from books that are increasingly being commissioned by them; this has led to a proliferation of a new kind of world literature that is easily available in translation and marketed in massive numbers but lacks the aesthetic values an enlightened readership might expect (2004).

Taking these perceptions into account, we could be tempted to consider literature as one more financial asset in contemporary market-oriented societies, leading us to ponder the possibility that lists and prizes have become one more element in the reification of culture. In this respect, it is significant the way both Nicolette Jones (1998) and Richard Todd (1996) have provided insightful accounts of the influence of the Booker Prize on sales. Seen from the management of the Booker Prize, the view seems surprisingly similar; thus, as a former chairman of the Booker Company,

Sir Michael Caine, praised the strategies of Martyn Goff as the administrator of the prize for his success in promoting it: "never saying sufficient to give an official view, but always sufficient to start the journalists hunting the hare" (1998) From a different perspective, Robert McCrum talks about the emergence of new forms of writing, attuned to the whims of the prize circuit: "The Booker novel, new fiction's mutant cousin, has come to dominate the landscape. And the Booker genre (which is what it is) has become disproportionately influential on The Way We Read Now" (2007). Furthermore, Mark Lawson considers that many publishing decisions now rest on the presence in awards lists: "The frightening consequence of these cultural changes is that serious fiction is now almost entirely dependent on judging panels" (2008).

However, in spite of the commercial implications of the awards system, there is no doubt that if we go over the lists of nominees of the most prestigious and well-known prizes, most of them belong to what we might call serious literature, complying with Pierre Bourdieu's model of "works produced by the field of restrictive production" (1985).[3] In the wake of the 2007 Booker controversy, Mark Lawson stated that the prize has helped to consolidate the careers of major writers although, paradoxically enough, sometimes by failing to get the award (McEwan, Barnes); on the contrary, in other cases it has rescued from oblivion books that might otherwise be neglected by the general public, for not complying with the tastes of the bourgeoisie (2007).

Likewise, we can take into consideration the importance of the Nobel Prize and its impact on scholarly circles. In many instances, the Nobel awards have been taken as indications of the vitality of national literatures. Thus, Carol P. Marsh-Locket and Paula Burnett have stressed the importance for Caribbean literature of Derek Walcott's award in 1992 (Marsh-Locket 1993; Burnett 1993). Ken Gelder and Paul Salzman have similarly considered the impact in Australia of the Nobel Prize awarded to Patrick White (Salzman 1989), and Ezenwa Ohaeto that of Soyinka's prize in African literature (1993, 26). David Lodge has expressed his view that the Nobel has sparked off the flame of literary prizes in the 20th century, adding that "the Nobel still commands enormous cultural prestige. I suppose it must be regarded as the highest award you can win as a writer in spite of the many mistakes the judges may have made in the past."[4]

---

[3] Here he endows these works with qualities such as "purity", "abstract" and "esoteric", because they demand of the receiver a certain aesthetic disposition, an ability to understand their multiplicity of approaches as well as the references enshrined in cultural tradition.

[4] This was Lodge's answer to a question by J. Varela-Zapata.

	LIFE SPAN	NOBEL AWARDED (YEAR)	MLA ENTRIES PREVIOUS TEN YEARS	MLA ENTRIES SUBSEQUENT TEN YEARS	% INCREASE IN MLA RECORDS
SAMUEL BECKETT	**1906-1989**	**1969**	**298**	**693**	**132.55**
ARTHUR MILLER	1915-2005	---	198	234	18
SAUL BELLOW	**1915-2005**	**1976**	**205**	**429**	**109.26**
RALPH ELLISON	1913-1994	---	153	172	12.41
WOLE SOYINKA	**1934-**	**1986**	**222**	**303**	**36.48**
CHINUA ACHEBE	1930-	---	229	236	3.05
DEREK WALCOTT	**1930-**	**1992**	**80**	**226**	**182.5**
EDWARD K. BRATHWAITE	1930-	---	15	41	33.3
SEAMUS HEANEY	**1939-**	**1995**	**236**	**317**	**34.3**
PHILIP LARKIN	1922-1985	---	132	118	-10.6

Fig. 3. Impact of Nobel Prize on scholarship (MLA Database)

In this sense, we have inquired for this article whether prizes such as the Nobel have a real impact on the academic realm, by considering the number of scholarly articles quoted in the MLA database over ten-year periods (before and after the award).[5] We have compared the figures for the recipients of this Prize (in bold type, in the table in Figure 3) to those for other writers of a similar background, regional origin and genre. It is interesting to note that recognition of writers among scholars has always been on the rise after the award, in clear contrast with non-recepients whose data tend to remain stable.

We can compare, for example, the critical production on two playwrights, Beckett, from Ireland, and American Arthur Miller; both were born in the early 20th century and died after a long and fruitful career, both

[5] MLA International Bibliography. http://collections.chadwyck.co.uk/marketing/home_mla.jsp.

also enjoyed much popularity and saw their plays performed all over the world. The critical acclaim seems to have favoured Beckett, even before he was awarded the Nobel Prize (298 hits, against 198). However, the distance becomes more than three times greater once the award goes to the Irish writer.

We can also consider two American writers with parallel life spans: Bellow (1915-2005) and Ellison (1913-1994). Both had drawn comparable critical attention for the first ten-year period and came from what we could call social minorities; Ellison is an Afro-American and Bellow a Jewish writer who was awarded the Nobel Prize in 1976. In the previous decade, we find in the MLA database 205 entries for Bellow and 153 for Ellison. The impact of the Nobel is clear when we check these results against those in the decade after the award: Bellow is clearly ahead with 429 entries while Ellison lags behind with 172. For the first author we have an increase in critical production over 100%, while this is a mere 12% for Ellison.

Similar results can be obtained in all the other cases analysed. Nigerian Chinua Achebe, the author of *Things Fall Apart*, arguably the most read African novel, and Wole Soyinka, also born in Nigeria in the 1930's and the most famous African playwright, received a comparable critical attention before 1986. This year is marked by Soyinka's Nobel Prize and the subsequent lead in MLA entries hereafter. If we consider the impact of the Nobel on the critical production devoted to Derek Walcott (vs. Braithwaite) and Seamus Heaney (vs. Larkin) the outcome is the same.

Therefore, as a conclusion, we can say that canon formation is one of the most controversial and debated issues in contemporary literary studies. It is now clear that the canon is a continuous process whereby some authors are progressively neglected by readers and academics, while others come to the fore. Interest in defining the canon dates back to Victorian times and the earliest decades of the 20th century and has continued up to the present. Some scholars avoid the inclusion of present-day literature in canonical surveys because they believe that only a temporal perspective is a guarantee of reliability. This is not the case with a number of non-academic sources such as surveys carried out by assorted journals, publishing houses or reader's clubs that are also significant in the identification and consolidation of a canonical list. The sources we have considered above are especially relevant to inquire about the present-day canon; in fact most of the surveys we have analysed have a contemporary scope and limit the period of research to 20th century literature.

On the other hand, although literary prizes can be considered as commercial approaches to literature and they have an influence on sales we also become aware of their influence on the number of scholarly publications, as the rise in entries in the MLA database for Nobel Prize winners indicates. We have further emphasized the remarkable coincidence between Harold Bloom's selection and the lists of Nobel Prize winners. The parallelism between both lists is clear, and if we further check the coincidences with the assorted surveys mentioned above it is clear that the same writers are represented in most of them. Therefore, although no single source, be it a single author, anthology, survey or literary award can be taken in itself as an ultimate reference on canonicity, these combined results should be seriously considered as such.

Bibliography

Amis, Martin. 2000. *Experience*. (New York: Hyperion, 2000), 46n. New York: Hyperion.

Bloom, Harold. 1995 [1994]. *The Western Canon*. London and Basingstoke: Macmillan.

Bourdieu, Pierre. 1985. "The Market of Symbolic Goods." *Poetics* 14.

Burnett, Paula. 1993. "Hegemony or Pluralism? The Literary Prize and the Post-Colonial Project in the Caribbean" *Commonwealth* 16.1 16 (1):1-19.

Caine, Michael. 1998. "The Booker Story." In *Booker 30. A Celebration of 30 Years of the Booker Prize for Fiction 1969-1998*. London Booker Plc.

Casanova, Pascale. 2004. *The World Republic of Letters*. Translated by M. B. DeBevoise. Cambridge, Mass. and London: Harvard UP.

Cowley, Jason. 2009. "And the winner is?". *The Observer* (Sunday October 22, 2006), http://books.guardian.co.uk/manbooker2006/story/0,,1928489,00.html.

Crawford, Robert. 1998. *The Scottish Invention of English Literature*. Cambridge: Cambridge UP.

Forgacs, D., ed. 1988. *A Gramsci Reader*. London: Lawrence & Wishart.

Jones, Nicolette. 1998. "Read All About It." In *Booker 30. A Celebration of 30 Years of the Booker Prize for Fiction 1969-1998.* . London: Booker Plc.

"Judging Britain's Booker Prize." 1997. The Economist, 2 October 1997.

Kermode, Frank. 1985. *Forms of Atttention*. Chicago and London: U of Chicago P.

Kiernan, Brian. 1997. *Studies in Australian Literary History*. Sydney: Sydney Studies.

Kolbas, Dean. 2001. *Critical Theory and the Literary Canon*. Boulder, Co: Westview Press.

Lawson, Mark. 2007. "Accounting for Taste" *The Guardian* (October 20, 2007), http://www.guardian.co.uk/Columnists/Column/0,,2195590,00.html

———. 2008. "How Fiction Lost the Plot" 2008 [cited 5 January 2008]. Available from http://www.guardian.co.uk/commentisfree/story/0,,2235794,00.html

Lodge, David. 2006. "The Author's Curse.". *The Guardian* (20 May 2006), http://books.guardian.co.uk/departments/generalfiction/story/0,,1779181,00.html

———. 2007. "A Mixed Blessing: A Writer's View of Literary Prizes." In *Pre-and post-publication itineraries of the contemporary novel in English*, edited by V. Guignery and F. Gallix. Paris: Editions Publibook Université.

Lubbock, John. 1886. "On the Pleasure of Reading" *The Contemporary Review* 49 (Jan.-June).

Marsh-Locket, Carol P. 1993. "Centering the Caribbean Literary Imagination" *Studies in the Literary Imagination* 26 (2).

McCrum, Robert. 2007. "It's Time to Ditch the Prize Guys" *The Observer* (October 21, 2007), http://books.guardian.co.uk/manbooker2007/story/0,,2195896,00.html.

Ohaeto, Ezenwa. 1993. "Reflections and Reactions: Literature and Wole Soyinka's Nobel Prize in Nigeria." *Commonwealth* 16 (1).

Ohmann, Richard. 1975. "The Shaping of a Canon: U.S. Fiction, 1960-1975" In *Canons*, edited by R. v. Hallbert. Chicago: U of Chicago P.

Phelps, Gilbert. 1992. "Literature and Drama". In *Modern Britain. The Cambridge Cultural History.* , edited by B. Ford. Cambridge: Cambridge UP.

Pons, Xavier. 1993. "'And the Winner is…' Literary Prizes in Australia." *Commonwealth* 16 (1).

Rees, Cees J. Van. 1985. "Empirical Sociology of Cultural Productions." *Poetics* 14.

Salzman, Paul. 1989. *The New Diversity. Australian Fiction 1970-88*. Melbourne: McPhee Gribble Pub.

Todd, Richard. 1996. *Consuming Fictions. The Booker Prize and Fiction in Britain Today.* . London: Bloomsbury.

Drawbacks in the Process of Editing a Non-Canonical Chaucerian Text

The Case of Yonge Gamelyne of the *Canterbury Tales*

Nila Vázquez[1]

Introduction

With scholars such as Bédier (1928), Pasquali (1934) and Bowers (1959), the process of editing arrived, during the 20th century, at an intermediate position between *emendatio ope ingenii* or *divinatio*[2] (the editor guesses what needs to be changed in her/his text) and *recensio sine interpretatione*[3] (the editor sticks to the text), allowing for a balanced combination of sources' authority and editor's judgement in *l'art d'éditer les anciens texts*[4] ("the art of editing old texts"). More recently, Greg has asked for eclectic editing, against "the fallacy of the "best text" and "the tyranny of the copy-text" (1950-1, 19-37) and McGann has considered the text as a social construct and has focused on the cooperation process involved in the production of a literary work (1992, 1-13). When I started preparing my edition of *Gamelyn*, I had to review a great amount of literature on textual criticism and critical editing to decide what kind of outcome I wanted to produce. I found many interesting ideas as regards the process of editing but I have to say that I agree, most of all, with Peter Robinson (2000, 5-14) when he states that the main aim of the editor should be to offer a useful tool so that readers can make a connection between variation and meaning. As he says, a scholarly edition is more than simply presenting an archive of variants, and a critically edited text accompanied by "the many texts" is the best instrument a reader can be offered. With this principle in mind, together with Housman''s idea that the best scholarly editor must be notable by her/his "absence" and must keep a balance between authorial intent and textual

---

[1] Dr. Nila Vázquez is part of the Research Project "Variation, Linguistic Change and Grammaticalization", grant HUM2007-60706 (Spanish Ministry for Science and Innovation). This grant is hereby gratefully acknowledged.

[2] This method of editing was used until the 18th century by the humanists.

[3] Scholars such as Karl Lachmann and Friedrich Wolf used this procedure in their editions (Lachmann 1846, Wolf 1884).

[4] This is a reference to Bédier's work (1928, 161-96, 321-56).

precision, I undertook the task of editing the romance of "Yonge Gamelyn" of the *Canterbury Tales*.

One of the main drawbacks I had to face once I had decided to edit this text was the fact that it was considered a spurious text which had been inserted in some manuscripts of the *Canterbury Tales*, probably because it was found among Chaucer's belongings at his death. As some scholars say, "it is possible that Chaucer did intend to write a version of it for use as the Cook's tale" (Drabble 1995, 378), but no one except Norman Blake,[5] when I came to meet *Gamelyn*, dared insinuate a possible Chaucerian authorship for the *Tale* or, at least, suggest that more research had to be done on the subject. However, to determine whether this tale was written by Chaucer or whether it is a spurious text is far from the aim of the present piece of work and I will focus now on its relationship with the *Canterbury Tales*.

1. Gamelyn and the Canterbury Tales

The *Tale of Gamelyn* is a verse romance written in 902 lines, arranged in rhyming couplets. It does not occur anywhere else other than in manuscripts of the *Canterbury Tales*. Using Manly and Rickert's classification of the manuscripts of the *Tales* (1940, 2:49-77), the twenty-five witnesses which include *Gamelyn* are the following:[6]

- Bodleian Library MS Barlow 20c (Bw), type ~d[7]
- Christ Church Oxford MS 152 (Ch)
- Corpus Christi College Oxford MS 198 (Cp), type c
- Takamiya MS 32: Delamere (Dl), type d
- British Library MS Egerton 2863 (En^2), type d
- Fitzwilliam Museum McClean 181 (Fi), type ~d
- Glasgow Hunterian Museum U.1.1 (Gl), type d
- British Library MS Harley 1758 (Ha^2), type d
- British Library MS Harley 7334 (Ha^4)
- Bodleian Library MS Hatton Donat. 1 (Ht), type ~d

---

[5] It was he who encouraged me to edit the *Tale of Gamelyn* and who introduced me to the *Canterbury Tales* Project.

[6] *Gamelyn* appears in twenty-five out of eighty-four copies of Chaucer's work. However, if we take into consideration only those copies of the *Tales* which are complete (fifty-five), *Gamelyn* appears in forty-five percent of the volumes.

[7] The symbol ~ plus the letter <d> means that the MS shows an order of the d type but with some variations. When no indication of type ordering appears, the MS shows a unique arrangement of the tales.

- Cambridge University Library Ii.3.26 (Ii)
- British Library MS Lansdowne 851 (La), type *c*
- Bodleian Library MS Laud Misc. 600 (Ld^1)
- Bodleian Library MS Laud Misc. 739 (Ld^2), type *d*
- Lichfield Cathedral MS 29 (Lc), type *d*
- Cambridge University Library Mm.2.5 (Mm), type *d*
- Pierpont Morgan Library MS 249 (Mg), type *d*
- Rosenbach Museum and Library 1084/1 (Ph^3), type *d*
- Petworth House MS 7 (Pw), type *d*
- Bodleian Library MS Rawlinson Poetry 149 (Ra^2), type ~*d*
- British Library MS Royal 17 D.XV (Ry^1), type ~*d*
- British Library MS Royal 18 C.II (Ry^2), type *d*
- British Library MS Sloane 1685 (Sl^1), type *d*
- British Library MS Sloane 1686 (Sl^2), type *c*
- Trinity College Oxford MS 49 (To^1)

As seen above, the *Tale of Gamelyn* appears only in manuscripts with a *c*, *d* or unique arrangement of the tales and, in most cases, it is placed between sections A (which contains GP, KnT, MiT, ReT and the CkT) and B1 (the MLT). The only two exceptions are manuscripts Hatton Donat.1 (Ht) and Rawlinson Poetry 149 (Ra2). In the former, the CkT and Gamelyn are displaced and appear between the MLT and its end-link. In the latter, it follows the MeT and precedes the WBT. Apparently, the editors of Chaucer's manuscripts did not hesitate when arranging this particular Tale. We do not discuss whether Chaucer had left any indication of where it should be placed, [or whether it was apparently intended to appear as the second tale told by the Cook (Knight and Ohlgren 1997, 184).⁸ The basic reason for this belief is that it is found following the introduction made by the Cook and, in some manuscripts, for instance Harley 7334, it appears with the label "The Cookes Tale of Gamelyn." Leaving aside the issue of which pilgrim this tale should be assigned to, it becomes clear that we are dealing with a poem connected to the Robin Hood ballads. The plot tells us about Gamelyn, the youngest of three brothers who is mistreated by his wicked eldest brother after their father's death. Gamelyn

---

[8] Although some scholars (Urry 1721, 36, Skeat 1893, xv and Snell 1901, 5) believe that the *Tale of Gamelyn* should fit better as the tale told by the Yeoman, perhaps the first editors decided to link it to the CkT, posibly because of the reference to a cook in line 92 where Gamelyn says "Go and bake it yourself, I will not be your cook!," and this initial arrangement was followed by others in later copies.

has to escape to the woods and becomes an outlaw. In the end, he takes revenge on his eldest brother and some men of the Church who wanted to have him hanged, recovers all that his father had given him and ends his days happily married.

2. Previous Editions of the *Tale*

Before starting the process of editing the *Tale*, I analyzed all the previous editions of *Gamelyn*. It has been printed on different occasions from the early eighteenth century to the present day.[9]

The first edition of *Gamelyn* is found in John Urry's 1721 volume on Chaucer's works. It shows the readings of nine manuscripts where the *Tale* appears, though Urry's spellings make it impossible to discern on which manuscript he based his text. In the late eighteenth century, John Bell (1782), in his book devoted to the work of the poets of Great Britain, and, later on, Robert Anderson (1795), take their texts directly from Urry's. Perhaps the most interesting difference between these two versions of the *Tale* is a note introduced in the latter arguing that the *Tale of Gamelyn* was not written by Chaucer.

Moving ahead into the nineteenth century, we find Alexander Chalmers' 1810 edition. This volume offers another replica of Urry's version and includes an inaccurate assertion by the author that the *Tale of Gamelyn* was added to Chaucer's canon by Stow.[10]

Thomas Wright is the first editor to depart from Urry's text. In his work on the *Canterbury Tales* (1847-51), he chooses British Library manuscript Harley 7334 as base text for his edition of the *Canterbury Tales* and presents *Gamelyn* in smaller type to distinguish it from the other tales.[11] On page 51 Wright says: "Tyrwhitt omits this tale [in his eighteenth century edition], as being certainly not Chaucer's in which judgement he is probably right." Thus, Wright accepts the widespread opinion of *Gamelyn*'s spurious character, though the use of the adverb "probably" (he could have chosen "certainly" or "absolutely") allows for discussion. This version skips three lines (563, 601 and 602), no doubt due to an unintentional mistake of the editor.

As was the case with Urry's edition, which was followed by later editors of the *Canterbury Tales*, Wright's text was reprinted by Robert Bell and

---

[9] A first draft of the discusión on previous editions of Gamelyn appeared in Vázquez and Conde Silvestre (2005, 161-73).

[10] John Stow was one of the first editors of the *Canterbury Tales* (1561), as well as one of the first scholars who devoted his studies to the figure of Geoffrey Chaucer.

[11] The change of type can be seen as a way to warn the reader that this particular tale is somewhat special, though the editor decides to include it anyway.

Richard Morris in the course of the nineteenth century. The former reproduces Wright's version in his edition of English Poets (1854-56). In fact, the reproduction is so literal that Wright's omission of lines 563, 601 and 602 also occurs here. Bell justifies the inclusion of *Gamelyn*[12] in his edition saying: "it is retained in this edition as a curious specimen of a species of composition long popular among the Anglo-Saxon peasantry" (vol. I: 238). On the other hand, Morris's version (1866) rectifies the omission of the lines and corrects some other mistakes.

In turn, the six-text edition of the *Canterbury Tales* presented by Frederik Furnivall (1868), offers the readings of Royal 18 C. II, Harley 1758, Sloane 1685, Corpus, Petworth and Lansdowne 851. It obviously omits Harley 7334 because it had been printed before three times.

Skeat's 1884 version is actually the only proper edition of *Gamelyn* so far. He follows Harley 7334 as base text, which is, for him, "much the best and oldest of the manuscripts containing the Tale" (1893, xxx), and collates it with Furnivall's readings in his 1868 edition. It includes an interesting introduction to the *Tale*, in which he examines some aspects of the romance, such as its metre, rhymes and lexicon (always through a non-Chaucerian prism) and mentions its connection with Lodge's *Rosalynde*, Shakespeare's *As You Like It* and the ballads of Robin Hood. The most important flaw of this quite good edition is, in my opinion, the overload of personal beliefs and comments when analysing the contents of the *Tale*. A couple of examples will suffice: "I cannot but protest against the stupidity of the botcher whose hand wrote above it *The Cokes Tale*" (xiv), when referring to the title *The Cook's Tale* used for *Gamelyn* in Harley 7334; or "which may easily have been a mistake for fourteenth, such mistakes being extremely common" (xxxv), when discussing Lindner's (1878-79) dating of *Gamelyn* and trying to excuse him for suggesting it was written in the thirteenth century.[13] Skeat dates the *Tale* ca. 1340, places it in the East Midlands and assumes that there must have been a French original from which it would have been translated. However, he does not offer clear evidence

---

[12] Since Robert Bell is reprinting Wright's version of the *Canterbury Tales*, which incorporates the *Tale of Gamelyn*, this tale has to appear in his edition and cannot be left out. However, his need to justify its presence reveals that the author believed it to be spurious and not written by Chaucer.

[13] Skeat agreed with most of Lindner's assertions on *Gamelyn*, but not with his dating of the *Tale* and, here, he tries to convince the reader that Lindner could have miswritten "thirteenth century" instead of "fourteenth century." However, a close reading of Lindner's article reveals that the same idea is suggested several times. On one occasion, he talks about dating *Gamelyn* 100 years before Chaucer's time (Lindner 1878-79, 98), thus leaving his intention clear.

for any of these assertions. Finally, one of the most outstanding benefits of Skeat's edition is that it includes a chapter with some explanatory notes and a small glossary at the end which provides grammatical information about some of the tokens.

Moving forward in time, we find Furnivall's transcription of the Harleian manuscript for the Chaucer Society (1885) and Skeat's revision of his 1884 edition (1893). Neither of these two works offers innovative details worth pointing out.[14] The version reached by Furnivall is the one used by French and Hale and by Sands. French and Hale include *Gamelyn* in their 1930 collection of medieval romances, though no further information is added. In turn, Sands' edition (1966), the most widely known version of the romance, as the *Oxford Companion* reads (Drabble 1995, 378), discusses the connections between Gamelyn, Robin Hood and Lodge's Rosader (the male character in *Rosalynde*). In his introduction to the text, Sands offers a brief summary of the plot and acknowledges that his edition combines features of several others. When compared with previously printed versions of the *Tale*, it becomes clear that we are dealing with a diplomatic edition based on that by French and Hale.

The most recent edition of *Gamelyn* is Knight and Ohlgren's 1997 version, which is included in a collection of outlaw tales. The editors decide to use the Petworth manuscript as base text because "editorial work on the *Canterbury Tales* has shown these two manuscripts [Corpus and Harley 7334] to be unreliable"[15] and "collation shows it [Petworth] to offer the best readings […] in this version *Gamelyn* on a significant number of occasions seems a better poem" (Knight and Ohlgren 1997, 184). In their introduction to the text they discuss briefly its style, focus on its plot and its narrative and emphasise its connections with the Robin Hood cycle. Knight and Ohlgren date the *Tale* ca. 1350-70, following the historians Keen (1961), Holt (1989) and Dunn (1967), and place it near Leicestershire.

The diachronic survey of previous editions of the *Tale* given above reveals that, in those works belonging to the eighteenth and nineteenth centuries, *Gamelyn* appears in editions of Chaucer's *Canterbury Tales*, whereas, in the twentieth century volumes, it is included in collections of romances

---

[14] It is worth noticing that Furnivall agrees with Skeat in his choice of Ha⁴ as base text in spite of considering this manuscript as generally unreliable (1885, viii).

[15] Knight is here referring to his edition of The Franklin's Tale for the *Variorum* Chaucer, for which he used Pw as base text and rejected the readings of Cp and Ha4.

of various kinds (Middle English Romances and Outlaw Tales). In the first case, even though the editors did not generally accept the *Tale* as Chaucer's, following Tyrwhitt's argument that "it is not to be found in any of the MSs of the first authority" (1775-78, 145), they decided to include it because it occurred in the manuscripts of the *Canterbury Tales* which they were using, i.e. Corpus, Harley 1758, Harley 7334, Lansdowne, Petworth, Royal 18 C. II and Sloane 1685. By the end of the nineteenth century, the position of Harley 7334 as one of the best manuscripts for the *Canterbury Tales* changed and Ellesmere (Huntington Library El. 26 C 9) and Hengwrt (National Library of Wales Peniarth 392 D) started to be regarded as better copies. Neither of these two manuscripts includes the *Tale of Gamelyn*, though the scribe responsible for both of them (Adam Pynkhurst, Mooney 2004, 3) leaves some space after the "unfinished" tale told by the Cook as if he were waiting for some material to be included there.

Finally, in the late nineteenth century some eminent scholars, such as Lindner (1878-79) and, then, Skeat (1893 [1884]), following Lindner's premises, resolutely argued against the possible Chaucerian authorship of the romance, on the grounds of grammar, lexicon and rhyme in the poem. From that moment on, *Gamelyn*'s position changed from being considered a "presumably spurious tale" to being completely rejected and omitted in subsequent editions of the *Canterbury Tales*. As a result, the only twentieth century versions of *Gamelyn* we find appear in collections of romances and ballads.

3. A New Edition of *Gamelyn*

As seen above, most of the editions of *Gamelyn* that have come to us are basically printed transcriptions of single manuscripts, very often reprinted by other editors of the *Canterbury Tales*. Thus, Urry's blurry eclectic version (an exception, for he says that he used nine manuscripts) was reprinted by John Bell, Anderson and Chalmers; Wright's version, using Harley 7334 as base text, was, in turn, reprinted by Robert Bell and also by Morris; Furnivall's edition, using Harley 7334 as base text, was also used by French and Hale and then by Sands, who took it through the latter; Skeat's version collates the readings in Harley 7334 with Furnivall's six-text version; finally, Knight and Ohlgren use Petworth for their edition. As can be seen, first Harley 7334 (in almost all the editions) and then Petworth (in one) are the preferred manuscripts for the printed versions of *Gamelyn*. As will become evident in the discussion of the best readings for the romance below, I believe, however, that neither of these manuscripts should be used as base text for this particular tale. In addition, all of these versions offer a modernised and extremely regularised text.

Furthermore, rather than focusing on the individual characteristics of the romance and their analysis, the different editors dwell on giving reasons for keeping *Gamelyn* outside Chaucer's canon. In my opinion, none of the reasons they allege constitutes conclusive proof that this is indeed the case. The refutation of each of their arguments is beyond the scope of the present piece of work. However, a couple of examples will suffice. Lindner's description of Gamelyn's brother's house (an Anglo-Norman house of the thirteenth century style) is given by this scholar as a reason to situate the romance in the thirteenth century (1878-79, 321), well before Chaucer's lifetime. In turn, Skeat asserts that the percentage of French loans in this tale is "very different from what we find in Chaucer" (1893, xxviii), using this weak argument (for Chaucer's versatility of the lexicon, depending on the type of work, style, discourse, etc., has always been recognised) as a proof to consider *Gamelyn* as non-Chaucerian. Moreover, Skeat affirms that false rhymes, such as those in lines 45-46: *two / goo*, or 575-576: *gate / scape*, could have never come out of Chaucer's hands (xxvi, xxvii). He explains the first "deficient rhyme" on the basis of the "potential" way of pronouncing *twoo* as /oa/ at that time, but this is a mere hypothesis. As for the second instance, Skeat neglects that rhymes of this kind including plosives /p, t, k/ are found in contemporary poems (e.g. in lines 2753/2754 of Chaucer's *Romaunt of the Rose* we can read *And trowe thei shulde nevere* **escape** */ Nere that hope couthe hem* **make**).[16] Finally, for him, rhymes such as those in lines 93-94: *nowe / nowe* and 445-456: *other / other* are "simple repetitions" resulting from the lack of proficiency of the author, without noticing that these sentimental rhymes were frequently used in the erudite poetry of the Middle Ages.

In conclusion, none of the examined editions of the *Tale of Gamelyn* is, from my point of view, completely exhaustive or reliable, and the most accurate one, Skeat's version, is too focused on personal beliefs and decisions and too much influenced by Lindner's article (1878-79) on the romance. In view of the obvious shortcomings of the existing versions of the tale, my goal was to attain a transparent edition that would treat *Gamelyn* as a separate piece of work.

---

[16] These rhymes are taken from the transcription of Chaucer's work found in MS Glasgow Hunter 409 (V.3.7), available at the URL of the *Romaunt of the Rose* Project: http://www.memss.arts.gla.ac.uk

3.1. Choosing a Base Text for the Edition

When preparing the edition of a text which has survived in a large number of manuscripts, it is essential to choose carefully the one that will be used as base text (i.e. the *codex optimus*, Blecua 1987, 33). As Greg (1950-51, 374), one of the fathers of modern textual criticism, states a copy text is an "early text of a work which an editor [chooses] as the basis of his own." It is also important to select a significant group of exemplars against which the selected manuscript will be collated, for "in a properly critical edition, the editor will produce a critical text which is based upon the copy text but into which has been introduced a series of emendations and corrections" (McGann 1992, 24). Bearing in mind that the oldest and most carefully written manuscripts very often contain closer readings to the original of an author, and following Manly and Rickert's dating of the manuscripts in which *Gamelyn* appears (1940), the prime candidates for becoming the base text of my new edition were Corpus, Harley 7334 and Petworth.[17] Let us analyze some examples in these three and some other valuable manuscripts which have been helpful in coming to a decision as to which text should be used as base text.

When lines 281-283 of *Gamelyn* are analysed in several witnesses, it can be seen that they appear in Ch, Cp, Ha[4] and La, whereas Pw, among others, lacks them, obviously because they were not included in the text from which they were copied. The scribes of Ht, Mm and Ry[2] decided not to interfere,[18] whereas the Pw scribe added a whole line as a new line 283. In manuscripts Fi and Lc, where these lines are missing as well, the scribes also added a new line 283, but none of these two manuscripts agrees with Pw.

L 281

Cp	And sayde haue gamelyn the Ring		and	the Ram
Ch	seiden		rynge	&
Ha[4]	seyden	Gamelyn	Ryng	
La	seide	Gamelin	ringe	&

Fi, Ht, Lc, Mm, Pw and **Ry**[2] omit the line

---

[17]   As seen above, Harley 7334 (in most cases) and Petworth (in one) have been chosen as base text in former editions of *Gamelyn*.

[18]   These lines are lacking in Mm. However, there is one *N*. for *Nota* on the left margin and an annotation on the right margin of line 284, saying *Hic deficit versus in copia*. At the end of the folio there is one *A*. for *Addenda* on the left margin, where a later hand adds the three missing lines, in agreement with the readings in Cp, Ch, Ha[4] and La.

L 282

Cp	For the beste wrastelere that euer heere cam	
Ch	wrasteler	here
Ha⁴	best wrasteler	here
La	best wrastelier that	here

Fi, Ht, Lc, Mm, Pw and **Ry²** omit the line

L 283

Cp	Thus wan	Gamely the	Ram and the Ryng
Ch		Gamelyn	&
Fi	And	Gamelyn that was so ginge	
Ha⁴		Gamelyn	
La	wanne	Gamelin rame &	Ringe
Lc	Saunt mercy seide Gamelyn anon withoute lettyng		
Pw	And	Gamelyn bithought him it was a faire thinge	

Ht, Mm, and **Ry²** omit the line

A similar example is found in line 377, where Pw offers a reading different from that in the group Cp, Ha⁴ and La, and also different from that in Fi:

L 377

Cp	Lat me bynde the bothe hand and foote
Fi	And therfore y doo hit and other wey I not
Ha⁴	now feet
La	honde &
Pw	This most be fulfilled my men to dote

Ch, Ht, Lc, Mm and **Ry²** omit the line

In line 246 we witness another intrusion of the Pw scribe, who replaced *oon arm* "one arm" by *owne arme* "own arm," in order to achieve a "better" reading (none of the other manuscripts shows that form).

L 246

Cp	And tharto his **oon** arm that yaf a gret crak
Ha⁴	And therto his **oon** arm that gaf a gret crak
Pw	And therto his **owne** arme that gaf a grete crake

In lines 251 and 267, we see the same scribe making mistakes and trying to amend them.[19]

---

[19] [del] and [add] are the tags used in the *Canterbury Tales* Project to indicate that the scribe has deleted or added a certain word respectively.

L 251

Cp	Than seyde the Frankelein that hadde his sone there
Ha⁴	Thanne seyde the Frankeleyn that had his sones there
Pw	Than seide the frankeley þᵗ had the sones [del]thre[/ del] there

L 267

Cp	Tuo gentil men that yemede the place
Ha⁴	Tuo gentil men ther were that yemede the place
Pw	Two gentile men [add]that[/add] ȝemed the place

Finally, in line 292, he first changes the word order of *was it* and then adds *strong* to repair the lost rhythm. Again Pw is the only manuscript that shows such a reading.

L 292

Cp	Than **was it** schett faste with a pyn
Ha⁴	And thanne **was it** schet faste with a pyn
Pw	And **it was** shett fast with a **strong** pynne

The illustrative examples discussed so far, in addition to some others,[20] convincingly prove that Cp and Ha⁴ are not as "unreliable" as Knight and Ohlgren suggest (1997) and that "collation" does not always show Pw "to offer the best readings," at least for this particular tale. Let us consider now some other exceptional readings in Cp and Ha⁴. The focus will be on additions, for omissions can easily be explained as simple scribal errors:[21]

- In line 144, Cp and Ha⁴ (together with Fi and Lc, the latter probably following Ha⁴'s text), insert a word to make clear the meaning of the sentence, but Ha⁴ does not succeed in obtaining a good rhythm.[22]

L 144

Cp	To haue hem **driuen** fro me þei wolde haue do me harmes
Fi	To haue hem **kepte** fro me þey wolde haue do me harmes
Ha⁴	To haue **I put hem** fro me he wolde haue do me harmes
Lc	To haue **put hem** fro me thei wolde haue do me harmes

---

[20] Similar examples from Pw can be found in lines 20, 37, 58, 98, 101, 105, 106, 134, 144, 165, 287, 292, 330, 426, 638, 696 among others.

[21] Cp and Ha⁴ are written by the same scribe.

[22] Likewise, Ha⁴ makes a mistake with the pronouns.

- In line 172, in both cases, the scribe adds *vp*, perhaps as a result of a personal interference related to his use of idiomatic expressions. In Cp, the scribe places *vp* before the main verb and also introduces the prefix *y-* before the past participle *set*, whereas in Ha[4] he puts *vp* after the main verb. The rhythm of the line is regularised in both cases, though, in the first one, it becomes more elegant.

    L 172
    Cp   And ther fore ther was   **vp y**set a Ram and a Ryng
    Ha[4]   And therfor ther was   sette **vp** a Ram and a Ryng

- In line 414 the Cp scribe adds *lose* (Fi and Lc add *hold* and *help* respectively) in an attempt to clarify the syntax of the sentence:

    L 414
    Cp   I wil holde the couenant and thou wil **lose** me
    Ha[4]   I wol hold the couenant and thou wil   me

- Ha[4]'s additions constantly break the rhythm, whereas Cp's tend to improve it. Some examples are:

    L 260
    Cp   And sayde if ther be moo lat he come to werke
    Ha[4]   And sayde if ther be **eny** mo lat hem come to werk

    L 267
    Cp   Tuo gentil men   yemede the place
    Ha[4]   Two gentil men **ther were that** yemede the place

    L 312
    Cp   He leet **hem** in all   that gone wolde or ryde
    Ha[4]   He lete   in all **maner men** that gon wold or ryde

    L 592
    Cp   For to helpe Gamelyn and goode strokes **he** ʒaf
    Ha[4]   For to helpe Gamelyn and goode strokes   ʒaf

Finally, Ha[4] is frequently the only manuscript with a reverse word order of elements in a sentence, as can be seen in line 119: *a staf had* instead of *had a staf*, line 232: me fynd instead of *fynd me* or line 570: *wordes two* instead of *two wordes*.

In view of the examples discussed above and some others,[23] it becomes clear that Cp can be regarded as the most reliable manuscript containing *Gamelyn* and, as such, it will be used as base text for my critical edition of the *Tale*.

3.2. Selecting Additional Manuscripts for the Edition

The manuscripts to be collated against the base text, Cp, were selected taking into account a combination of significant criteria: on the one hand, their nature as old (i.e. closer to Chaucer's lifetime) and valuable manuscripts; on the other hand, their representativeness within the general classification in the textual tradition of the *Canterbury Tales* and their textual affiliation.[24] Bearing all these criteria in mind, a first group of manuscripts, comprising Ha^4, La and Pw, was selected. They are the best old exemplars after Cp. Besides, Ha^4 shows a unique arrangement of the *Tales*, La represents type *c*, and Ha^4 and Pw were used as base text in previous editions of *Gamelyn*. A second group of manuscripts includes Mm, Lc and Ry^2, which, together with Pw, are some of the best representatives of type *d* (this group contains the largest number of witnesses in which the romance appears). Thirdly, Fi and exemplify type *d* with some variations. Finally, Ch was selected on account of its classification as another worthy manuscript with a unique structure and of its close relationship with the oldest exemplars Cp, Ha^4 and La.

As a result of the process of selection discussed above, an illustrative collection of ten manuscripts was achieved (Cp + Ch, Fi, Ha^4, Ht, La, Lc, Mm, Pw and Ry^2). Those late careless copies and those that were direct copies of other manuscripts were disregarded, since their readings would not be significant enough to be taken into account. The only inclusion of a somewhat "inaccurate" or "corrupt" manuscript is Fi. Nevertheless, since it has been suggested that "there is a possibility that in some tales it represents pre-*Canterbury Tales* versions and in others first drafts" (Manly and Rickert 1940, 1:163), checking its readings of *Gamelyn* against those of the other manuscripts might prove revealing in future research.

---

[23] More examples from Ha^4 can be found in lines 50, 69, 123, 131, 144, 146, 165, 168, 189, 212, 263, 312, 409, 450, 481, 563, 570, 588, 641, 681, 732, 777, 782, 804, 830, 851, 872 and 892 among others. In contrast, Cp offers the best readings for lines 43, 144, 147, 217, 287, 312, 408, 414, 519, 592, 606, 618, 641 and 715 among others.

[24] I have also taken into consideration Manly and Rickert's description of Chaucer's manuscripts (1940, vol. I) and Rogers' grouping of the manuscripts containing the Canterbury Tales (1959, 54-59).

3.3. Recensio and Emendatio of the codex optimus

After finishing the collation of the manuscripts, I analyzed all the variants found in the different witnesses. This was another challenging step in the process of editing the romance.

When dealing with texts such as the *Canterbury Tales*, in which all the extant witnesses derive from a single ultimate source, no authority can be given to a particular variant found in a particular manuscript, since we do not know how close any of the exemplars was to the spelling of their ancestor.[25] This accounts for the editorial decision of following mainly the base text and avoiding the extreme regularisation of spellings found in previous editions of *Gamelyn* which results in an artificial text, distant from the original Middle English version. As is well-known, the Middle English period is characterised by great variation in spelling and by showing important developments in the English language, from the fixed conventions of Old English to the advances of Early Modern English. Information of this type would obviously be lost in a modernised and regularised edition of the text. However, some amendments have been made in order to present an improved version of the *Tale* contained in the base text. As Robinson (2002, 54) asserts, even "authoritative texts [manuscripts] may contain scribal errors [...] this [the base text] is one text among many." A similar idea is found in Moorman (1975, 55): "no MS, whatever its authority, is faultless, nor can the MS itself be counted on to reveal its own errors." Thus, the readings in Cp have been corrected in those cases in which it showed a scribal mistake.[26] Some other changes in certain words are the result of single editorial decisions based upon the collation process (either *emendatio ope codicum* or *emendatio ope ingenii*, Blecua 1987, 34), also following the advice given by Moorman to the *novice editor* that "before making any change, the editor should (1) make every reasonable effort to justify the MS reading and (2) make no change without having a clear, articulate, and positive reason [...] for doing so" (1975, 57). In most cases, the editorial decision was clear because most of the valuable manuscripts agreed on a particular reading and that was included in the edited version of the text. However, on some occasions, none of them agreed and showed completely different readings. Then, the problem was worked out using the criteria of internal rhythm. Thus, the variant chosen was the one that suited best the rhythmical pattern of the line/s.

[25] The *ancestor* or *archetype* is interpreted here, following Thorpe's definition, as the manuscript that "most nearly approaches that from which all other MSS descend" (1972, 109).

[26] This happens only on a few occasions, for the Cp scribe was quite careful in his duty.

3.4. Displaying the results

This is one of the most important stages in the production of a scholarly edition. All the previous steps can be correct but if the results are not presented in a coherent way, the editor will fail in her/his main goal, which is, for me, attracting the interest of the reader.

As my intention was to offer the reader all the information available, I decided to render a synoptic edition of the *Tale*, together with my own edited version. The synoptic edition of a given work is made up of the different diplomatic editions of the manuscripts in which the text appears. In turn, a diplomatic edition consists in the transcription of the lines of a text as close to the original as possible. In Moorman's words a diplomatic edition entails "the faithfully transcribed reproduction as in a facsimile of a single MS including every spelling variant, every mark of punctuation, every scribal error" (1975, 48). This implies that any relevant feature observed in its lines should be reflected in the final output. Even apparently unimportant characteristics, such as tails in final letters are shown in the transcriptions included in my edition of *Gamelyn*. The reason for doing so is that the editor is not to judge what is or is not important to show. The aim is to provide the reader with as much information as possible, for she/he is the one who will decide what to concentrate on. For instance, although a final tail may not be significant at first sight, in some manuscripts it may stand for a final <e> which is no longer pronounced. Besides, the synoptic edition provided includes a large amount of information on specific features related to the general aspect of the manuscripts, including details about glosses, deletions, additions and so on. This way, the reader will be able to look for specific items depending on her/his research preferences.

On the other hand, in my edited text of the *Tale of Gamelyn*, "thorn" has been regularised into <th>, while "iogh" has been kept wherever it occurred in the base text. Moreover, abbreviations have been expanded, numbers appear in letters and specific characters used in the diplomatic transcriptions, such as tails, flourishes and macrons, have been disregarded. No further modernisation has been carried out, apart from the insertion of modern use of capital letters and punctuation marks. Finally, scribal word-division has been kept, except in the case of past participles with the prefix *y-/I-* (sometimes attached to the verb, sometimes standing independently before it), which appear as a single word starting with *y-*.

Concerning the notes to the text, these do not provide grammatical information, nor detailed explanations of meaning, nor information on the readings of other manuscripts, nor observations on similarities in content or language with other literary works. This is so because information of these kinds is already offered in other parts of my volume. Thus, the complete glossarial index includes grammatical information on each of the tokens in the text. Furthermore, the reader is provided with a translation of the *Tale* into Present-day English, while the *apparatus criticus* of the edited version of *Gamelyn* offers all the details regarding different manuscript occurrences. Moreover, the type of language used and the major coincidences with different authors in language and plot are discussed in a chapter on internal and external features of the text. Any other relevant *background* information on a certain word, phrase or sentence appears in a footnote attached to it.

Final Remarks

This oral-flavoured written romance is clearly an outlaw tale, but also an epitome of the "wicked brother's leit motif" common to the Latin and Scandinavian traditions. Evil characters are punished for their unfair deeds, whereas the hero and his companions are rewarded. The theme of the *Tale of Gamelyn*, however, is not that simple. It can also be regarded as one of the most ironic condemnations of the English Church ever presented in the Middle Ages or as a good source to analyse how medieval law worked (cf. Shannon 1951). In spite of its shortcomings, such as its rough, sometimes rather repetitive style, *Gamelyn* can be regarded as a proficient piece of work. After all, the prime aim of a narrative is to entertain, and the vividness of this romance holds the reader's attention until the final couplet. Moreover, its happy end inspires a rewarding feeling that, in the end, justice prevails.

The aim of my edition has been to provide the reader with some information about the *Tale of Gamelyn,* a small work of art included in some of the manuscripts of Geoffrey Chaucer's *Canterbury Tales.* In my study, I discuss the relationship between *Gamelyn* and the *Tales,* I offer some relevant information on the manuscripts containing the *Tale* and, finally, I present a new critical edition, accompanied by its translation into Present-day English and a glossarial index. The idea of reaching important conclusions was not in my mind when I started my research. This volume is practical in its essence, the result obtained from my research work being the work itself. Each part of the book is the outcome of months and months of study and analysis of the data obtained at the consecutive stages. The transcriptions of all the manuscripts, together with the results of the collation of all the lines, were necessary to achieve a critical edition in which the best possible readings for the *Tale of Gamelyn* have been reached. Finally, this new text was used as base text for the translation and the glossarial index.

Editing the *Tale of Gamelyn* has been an extremely interesting experience. I had to learn some essentials of Palaeography and Textual Criticism for the transcriptions and the codicological descriptions accompanying the individual diplomatic transcriptions and for the edited version of the *Tale*, respectively. I also had to learn how to use the programme COLLATE[27] to collate and regularise the lines of all the manuscripts and to achieve a "good" text of the romance. "Thought, method and decision," as Robinson (2002, 54) mentions when describing the process of undertaking a critical edition, accompanied me during the whole process of creating this new edition of *Gamelyn*. All the efforts, I believe, have been worthwhile, for I feel that we are now closer to the original text created by its author.

After such a long time working on the *Tale of Gamelyn* I am still uncertain about who wrote it and about the reason why it can only be found in manuscripts related to the *Canterbury Tales*. However, the real importance of this *Tale* lies in itself, in its own identity as a separate unit. It tells us an interesting story, related to some of the most popular romances and ballads written in contemporary and later periods in England and abroad. There is something special about it, perhaps its intensity in the narration of the plot, perhaps the way in which Justice prevails and natural order is restored. This may be the reason that led Thomas Lodge to base his *Rosalynde* upon it, perhaps the same reason that led Shakespeare to recreate it in his *As you like it*. Be that as it may, it is certain that, in spite of all the controversy surrounding its creation, *Gamelyn* will continue being studied as a valuable piece of work by later generations.

Bibliography

Anderson, Robert, ed. 1795. *The Works of the British Poets*. London: Robert Anderson.

Bédier, Joseph. 1928. "La tradition manuscrite du *Lai de l'Ombre*: réflexions sur l'art d'éditer les anciens textes." *Romania* 54: 161-196, 321-356.

---

[27] COLLATE is a computing tool developed by Peter Robinson.

Bell, John, ed. 1782. *The Poets of Great Britain Complete from Chaucer to Churchill*. London: John Bell.

Bell, Robert, ed. 1854-56. *Annotated Edition of English Poets. Annotated by John M. Jephson*. London: John W. Parker and son.

Blecua, Alberto. 1987. *Manual de Crítica Textual*. Madrid: Castalia.

Bowers, Fredson. 1959. *Textual and Literary Criticism*. Cambridge: Cambridge University Press.

Chalmers, Alexander, ed. 1810. *The Works of the English Poets from Chaucer to Cowper*. London: J. Johnson.

Drabble, Margaret, ed. 1995. *The Oxford Companion to English Literature*. Oxford: Oxford University Press.

French, Walter Hoyt and Charles Brockway Hale, ed. 1930. *Middle English Metrical Rom*ances. New York: Prentice Hall.

Furnivall, Frederick James, ed. 1868. *A Six-Text Print of Chaucer's Canterbury Tales*. The Chaucer Society. London: Kegan Paul, Trench, Trübner and Co.

———, ed. 1885. *The Harleian MS 7334 of Chaucer's Canterbury Tales*. The Chaucer Society. London: Kegan Paul, Trench, Trübner and Co.

Greg, Walter W. 1950-1. "The Rationale of Copy-Text." *Studies in Bibliography* 3: 19-37.

Housman, Alfred Edward. 1921. "The Application of Thought to Textual Criticism." *Proceedings of the Classical Association* 18: 67-84.

Knight, Stephen and Thomas Ohlgren, ed. 1997. *Robin Hood and Other Outlaw Tales*. Middle English Text Series. Kalamazoo, Michigan: Western Michigan University for TEAMS: 184-226.

Lachmann, Karl, ed. 1846 [1831]. *Novum Testamentum Graece, ex recensione Caroli Lachmanni*. Berolini: G. Reimer.

Lindner, Felix. 1878-79. "The Tale of Gamelyn." *Englische Studien* II: 94-114 and 321-343.

Manly, John Matthews and Edith Rickert, ed. 1940. *The Text of the Canterbury Tales, Studied on the Basis of All Known Manuscripts*. 8 vols. Chicago: University of Chicago Press.

McGann, Jerome J. 1992. *Critique of Modern Textual Criticism*. Chicago: University of Chicago Press, 1983. Repr. Charlottesville: University Press of Virginia.

Mooney, Linne. 2006. "Chaucer's Scribe." *Speculum: A Journal of Medieval Studies* 81: 97-138.

———. 2004. "Chaucer's Scribe: New Evidence of the Identification of the Scribe of the Hengwrt and Ellesmere Manuscripts of Chaucer's Canterbury Tales." Presented at the 14th Biennial Congress of the New Chaucer Society, University of Glasgow, 17 July 2004.
Moorman, Charles. 1975. *Editing the Middle English Manuscript.* Jackson: University Press of Mississippi.
Morris, Richard, ed. 1866. *The Poetical Works of Geoffrey Chaucer.* 6 vols. London: George Bell and Sons.
Pasquali, Giorgio. 1934. *Storia della tradizione e critica del testo.* Florence: Le Monnier.
Robinson, Peter M. W. 2000. "The One Text and the Many Texts." In *Making Texts for the Next Century,* edited by Peter M. W. Robinson and Hans Walter Gabler. *Literary and Linguistic Computing* 15.1: 5-14
———. 2002. What is a Critical Edition? *Variants* 1: 43-62.
Sands, Donald B., ed. 1966. *Middle English Verse Romances.* New York and London: Holt, Rinehart and Winston.
Shannon, Edgar F. Jr. 1951. "Medieval Law in The Tale of Gamelyn." *Speculum* 26: 458-464.
Skeat, Walter William, ed. 1893 [1884]. *The Tale of Gamelyn.* Oxford: Clarendon Press.
———, ed. 1963 [1894-97]. *The Complete Works of Geoffrey Chaucer.* 7 vols. Oxford: Clarendon Press: Vol. IV.
Snell, Frederick John. 1901. *The Age of Chaucer.* London: G. Bell.
Stow, John, ed. 1561. *The Workes of Geoffrey Chaucer, Newlie Printed, with Diuers Addicions, Whiche Were Never in Print Before.* London: Kyngston for Wight.
Thorpe, James. 1972. *Principles of Textual Criticism.* San Marino, CA: Huntington Library.
Tyrwhitt, Thomas, ed. 1775-78. *The Canterbury Tales of Chaucer.* 5 vols. London: Payne..
Urry, John, ed. 1721. *The Works of Geoffrey Chaucer, Compared with the Former Edition and Many Valuable Manuscripts.* London: Lintot.
Vázquez, Nila and J.C. Conde Silvestre, ed. 2005. *Editing Middle English Texts in the 21st Century: New Techniques and Approaches.* Murcia: Servicio de Publicaciones de la Universidad de Murcia.
Wolf, Friedrich August, ed. 1884 [1795]. *Prolegomena ad Homerum.* Halle: Orphanotrophei.
Wright, Thomas, ed. 1847-51. *The Canterbury Tales of Geoffrey Chaucer. A New Text with Illustrative Notes.* 3 vols. Percy Society. London: Richards.

Missing Link

The *V.* Galleys at the Morgan Library and the Harry Ransom Center

Luc Herman, John M. Krafft and Sharon B. Krafft

The famously private contemporary American novelist Thomas Pynchon — best known for the gemlike *Crying of Lot 49* (1966) and the monumental *Gravity's Rainbow* (1973) — has afforded readers few glimpses into his processes of composition. Even the seemingly revelatory introduction to the collected edition of all but one of his early short stories, *Slow Learner* (1984), is extremely, if subtly, guarded. So the surfacing in 2001 of a draft of his first novel, *V.* (1963), was a boon to scholars. In an earlier essay we surmise that this draft, a typescript now held by the Harry Ransom Humanities Research Center in Austin, Texas, was the working copy used by a typist in 1961 to prepare a clean copy for initial submission to J. B. Lippincott, the publisher that had contracted for *V.* Although we have not seen that clean copy, we infer that it was identical in content to the Ransom typescript, since the editorial correspondence about the former can be followed in detail by referring to the latter (Herman and Krafft 2007). Comparing the Ransom typescript with the published novel as we have done reveals much about how Pynchon reorganized his text, clarified its focus, eliminated some self-indulgent passages — reveals, in general, how and how quickly Pynchon matured as a writer. But the Ransom typescript alone does not tell the complete story of the evolution of *V.* So here we step back to examine more of the intermediate stages by which the one became the other.

By the early fall of 1962, Pynchon was at work with Faith Sale on the galley proofs of *V.*, which would be published the following March. Sale, an old friend of Pynchon's from their student days at Cornell, worked at Lippincott at this time. She probably took editorial charge of the novel after Pynchon's first editor, Corlies Smith, had moved from Lippincott to Viking around Labor Day in 1962. Sale's suitability for this task may have been determined by the fact that she was already quite familiar with the novel. Indeed, Pynchon had sent her a discarded draft — the Ransom typescript — of the novel's first version, which he had submitted to Lippincott in late June or early July of 1961. He rewrote the novel in the spring of 1962, cutting more than one hundred typescript pages, combining and reordering the chapters, but producing relatively little wholly new text in the process.

Yet even after this extensive revision, which did away with a lot of inferior material and led to an extraordinary new version of the chapter (nine) set in German South-West Africa, Pynchon does not seem to have been entirely happy with the result (Herman and Krafft 2006).

Two sets of unbound long galleys of *V.* (one held by the Morgan Library in New York as part of the Carter Burden collection,[1] and the other held by the Harry Ransom Center, which acquired it in the late 1960s) show that Pynchon made further cuts, totaling some four hundred and fifty lines, to the novel — and even produced a few new lines for it[2] — down to the wire. The galleys, therefore, constitute a missing link between the earliest known — Ransom — typescript version and the published novel. While the final cuts are most often far less substantial than those made during the spring 1962 rewriting, the galleys, especially viewed alongside an October 1962 letter from Pynchon to Sale written after he had finished proofreading the galleys, further contribute to an understanding of how *V.* came about. They even shed light on some problems left unsolved when considering the transition from the typescript to the final text. The Morgan galleys also provide a fascinating insight into the proofreading process.

Both sets of galleys, the Morgan and the Ransom, consist of 196 numbered leaves of text, printed on rectos only. The numbering goes up to 195, but a page 116A brings the total to 196. Each leaf is 28 inches long by 7 inches wide. A typical page contains 96 lines of text, the lines running approximately 5 inches. The lineation (though not, of course, the pagination) matches that of the Lippincott first edition — and the 1986 Harper Perennial paperback reprint. The Ransom set also has three separately numbered pages of front matter, which includes both the table of contents and a brief "cast of characters" — in its entirety, "Benny Profane,

---

[1] This collection also contains more than one hundred letters written by Pynchon to his first agent, Candida Donadio, which, out of regard for Pynchon's privacy, will not become available to scholars until five years after his death.

[2] For example, an additional short paragraph about the famous nose job Esther undergoes in chapter four: "No one had told Esther that anything about the operation would hurt. But these injections hurt: nothing before in her experience had ever hurt quite so much. All she had free to move for the pain were her hips. Trench held her head and leered appreciatively as she squirmed, constrained, on the table" (Thomas Pynchon 1963, 105). This passage is missing from typescript page 84 and galley page 38.

a schlemihl / Herbert Stencil, a quick-change artist" (g. [ii])[3] — that was omitted from the published novel. The Ransom set, unmarked, shows no evidence of having been used for proofreading. The Morgan set, stained here and there with what may well have been hot cocoa, features dozens of handwritten questions, suggestions and corrections (none, to the best of our judgment, by Pynchon) in black, blue and red. Proofreading signs and comments in the margins abound, but these notations do not continue beyond the end of chapter thirteen (g. 152), which indicates that the Morgan galleys cannot have been the definitive source for the subsequent production of page proofs. We believe the Morgan galleys must have been used to help prepare another, entirely marked set, the master proofs or author's copy, to be sent to Pynchon for checking, or else were proofread in house in parallel with Pynchon's checking of the master proofs.

Let us pause here to enumerate the five documentary stages, known and presumed, we have cited as constituting the genealogy of *V.*: (1) the Ransom typescript, (2) the 1961 clean typescript first submitted to Lippincott, (3) the 1962 revised typescript, (4) at least three sets of galleys — (a) one, held by the Ransom, unmarked, (b) one, held by the Morgan, only partially marked, (c) one, whereabouts at present unknown (to us), fully marked by the publisher and then by Pynchon — and (5) the published novel. We have studied 1, 4a, 4b and 5; we have Corlies Smith's evidence for the existence of 2 and 3;[4] we have the evidence of a letter by Pynchon as well as the knowledge of common publishing practice for the existence of 4c.[5]

---

[3] We abbreviate "galleys" as "g." and "typescript" as "ts." In the galleys' table of contents and text, the phrase that becomes "gets to an apocheir" in the title of the published novel's first chapter (Pynchon 1963, 5, 9) is "attains apocheir" (g. [ii], 1); the corresponding phrase in the title of the typescript's second chapter is "arrives at apocheir" (ts. 18). As we discuss further below, the galleys (in the table of contents, but, curiously, not in the text) identify "Epilogue, 1919" (Pynchon 1963, 6, 456) as "chapter seventeen" (g. [ii], cf. 181).

[4] Smith returned a copy of the first typescript version of the novel to Pynchon, at his request, for rewriting (Herman and Krafft 2007, 3), but we do not know whether that copy was marked with the kinds of revising suggestions contained in the editorial correspondence between Smith and Pynchon. We assume that a copy of the second typescript version of the novel was copyedited in preparation for composition of the galleys, but we have no direct knowledge of that document.

[5] To be sure, as noted in *The Chicago Manual of Style*, for example, publishers' practices in handling galleys vary. Some keep the true master proofs in house, sending copies of the masters to authors for checking, then transferring authors' corrections from those copies to the master

In both the Morgan and the Ransom galleys, all the text pages have the same header, "V.–10/13/25 Elec. W/curs. OS (Lippincott) 3920," except for page 116A, where the header is "V.– 10/13/25 Electra–(1.2)–3920." Compared to the previous page numbers, 116A is slightly smaller and not in boldface. Page numbers 117 and 118 are like 116A, but 119 and 120 revert to the larger font and boldface. The numbers on pages 121-135 again resemble 116A, while 136-142 return to the original font size and style. Page numbers from 143 through the end of the galleys are once more in the type of 116A. All this may mean that the job of typesetting *V.* was split, or that typesetting most of the latter half of the galleys was a complicated affair, perhaps requiring extensive recomposing. Did an intervention by Pynchon require the insertion of 116A, or did a compositor goof, and did many of the following pages have to be changed accordingly? Are the differing fonts of the page numbers a mere meaningless inconsistency? At this point, we have no way to know. The passage on galley page 116 A is the end of chapter ten (Pynchon 1963, 302-303). It occurs already in the typescript (ts. 480-481) in essentially its final form, although there it still has Stencil speaking of himself in the first rather than the third person — as he does everywhere else in the typescript. Even if the change of person here had somehow been overlooked during the spring 1962 rewriting, correcting the lapse would not have required adding a page to the galleys.

How can we be sure Pynchon worked on the galleys represented by the sets at the Morgan and the Ransom? First, it is highly unlikely that a publisher at the time would have gone to the trouble and expense of producing more than one version of long galleys, although the differing page-number fonts of the *V.* galleys might indicate at least a partial exception to this rule. Second, however, Pynchon himself offers direct evidence. In a letter of October 1-2, 1962, written from Seattle, he tells Sale she should "by now . . . have the last batch of galleys,"[6] and goes on

---

proofs. We do not know what Lippincott's practice was; it is possible that two or more copies of the galleys, more or less fully marked, existed or still exist somewhere. About a number of other points concerning the galleys we can also only speculate. Why was one set, the Ransom galleys, left unmarked? Unmarked galleys are customarily sent to authors for their convenience along with the master proofs for correcting, but more than that we cannot venture. Why was one set, the Morgan galleys, marked only partially? We do not know, although we can see that the marking, partial as it was, did influence details in the published novel. What became of the master proofs or author's copy containing Pynchon's corrections? We wish we knew.

[6] Thomas Pynchon, letter to Faith Sale, 1-2 Oct. 1962 (Harry Ransom Humanities Research Center, The University of Texas at Austin).

to consider various aspects and details of the novel, sometimes referring to galley page numbers which correspond to those in the Morgan and Ransom sets. For example, when he addresses whether to hyphenate "siege party" (he explains that it "was meant, I think, to sound Germanic or something"), he refers to galley page "106, paragraph 3," where the phrase actually occurs for the last time (cf. Pynchon 1963, 277).[7] Addressing the list of events he "copied straight out of a World Almanac," Pynchon refers to "111," the galley page on which the list begins. Concern over the spelling of the Mexican city Oaxaca leads him to a typical moment of mock self-deprecation: "Who cares, nobody's going to read it anyway." The spelling is correct in the published novel (Pynchon 1963, 290).

A final galley page number in the letter is somewhat more problematic. After "139," Pynchon writes, "the Duet to which I refer is one I was going to write, but haven't been able to work out the chord changes for, so to hell with it." On page 139 of the galleys, however, there is no mention of a Duet, so perhaps Pynchon is referring to a note he made on the proofs he had returned to Sale, or to a point he had made about this passage in an earlier letter. Nonetheless, the text on galley page 139 does differ markedly from that on the corresponding pages of the published novel, 357-359. When Benny Profane and Rachel Owlglass finally make physical contact in this scene, the galleys still include the following passage:

> Not having any idea whether he meant them or not, only knowing these words hadn't been practiced either, Profane would say things like: "Curse everyone, even the fond relatives who stood around, smiling, at my bris, who let the world take even a little something from me which might have been yours. And also curse anybody who ever tries to take from me anything which is mine, only, only because it is now yours by this touching."
>
> And "This heart is like a scungille whose shell is beautiful, but a shell that has to be broken now, knocked apart for you to look at and if you want eat the conch-flesh which is passion's but maybe only passion's food; don't argue, Rachel, take."
>
> At least it was what he wanted to say. And therefore, like all our post-mortems, what he did say. (g. 139)

These lines were probably dropped because they exemplify the "internal blithering" of Profane, whose subjectivity was in the process of being muted and his character "attenuat[ed]" between original typescript and

---

[7] Pynchon cedes the decision whether to hyphenate the phrase to Sale.

published novel.[8] Perhaps they were dropped also because they were to have been part of a scene involving a never-completed Duet sung, in operatic fashion, by the lovemaking protagonists of the moment. Whether Pynchon or Sale decided to remove these lines, he or she also, inadvertently perhaps, cut a connection with the intricate scungille image in the introduction to chapter three, the Egypt episode — an introduction, added during the spring 1962 rewriting, in which Pynchon seems to reflect on his historiographical method (Herman 2005).

It seems fitting that the opera-loving Pynchon would want to try his hand at a Duet when the plot permitted (Cowart 1980, 63-5 and *passim*; Weisenburger 1990). But time had the better of him in this case, and either he or Sale must have felt that Profane's lines above, adding as they did to a subjectivity that was being diminished elsewhere in the novel, also had to go. The typescript, which contains an earlier version of the lines removed at the galley stage, seems to confirm the speculation that Pynchon was thinking "Duet" at that point in the plot. Just before the beginning of the passage quoted above, the typescript reads, "'Your turn,' [Rachel] said to his chest" (ts. 551). The Duet, incidentally, may also be what Pynchon refers to in an April 19, 1962, letter to Smith that accompanied the rewritten version of *V.* as "a song which ought to go in about page 400."[9] At that moment the manuscript was "short" (Pynchon's word) not only that song but also chapter nine, which, unlike the duet/song, Pynchon provided within a few weeks. Given the pages in the published novel (Pynchon 1963, 357-359) where, judging by the October 1-2 letter to Sale, the duet/song might have been inserted, the mention in the April 19 letter to Smith of page 400 in the revised typescript may well indicate that "song" and "duet" indeed refer to the same never-written piece of the novel.

Another comment in the October 1-2 letter also corroborates the assumption that Pynchon used a set of galleys identical to the Morgan and Ransom copies when proofreading *V.* He reminds Sale that he has "suggested going back to" the typescript's title "June Disturbances" for the chapter set in 1919 Malta that now concludes the novel; but "having seen [her] ideas" in the letter he received after returning the last batch of

---

[8] Thomas Pynchon, letter to Corlies M. Smith, 13 Mar. 1962. We are grateful to the late Cork Smith for giving us photocopies of his editorial correspondence with Pynchon about *V.* (see Herman and Krafft 2007 for more details).

[9] Thomas Pynchon, letter to Corlies M. Smith, 19 Apr. 1962.

galleys to Lippincott, he is "not so sure" anymore. The galleys identify this section of the novel as "chapter seventeen" (see note 3, above) and title it "Epilogue, 1919," but Pynchon insists that "chapter 17 [sic]" be removed. He even suggests dropping "1919" too and thus letting the reader "be confused," but Sale must have decided to keep the date in.

In the October 1-2 letter, Pynchon also responds — sometimes a little defensively, sometimes appreciatively — to Sale's questions and suggestions about the Paris chapter (fourteen). He admits that "the spear in the crotch" of the young dancer at the center of the chapter "bothers [him] too," but he explains (as he says he did in a previous letter we do not have) that the scene cannot be changed "without doing a wall-to-wall rewrite."[10] Sale must have objected as well to the/a narrator's sudden intrusion two-thirds of the way through the chapter and specifically to the clause "If we've not already guessed" (g. 159 / Pynchon 1963, 406; cf. ts. 622), but Pynchon does not give in. He also rejects Sale's "Valerie idea," which was probably a suggestion to give this chapter's "lady V." a full first name. On another point he is "neutral": if Sale does not like "the looming bed," she can "chop it out." The reference is probably to "The bed was a great four-poster and Mélanie might have known even then that it loomed large in her future" (g. 159 / ts. 622), of which only the first clause survives in the published novel (Pynchon 1963, 406). But Pynchon is grateful to Sale for catching his mistake of "instep" (g. 155 / ts. 607) for what should be, and does become, "calf" (Pynchon 1963, 400). This discussion of the Paris chapter concludes abruptly as follows: "(Let me know what you think about the real big deletion in this chapter — all that bouillon d'onze heures nonsense.)."

Pynchon made many last-minute cuts, small and large, totaling approximately one hundred and seventy lines, from chapter fourteen. The majority of those lines form this one passage. A *bouillon d'onze heures* (literally, a cup of broth drunk at eleven o'clock [PM]) is a poisoned drink. In the deleted scene, Mélanie, the young dancer, and Porcépic, the avant-garde composer of the ballet in which she will star, are eating soup around eleven (AM) at a *Bouillon Duval*, a downscale chain restaurant frequented by tourists who brag about the upscale places they ate the night before. Porcépic dominates the conversation, which deals with issues such as the decadence

---

[10] Pynchon uses the same phrase, "a wall-to-wall rewrite," for what he decided against doing with his early stories when he republished them (1984, 3).

of tourism, French idioms, anarchism and the nature of history, some of which he combines in a more or less original way. Here he is on history and the *bouillon*:

> "We all drink the eleventh-hour broth which had been brewed for us, though not by the hands of history. That has no hands. We sup unknowing, amiable victims in the poison plot. Who is to say where its formula evolved, what apothecary hands have stirred it, or from what dark alembics it came to be poured like the rain of heaven on our world." (g. 158 / ts. 617)

The suggestion that history has no hands plays off the metaphor of history as a woman earlier in the passage, "a towering and timeless female wielding a lash" (g. 157 / ts. 616). Porcépic scorns what he considers the stupid anthropomorphizing and the effeminate metaphysics of the expatriate Russian revolutionaries who meet at the café L'Ouganda and have come up with this comparison; and he disputes the validity of the metaphor not only by rejecting it wholesale ("How can anyone sane live with a philosophy like that?" [g. 158 / ts. 616]) but also by developing it in a dismissive way:

> "History is no more a woman than the gouine in the street. If she were in an endless street, empty except for monuments, buildings, lampposts or broken masonry; if her pace were kept steady to the horizon, then we might compare history to the rolling of her rump, ha-ha. Because she would become part of the street, which is: automaton or soulless. But add to the scene one gouin — one slovenly sailor — and allow our streetwalker to break her stride, deviate once from course, smile, feel the least response to him: and gouin and gouine will rollick rakehell, arm in arm away, and the street will have lost her." (g. 158 / ts. 616-617)[11]

"Nonsense," Pynchon's characterization of the whole of this deleted passage, is perhaps too strong a word for this part of it, but Pynchon may have had good reasons for dismissing it. A *gouine* is a lesbian; *gouin* seems to be Pynchon's invention. History, according to Porcépic's counterargument, is no more a woman than a streetwalking lesbian is a woman. If this

---

[11] If the metaphor of the lash-wielding woman had been retained, it would have linked nicely with the first song engineer Kurt Mondaugen hears after his arrival at Foppl's siege party in the South-West Africa chapter: "Love's a lash / Kisses gall the tongue, harrow the heart; / Caresses tease / Cankered tissue apart" (Pynchon 1963, 238). Love is a lash, and history's lash may well be love. Likewise, Porcépic's image of history's empty street would have connected with Fausto Maijstral's "nightmare" "street of the 20th Century" (Pynchon 1963, 323-324).

lesbian were to mechanically work an empty, soulless street — one perhaps inspired by the paintings of Di Chirico (to whom Pynchon refers and alludes elsewhere in the novel [esp. Pynchon 1963, 303, 307, 323-324]) — then history might be compared "to the [automaton-like] rolling of her rump." But, Porcépic contends, introducing a randy sailor into the scene will necessarily provoke a human response, commercial and/or sexual, on the lesbian's part, and so much for the Russians' notion of history as omnipotent dominatrix. In the next paragraph, quoted earlier, Porcépic emphasizes his own, materialistic understanding of history by saying it has no hands and cannot be thought to poison our lives. The *bouillon d'onze heures* is prepared by another, unknown but distinctly nonhuman force.

Pynchon must have come to feel he could do without Porcépic's musings, especially his ruminations on history, perhaps because they too exemplify what he had told Smith in his March 13 letter he intended to cut when rewriting the novel: discussions of "General Principles," or "a hell of a lot of introspective material." Even though Porcépic here undercuts the comparison of history with an overbearing woman, the metaphor is so explicit that it might tempt readers to see *V.*/V. as a mere allegory of history subjugating and destroying (the male element in) society. On the other hand, such a concern did not prevent Pynchon from letting the "homicidal [Russian] tailor" Kholsky speculate about "History" that "Perhaps she is a woman; women are a mystery to me. But her ways are at least measurable" (g. 157, 159 / *V.* 405). So perhaps the problem Pynchon saw with the *bouillon d'onze heures* passage was partly one of duplication or overdetermination. Retaining Kholsky's speculation quoted above, Pynchon deleted yet another scornful mention of woman and history just before it, this time by the French impresario Itague. The final clause of "Because we are less human, we foist off the humanity we have lost on inanimate objects and abstract theories and [thus] history becomes — 'snorting' — a woman" (g. 159 / ts. 620; cf. Pynchon 1963, 405) is removed.

While rewriting much of the novel in spring 1962, Pynchon had produced two pages on Stencil's historical imagination as it crystallizes around the concept of V. to introduce chapter three. Working on the galleys, he may have realized that the sophistication of that late addition made the *bouillon d'onze heures* scene seem, by comparison, too heavy-handed, and ultimately also suggestive of a determinism that remained insufficiently relativized. Furthermore, the novel's critique of tourism is already prominent as early as chapter three; since there are hardly any new thoughts on the subject in the conversation between Mélanie and Porcépic, the scene may have seemed expendable for that reason too. Finally, Mélanie's role in the episode does not go beyond that of a mere *raisonneuse*, which diminishes her characterization in the rest of the chapter, mostly passive though she indeed is. As for what the passage contributes to the characterization of Porcépic, Pynchon actually salvaged a seven-line paragraph from the hundred and two lines that make up the entire scene. Opening with "The Russian influence in Porcépic's music," it leads into the dramatization of the composer's connections with the group "of Russian expatriates led by . . . Kholsky" (g. 157 / Pynchon 1963, 404; cf. ts. 611).

The final long cut from the Paris chapter has two parts. The first is the end of a discussion at L'Ouganda involving speculation about the lovemaking roles of Mélanie and the lady V. Where the scene ends in the published novel (Pynchon 1963, 408), in the galleys Porcépic recites a limerick about lesbian love:

> There once was a lesbian named Hume,
> Who took a queer up to her room.
> They argued all night
> Over who had the right
> To do what, and with what, to whom. (g. 160 / ts. 624)

Pynchon would go all out on (rocket) limericks in *Gravity's Rainbow* (1973, 305-35), but perhaps he dropped this single limerick from *V.* because it jarred with the more or less sympathetic (if somewhat mysterious) representation of lesbian sexuality in the chapter. The men at L'Ouganda do make fun of lesbians, but apparently the limerick was stooping too low. In the rest of this deleted conversation, Kholsky imagines politics as another example of such combinatory roles as the assembled intellectuals have envisioned for the lady V. and Mélanie. The thought leads him to yet another declaration about history Pynchon must have been eager to eliminate: "History would break down into a chaos of ambiguous roles" (g. 160 / ts. 624).

The second and much larger part of the final long passage removed from the Paris chapter concerns the figure of the "Italian poet-agitator" Sgherraccio (g. 160 / ts. 624). Elsewhere we have described just how complicated the transition from typescript to published novel was in connection with this minor character, who appears twice and is mentioned half a dozen times in the typescript (Herman and Krafft 2007, 8-9). Cutting his cameo appearance at L'Ouganda meant he would not emerge in the Paris chapter until the very last paragraph, where he is connected with V.: "Rumor had it that a week or so later the lady V. ran off with one Sgherraccio, a mad Irredentist" (Pynchon 1963, 414). Instead of "a mad Irredentist," he is identified at the corresponding point in the galleys (163) and the typescript (634) as "the young Italian." Irredentism (advocating, in Sgherraccio's case, Italy's annexation of Malta — as the "first step" toward a federated Europe [g. 160 / ts. 625]) is only one part of his politics as he explains them to the other patrons at L'Ouganda: "Radical, Social-Monarchist, Republican, Christian, Pornocratic" (g. 160); or, according to the typescript, "Radical Social-Monarchist and Republican-Christian Pornocratic" (ts. 625). But the reductive characterization of him as "a mad Irredentist" at the end of the Paris chapter motivates or is motivated by his later presence on Malta along with V. (Pynchon 1963, 472).

In all, Pynchon made more than seventy-five deletions from the *V.* galleys, ranging from short single sentences to a passage of more than a hundred lines. Often he did away with what he must have deemed superfluous, as in chapter one, where he cut a passage about "an ex-juvenile delinquent from New York named Facciabrutta" (g. 2 / ts. 10) and also some slightly labored historical background on the 1954 French antiwar ballad "Le Déserteur," by Boris Vian, which Paola has just sung (g. 5 / ts. 19-20). The novel became snappier as a result of each such cut. While the cuts from the Paris chapter of the galleys were the most substantial, others are worth a closer look as well.

As we explain in our overview essay on the *V.* typescript at the Ransom Center, one page of the typescript, 343, at what became the end of the published novel's chapter eight, is missing; however, we can infer the likely content of the missing page from a passage in the galleys that was deleted from the published text (Herman and Krafft 2007, 18-19). The passage in question, on galley pages 86-87, sets up the celebrated South-West Africa chapter, "Mondaugen's Story." Mondaugen and Stencil have met at the Rusty Spoon, where in the published novel, "over an abominable imitation of Munich beer," the German engineer tells Stencil a story "about [his] youthful days in South-West Africa" (Pynchon 1963, 228). In the galleys the ersatz beer is present, but Mondaugen and Stencil are "arguing . . . the dilemma of the scientist or positivist in today's decadent world" (g. 86). When Mondaugen happens to mention "old Captain Godolphin" (g. 87), who has already figured in the Florence episode Stencil narrated to the dentist Dudley Eigenvalue, Stencil is all ears. Mondaugen identifies Godolphin as the surrogate father against whom he had revolted as a young man, though the outcome of the revolt was only his own disenchantment: "At the end of it, I had to admit that I knew nothing; and all that would happen henceforth — as I had admitted previously in theory but never emotionally — would be governed by Fortune or, if you will, the stars" (g. 87).

This passage, totaling twenty-six lines, was probably cut because it offers too simplistic a reading of events and interpersonal relations in the South-West Africa chapter — a reading more appropriate to the original typescript version of that chapter. The rewritten version features a Godolphin who is much more complex than Mondaugen's casual dismissal of him here — "He isn't important really" (g. 87) — suggests. For one thing, in the published novel Godolphin does not provoke Mondaugen's filial revolt but inspires his filial regard. An already-mentioned comment in the October 1-2 letter to Sale may furnish yet another, if slighter, reason for deleting this galley paragraph. Forgoing further efforts to contextualize the historical chapters more clearly, as Smith had asked (Herman and Krafft 2007, 5-6), Pynchon tells Sale he is no longer concerned about confusing the reader: "to hell with him, let him be confused." Dropping Godolphin from the setup of the South-West Africa chapter does not create confusion; but Godolphin's (and his actual son's) appearances in several chapters of the novel do necessitate an effort of memory and coordination on the reader's part.[12]

Other considerable deletions from the galleys were made in chapter eleven, the "confessions" of Maltese poet-priest Fausto Maijstral. After Maijstral explains how his Maltese part maintained "a working relevancy to God" during the air-raids on Malta of the Second World War — "made do" — while his "English part" was "keeping up [his] journal" (Pynchon 1963, 330), the galleys and the typescript both feature a long passage on "a common enemy whose name is not Mussolini nor Hitler nor even Satan" (g. 127 / ts. 516). Maijstral's speculation about this enemy — "he" — might seem at first to turn, ironically, toward Woman: "Does the Bad Priest [a transvestite] know his face? Perhaps we've been wrong about the Dark One all this time; thinking only of the manlike being who tempted

---

[12] See Herman and Krafft (2006, 108-109), for more details on this passage, notably on the remark in the galleys and the published novel that when Stencil retells Mondaugen's story to Eigenvalue a few days later, it has "become . . . Stencilized" (g. 87 / Pynchon 1963, 228).

Our Saviour" (g. 127 / ts. 516). By the end of the passage, however, it has become clear that "manlike" is meant as a synonym for "human." The enemy is (the) inanimate:

> Who then is the Enemy?
> Who. It all hinges on the misuse of a pronoun. Before Fausto came fully aware of his "mission" as a poet, he could on occasion be as deluded as the rest. Fausto had accepted his own words "force" and "energy" intellectually; but not emotionally. Not yet. (g. 128 / ts. 516-517)

Since *V.* as a whole narrativizes twentieth-century dehumanization, and since Maijstral later in the chapter reveals that the lady V. herself has evolved into a kind of robot (to be disassembled by Maltese children), Pynchon may have thought this passage unduly explicit, or simply unnecessary, especially in conjunction with the already-noted split between Porcépic and the Kholsky faction in the later Paris chapter. To read History in terms of a human adversary (as Maijstral says he had erroneously done) or, more specifically, in terms of a female punisher (as Kholsky is said to do, echoing the other V.-narratives imagined by Stencil, in which men continue to fall victim to the novel's titular woman) is to buy into an illusion of human agency and to misunderstand the development toward the inanimate that runs far deeper than a gender conflict and threatens to destroy humankind altogether.

The matter of gender conflict is also downplayed later in Maijstral's confessions by the removal of a passage on marriage:

> Marriage can only grow or progress on a negative basis. Two souls can only come to know one another by a process of elimination. Never must a positive statement be made: for a young man might blurt "I love you" and then have to spend the rest of his life qualifying his statement.
> As a form which gradually emerges from a block of marble by thousands of tiny chippings and carvings is more permanent than a clay figure built up from small additions to a wire armature, so is a marriage founded on Negativism more lasting than one which must depend on the protean impossibility of "commitment." (g. 132 / ts. 529-530)

No longer one who develops this kind of conflictual argument, the Maijstral of the published novel may appear wiser than his counterpart in the galleys and the typescript. Of course Pynchon may also have cut the marriage passage because he felt it was just too sharp a criticism of an institution he was not experienced enough yet to judge at the age of twenty-five. There is even a chance, as we can tell from the marked Morgan galleys (see below), that this cut was not Pynchon's idea but that he simply went along with what he thought must be sound advice.

In his letter to Sale of October 1-2, Pynchon devotes a short paragraph to the subject of copyediting. We know no one now who can confirm for us the specific details of Lippincott's practice at the time, but custom would have been for Pynchon to be sent the copyedited manuscript, from which the typesetter had composed the galleys, along with the marked galleys to proofread.

> I am not mad at the green fountain pen, alias Catharine Carver. The business with the hyphens, for example, made me aware for the first time that I come on like I invented the attributive noun, which is a fault and one I should get rid of — I mean I use too many of them. Her copyediting, besides improving the quality of the text (no kidding, it did — it looked entirely different) also served in many ways as a diagnosis, and that always helps.

The Morgan galleys feature abundant evidence of proofreading, none of it in green fountain pen. However, nearly all the marked pages are signed off "CC" in the bottom right-hand corner,[13] which seems to indicate that Catharine Carver, having copyedited the manuscript, was also responsible for the in-house proofreading of the galleys. Responsible, but not exactly in charge. More than one person appears to have been involved. No fewer than three pencils were used: a black one, up to page 152; a blue one, sometimes reacting to black, sometimes adding new corrections and suggestions; and a red one (which does not begin until galley page 82), sometimes in conjunction with blue, to which it may react. While one editor could have used more than one color, it seems unlikely that Carver used all three here, given the nature of their interaction. The initials CC are in

---

[13] There is no CC on Morgan galley page 9, but then it does not have a single correction on it. A brief passage was dropped from this page for the published version ("A mechanized centaur, making love to itself. What could he say?" disappeared from between "No one interrupted him" and "He felt like the angel of death" [Pynchon 1963, 29]), but this is the kind of content-related deletion that can logically be ascribed to Pynchon. Also on galley page 9, a comma was removed between "tonight" and "mnemonic" for the published version; Pynchon may have done this too. There is no CC on galley page 58 either, but it nevertheless features a few black-pencil corrections in what appears to be the usual hand. The absence of sign-off initials on this page may therefore be a mere oversight.

black, but black is often overruled by blue and red. Let us reiterate that the Morgan galleys cannot represent the complete job of proofreading that would have been done in house by Lippincott either in preparation for or in parallel with Pynchon's proofreading. Neither, of course, can they be the set Pynchon himself proofread.

Signs and notes in black with a question mark that remain unanswered by either blue or red may have gone to Pynchon (albeit indirectly) for resolution. On galley page 47, the sentence "There being only the single proposition: the world can only be rescued from certain decay through Heroic Love" draws the question "vary?"; and indeed, in the published novel the first "only" is replaced by "but" (Pynchon 1963, 125). Often, however, such questions do not lead to anything. On galley page 6, there is a question mark in the margin by "chang music," but the words remain the same (Pynchon 1963, 23). On galley page 10, a suggestion to capitalize "snap" is not taken up (Pynchon 1963, 33). Sometimes plausible black suggestions without a question mark (and not responded to by blue or red) do not make it into the published novel either. On galley page 23, a suggestion to add "one" between "gross" and "smiled" in "'Ah,' the gross smiled, 'coffee then'" is not taken up (Pynchon 1963, 64). Similarly, on galley page 25, the black pencil proposes "a" between "lay" and "while" in "Porpentine extracted a cigarette and lay while smoking where he'd come to rest," but to no effect. Occasionally, the black pencil calls for action. On galley page 139, the notation "see copy,"[14] accompanied by a circled question mark, queries the unlikely-seeming word "own" in the phrase "this own breed." The phrase nevertheless remains as is (Pynchon 1963, 358).

Most of the black pencil marks concern typesetting errors — or even what amount to belated copyediting issues: omissions and transpositions; spelling and capitalization; punctuation and diacritical marks; italicizing and other font changes; pronoun usage, and so on. On galley page 2, "lights out" has the l and o circled, with "caps?" in the right margin. Indeed, the phrase appears as "Lights Out" on the corresponding page of the published novel (Pynchon 1963, 12), although it appears as "lights out" much later (g. 146 / Pynchon 1963, 375), unremarked in the galleys. On galley page 16, black suggests changing "have a piece of fruit" (presumably to make it more Yiddish-sounding) to "have a piece fruit," which is how the phrase appears in the published novel (Pynchon 1963, 47). On galley page 26, "listening to Victoria but ge off somewhere else" elicits a

---

[14] Presumably a reference to the copyedited manuscript.

question mark and again the note to "see copy"; and "ge" becomes "yet" (Pynchon 1963, 73).

The blue pencil seems to have been wielded by a different hand. It reacts to the notations in black pencil, but not systematically so. On galley page 119, blue validates one routine black correction (with a characteristic and pertinent V-shaped checkmark), but leaves two others untouched. About half of the blue notations are simple validations, but many others are negative reactions to black. On galley page 149, blue validates one black correction, leaves another untouched, and says literally "no" to a black suggestion (with circled question mark) to change from "resistor" to "resister." The word keeps the ending "–or" (Pynchon 1963, 385). Elsewhere, too, blue carries the day. On galley page 70, "out on ms" in blue argues against the black suggestion to insert "a" into "steering sinuous course." We assume "ms" refers to the copyedited manuscript. Interestingly, the Ransom typescript, which was in Sale's possession while the galleys were being proofread, has "steering a sinuous course," but with the "a" marked out (ts. 283). So that particular "a" probably did not occur in the clean typescript Pynchon submitted to Lippincott in 1961 or in the revised typescript of 1962 which would have become the copyedited manuscript. The published novel also omits it (Pynchon 1963, 185). On galley page 81, black asks whether a word is missing between "does" and "go" in "ever does go out of himself"; blue answers, "I don't think so," given the appropriate emphasis on "does," and blue's reading stands (Pynchon 1963, 214). On galley page 150, where black suggests replacing "in" in "the tallest wind in the earth" with "on," blue writes "stet," and "in" remains (Pynchon 1963, 386). On at least two occasions, blue is downright dismissive of black: galley pages 61 and 80 feature big blue X's, one over the suggestion to respell the Italian "piango" (Pynchon 1963, 160), and one through the suggestion to insert "Why?" between "He called it off" and "How should I know?" (Pynchon 1963, 211).

The red pencil, in yet another hand, mostly validates black notations. Once it also reacts to the blue pencil: on galley page 82, red validates one affirmation and one contradiction of black by blue. Therefore, it seems safe to say that the red pencil was the final one to be used in the Morgan galleys. Since red does not react anywhere else to blue, and since its validation of blue here happens to be its first appearance in the galleys, this validation may well be a slight error on the part of someone who had been asked to double-check the proofreading by black but started off addressing blue's as well. Otherwise, red may simply have realized immediately that blue's double-checking had been so thorough that it did not need extra consideration. Overall, red is a little more active than blue, but, like blue, red does not systematically address the work done by black. Thus on galley page 93, red validates one simple black correction, to (re)insert the comma between "cried" and "fondled" (ts. 379 / Pynchon 1963, 244), but does not react to the black correction/suggestion to capitalize the beginning of "it's indefinite," which remains lower case (Pynchon 1963, 242). Since neither blue nor red does things systematically, on some galley pages (for example, 96, 106, 109 and 120) some black corrections and suggestions are addressed by blue while others are addressed by red. By no means, however, do blue and red between them deal with all the black notations on a page. Furthermore, it seems impossible to tell why red and blue address certain matters and ignore others.

What is most interesting about the red pencil is that it indicates several of the passages that would be dropped from the published novel. Since this is a content-related rather than strictly a proofreading issue, we might infer that red is Sale (despite our noting a hint earlier that blue might be), but we currently have no corroborating evidence. On galley page 110, red marks a fourteen-line passage of Profane's internal blithering (about mortality, Rachel and "love") to be removed from between "butyrate head" and "It was time" (Pynchon 1963, 286). Red also validates two black corrections on this page, but the red line indicating the deletion has "but" next to it, possibly to suggest that one of the validated black corrections is no longer relevant since the passage will be dropped. On galley page 112, red indicates a short passage to be dropped, two concluding lines about the dog days (Pynchon 1963, 291), and again writes "but" to suggest there is no more need for a validated black correction in it. On galley page 113, black has already suggested cutting the opening lines of a conversation between Profane and SHROUD (Pynchon 1963, 295), since Profane asks a question about Stencil although, as black notes, "They haven't met yet." Red validates this suggestion and lengthens by half a line the passage to be cut. Red does not indicate an earlier passage on galley page 113 — two lines setting the scene between Esther and Schoenmaker (Pynchon 1963, 294) — that will be deleted as well from the published text. On galley page 132, red does indicate the sixteen-line passage containing Maijstral's comments on marriage, discussed above, that will be deleted,[15] but this time does not indicate the black correction that becomes irrelevant as a result.

All the passages in the Morgan galleys marked by black and/or red for deletion were eliminated from the published novel. Does this fact suggest that Pynchon himself did not single-handedly make the cuts? Were notations in the Morgan galleys of passages to be deleted transferred to the master proofs sent to Pynchon? Did he have such confidence in the judgment of Lippincott's editorial staff that he accepted all such recommendations without balking? Or did Sale (if red was Sale), carrying on a more extensive editorial correspondence with Pynchon than we have been privy to, receive instructions or permission from Pynchon outside the formal proofreading process and mark the Morgan galleys accordingly? As of now, we can only speculate.

For a publisher to devote the services of at least three in-house proofreaders to a first novel, at the relatively late stage of long galleys at that, may seem extraordinary. Similarly, allowing Pynchon to cut a total of nearly five galley pages (the equivalent of twelve pages of published text) may seem an expensive indulgence. We did not have the opportunity to question Corlies Smith about this specific aspect of the culture at Lippincott, but we gather Lippincott was simply that kind of house. On the other hand, Faith Sale's friendship with Pynchon may account for some of the latitude he was given. In any case, making numerous and extensive cuts at the galley stage is much less troublesome than it is in page proofs. None of the editorial or personal correspondence we have seen even hints at any difficulty over these revisions. Pynchon did become unhappy with Lippincott, but apparently not over any reluctance on the publisher's part to go to great lengths to accommodate him when it came to a novel about which the house was evidently quite enthusiastic. A few weeks before the March 1963 release of *V.*, paperbound advance copies were sent to reviewers. These appear to be identical to the first edition except for the binding and an extravagant promotional blurb on the cover ("what will almost certainly be the most original novel published in 1963"; "the most important piece of fiction written since *Ulysses*"). Hyperbolic and anything but objective as such a blurb might seem by nature, especially in the case of a first novel, the publisher's enthusiasm was amply justified.

---

[15] Maijstral's marriage passage seems liable to the same implication of misogyny Pynchon responds to in the October 1-2 letter to Sale. If red took the initiative in recommending the deletion of that passage, the fact might be seen as reinforcing the identification of the red pencil as Sale.

We have focused here on the Morgan and Ransom galleys as a missing link between the Ransom typescript of *V.* and the published novel, but, as we have explained, they are not the only missing link. The galleys provide insights into the final stages of the novel's evolution, but many further questions remain about the entire process. We are confident that the Ransom typescript's contents are virtually identical to those of the clean copy submitted to Lippincott in 1961, but as of now we can only infer the contents of the 1962 rewrite. The copyedited manuscript; the master galley proofs containing (1) the complete set of agreed-upon proofreaders' corrections and queries, and (2) Pynchon's responses as well as his own proofreading notations; more letters between Pynchon and Sale written while the galleys were being proofread and their points discussed; page proofs, which must have been made up and checked after correction of the galleys: if any of these are still extant, they no doubt have even more to contribute to our understanding of how a most remarkable first novel came into being.

Bibliography

Cowart, David. 1980. *Thomas Pynchon: The Art of Allusion*. Carbondale: Southern Illinois UP.

Herman, Luc. 2005. "Thomas Pynchon's Appeal to the Canon in the Final Version of *V.*" In *Reading without Maps? Cultural Landmarks in a Post-Canonical Age*, edited by C. Den Tandt. Brussels: Peter Lang. 291-303.

Herman, Luc, and John M. Krafft. 2006. "From the Ground Up: The Evolution of the South-West Africa Chapter in Pynchon's *V.*" *Contemporary Literature* 47 (2):261-88.

———. 2007. "Fast Learner: The Typescript of Pynchon's *V.* at the Harry Ransom Center in Austin." *Texas Studies in Literature and Language* 49 (1):1-20.

Pynchon, Thomas. 1963. *V.* Philadelphia: Lippincott. Reprinted 1986, New York: Perennial.

———. 1966. *The Crying of Lot 49*. Philadelphia: Lippincott.

———. 1973. *Gravity's Rainbow*. New York: Viking.

———. 1984. *Slow Learner*. Boston: Little, Brown.

Weisenburger, Steven. 1990. "Thomas Pynchon at Twenty-Two: A Recovered Autobiographical Sketch." *American Literature* 62.4: 692-697.

From Argument to Design

Editions in Books and Beyond the Book

Hans Walter Gabler

The invention of printing constituted, as we know, a medial watershed.[1] Essentially, too, the invention of printing brought with it the invention of the book as we know it; even while the codex already existed for hundreds of years in the times of manuscript culture. A function common to both manuscripts and books is that of transmitting written testimony to human imagination, knowledge, culture and thought. We sometimes tend to make a categorical distinction between "texts" and the contexts of knowledge that we subordinate to them. But this we should beware of doing. For such a distinction is dubiously biased towards dimensions of the aesthetic in what has come down to us in writing, whereby the notion of "text" gets narrowed down to entities of the literary and poetical in transmissions. Yet "transmission" denotes throughout "transmission of texts", be they aesthetic or discursive; and it is to transmission in such a comprehensive sense that historical scholarship in general is committed, and scholarly editing in particular is dedicated.

As a literary scholar and critic, I am an editor myself, and what I profess is to uphold and carry forward the traditions of networking texts into relationships of mutuality between text and context — which is one way of defining the cultural practice of editing transmissions. Or, put simply: I am among those who materially make books out of books (or out of transmissions in manuscripts or in non-scripted media, too, if such be the call of the day). As a maker of books out of books, I construct in each instance a many-stranded argument, taking the shape of a complex of discourses

---

[1] My considerations as reflected in this paper were first voiced in a John Coffin Memorial Lecture in the History of the Book, titled "Argument into Design: Editions as a sub-species of the printed book", that I gave as a Senior Research Fellow of the Institute of English Studies, School of Advanced Study, University of London on 15 July 2008, on the occasion of the 2008 London Rare Books School. The lecture has been published on the Institute's website, with a full complement of illustrations. The present paper was given on two subsequent occasions, as a keynote at the SHARP Conference "Published Words — Public Pages", A Nordic Conference on International Print Culture, 10-12 September 2008, at the Danish Royal School of Library and Information Science, Copenhagen, Denmark, and also as an invited lecture in the Scholars' Lab at the University of Virginia Library, Charlottesville, Va., on 2 October 2008; it has been only slightly modified for publication.

that involves an edited text, a surround of contexts, and a presentation text of my own, all in the service of supporting (textually and contextually) the transmission I am treating, and so rendering anew, in the edition I provide. But in order to provide it, I naturally depend on the medium in which I set out my message. How can, how does an edition become a book? How — before the invention of printing — did a manuscript culture deal with presentations of editorial complexity? How, in the face of the medial watershed of our day, may the electronic medium be harnessed to the service of scholarly editing?

A scholarly editor does well to reflect carefully on the design potential of the medium in which the scholarly edition goes public. Throughout the Gutenberg era, this has been the book. We perceive this with all the greater clarity today when we are progressively exploring the digital alternative. What we perceive, too, is that not only has the outlet in books conditioned the task of editing. Conversely, it is also true that the ever ongoing cultural enterprise of editing and re-editing textual transmissions has significantly contributed to shaping and enhancing the potential of "the book" as a cultural artefact.

What I find particularly fascinating about the moment of the invention of the book in print is the circumstance that the very first printers of books were at once also editors. With the printed book comes a new awareness of transmission, an awareness that springs, in its turn, from a Renaissance spirit of renewal out of which the novel technique of printing is put into the service of a proliferation of cultural texts. The technique, we know, acted as a major stimulus to the printing trade at first in Venice. From there was created a market for the texts on which so much of the intellectual renewal of the period depended. Those were the texts, in Greek and Latin, of the Ancients. Foremost among Venetian printers, Aldus Manutius organised systematic searches for manuscript copy from which to print editions of ancient texts. They are quite properly termed editions because they generally resulted from editorial surveillance by Humanist scholars. Here, by its title-page, is a book of 1515, (Figure 1), not from Manutius and Venice, but from the major Basle printer and publisher, Frobenius, with the age's and the new invention's spirit of exploration behind it: the edition in print of a then just freshly re-discovered political satire on the Roman emperor Claudius *Apocolocyntosis divi Claudii*, attributable to Seneca the Younger, and edited by Beatus Rhenanus, a close associate of Erasmus of Rotterdam.²

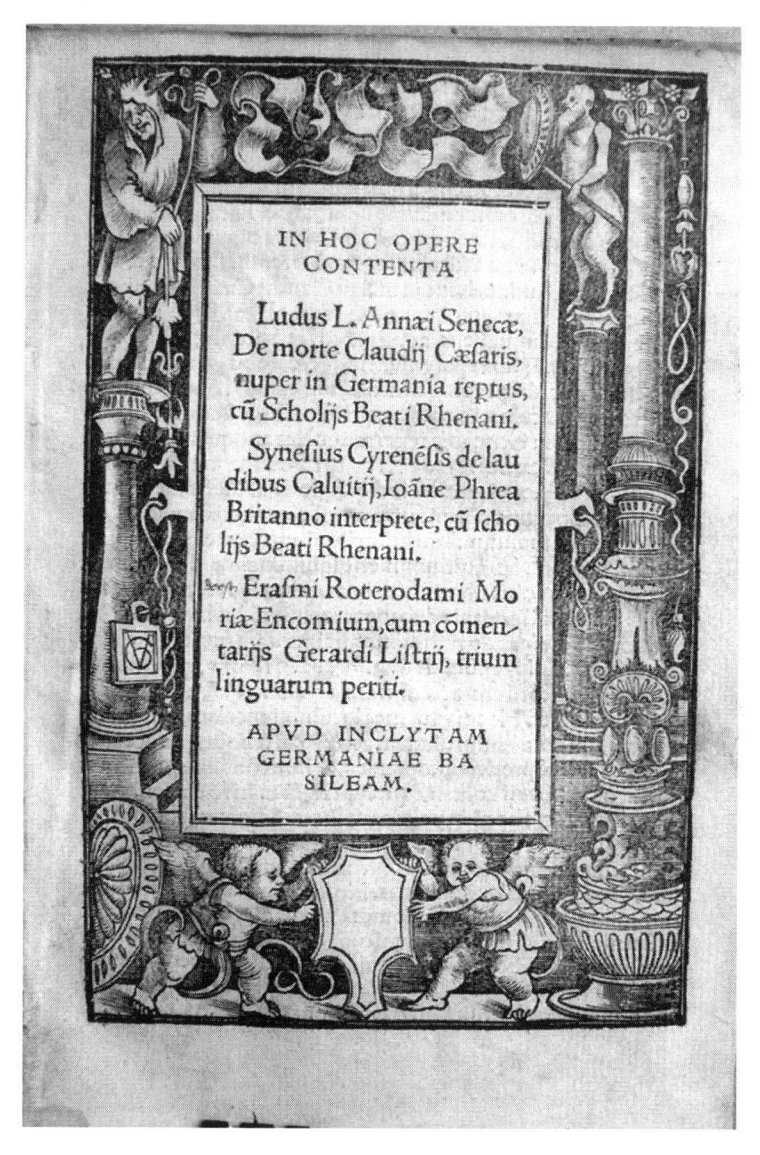

Fig. 1. Title-page of Frobenius edition of *Apocolocyntosis divi Claudi* (1515)

---

² With this are collected, as seen, Synesius of Cyrene's "Praise of Baldness", and Erasmus's "Praise of Folly".

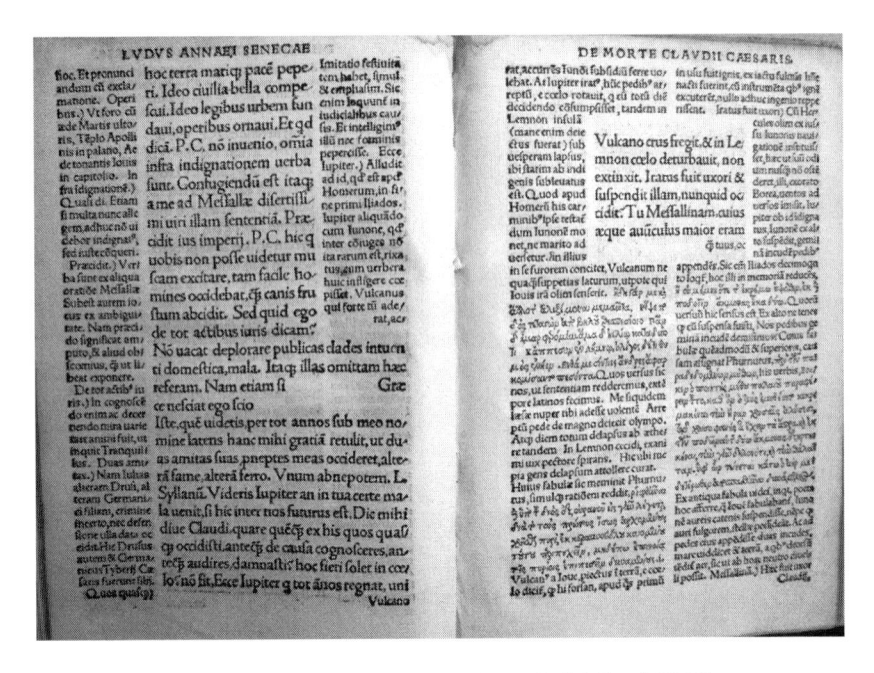

Fig. 2. Pages from Frobenius edition of *Apocolocyntosis divi Claudi* (1515)

The new beginnings in the new medium, then, went hand in hand with scholarly editing. What the book before us can tell, too, as shown in Figure 2,[3] in the lay-out in of two of its pages of text, variably sized in space and type-size, as well as variably surrounded by commentary columns printed in both Latin and Greek, is that the printing of books as editions went together with challenges of design: how to lay out books to express, and to harmonize with, the nature of their content.[4] Amazingly, as the example shows, early printing very soon proceeded to realising what in essence are hypertexts, laid out in the two dimensions of the book page that the reader is called upon to read not linearly only, but relationally, or in a manner of "radial reading", as Jerome McGann has termed such deployment of our reading skills.[5]

---

[3] The book from which these two images were taken lives in the library of my colleague and friend Werner von Koppenfels, who kindly allowed me to include them here.

[4] D. F McKenzie contends that "a book itself might be an expressive intellectual structure, in the way that a building directly manifests abstract intellectual forms[.]" (2002, 212.)

[5] Jerome McGann introduced his notion of "radial reading" at a conference on *New Directions in Textual Studies* at the University of Texas at Austin's Harry Ransom Humanities Research

Fig. 3. A manuscript page of Canonical Law text[6]

"Hypertext" is a buzz-word of the late 20th century. It is predicated on radial or relational reading, on cross-referencing a text both inside and outside the given book rather than merely taking it in consecutively from

---

Center in 1989 (1990).

[6] Gregor IX, *Decretium Liber V*. Bologna, third quarter of the 14th century; Vienna: Österreichische Nationalbibliothek, Cod. 2040, fol. 168r; Dr Norbert Ott kindly brought this folio to my attention, for which I am grateful, as I am for the stimulating conversations we have had over the years, and in preparation of this paper.

Hans Gabler From Argument to Design

upper left-hand corner to bottom right-hand corner of each page, and from cover to cover of the book. With intelligence to trigger it, "hyper-texting" is in truth a fundamental mode of organising knowledge in given medial environments. The mode is older than the book. We may observe it, for instance, in the Middle Ages long before the technique of printing was thought of (in Europe). We see it there, that is, if we cast our eye beyond the pale of transmissions of the genres of literature and take into account, too, say, the proliferation of the Bible in manuscripts, or of chronicles, or of law texts.

From the example of a manuscript page of Canonical Law in Figure 3 we perceive clearly the principle of hyper-texting. The typographical units of text, it is true, are hierarchically organised on the page. At the centre stands the Law Text itself in two larger-lettered columns, divided and framed by the white-space of gutter, margins and foot space: we register the off-setting function of this white space inside the page, even though, at the same time, it accommodates sets of marginalia in italic fine script. Columns of commentary to the full height of the page, next, frame the centre in its entirety. From the outside page-length margin beyond the right-hand commentary column, moreover, marginalia speak yet once more to the page's centre. We know how to read such an arrangement — we are culturally conditioned to reading not only consecutively, but relationally as well, and therefore to recognising the physical arrangement before us as a materialisation and enactment of the dialogicity of our own reading process.[7] Yet what this page assumes us to be capable of, too, is multi-medial reading. For what it offers us are not words only, is not merely the text of the Law, but a prominent image of a scene of a mass offering in supplication for justice. Far from being merely illustrative of the page's verbal content, as we in our modern logocentricity might misunderstand it to be, the image is to induce us, rather, yet further to contemplate that content — or else, to start our reading from *it*, and only then enter the verbal text for an intellectual grasp of the whole content of the page before us. Fully integrated into the process of relational texting and reading, the image refracts imaginatively the literal sense of the legal utterance — or, as we might perhaps say, hypertextualises the page before us multimedially.

---

[7] Since this lecture was given, my attention has been drawn to comparable practices of design in manuscript writing and book printing in Hebrew, as founded in traditions of Talmudic learning, of which I, however, have neither visual nor analytical experience.

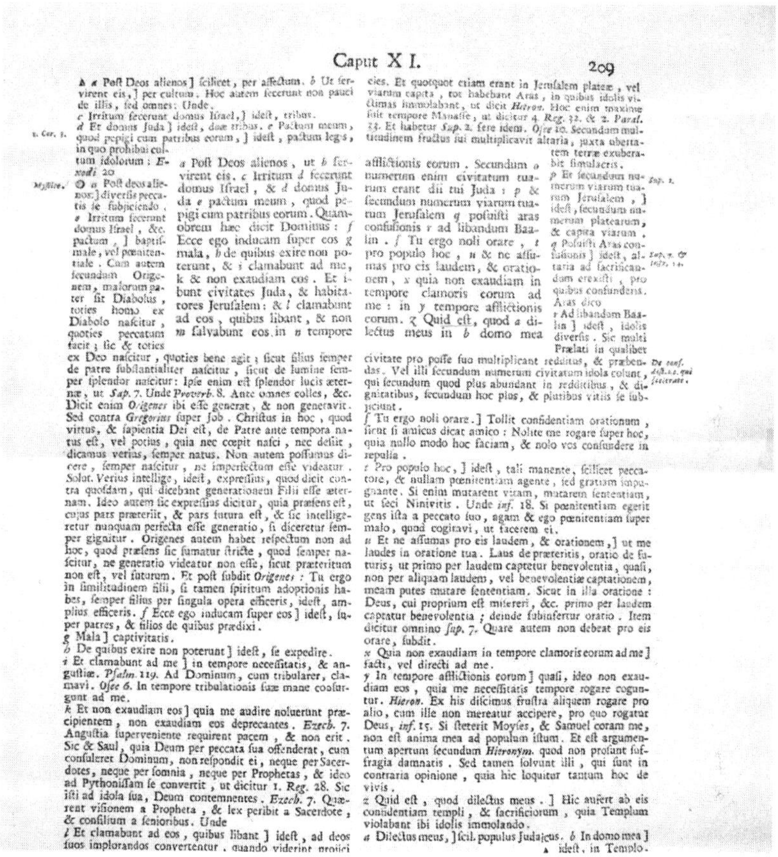

Fig. 4. A page from Hugo de Sancto Charo's biblical commentaries [volume IV], published by Nicolao Pezzana in Venice, 1754. I am grateful to Konrad Benedikt Vollmann for helping me to this example.

To return to the book: from the very beginnings of the techniques and art of book-making, as said, editions have been a definable class of books playing an important role in the emergence of conventions for shaping books, and designing book pages. The printer-publishers like Manutius, or (as in Figures 1-2) Frobenius, had templates to fall back upon when they fashioned the new medium into designs by which both to lay out editorial arguments, and to support processes of relational reading in and of editions. Behind the printers' designs lie not only conventions of page display older than the art of printing. Behind them lies also the intellectual force of editing. To be materially structured, or patterned, onto pages in manuscript and print, texts must have been pre-patterned by editors: that is, the editors' arguments must have been appropriately articulated materially and (as we would nowadays say) tagged into the source matter to be reproduced so as to generate the designs given at the interface of the edition page by scribes or typesetters.

At the level of appearance, the print surface, this could turn into something rather drearily explicit, as is apparently the case in Figure 4. Yet if we do not cling to the customary subordination of the commentary surroundings such as they here frame the text situated in the middle of the page's upper half, but instead, by way of experiment, reverse the perspective, we suddenly see something else. We perceive that the contents of what, in the page design, are the two main columns of the page before us (its notes), may be understood as a reservoir of knowledge from which the page's text could be said to be constructed. This may be a preposterous view to take of the actual text on which the page is centred. It is a biblical text, entitled (one would have thought) to priority at any time. Yet in truth, one could equally class it as a hermetic text condemned to utter incomprehensibility without such sources of knowledge — factual, theological, cultural, lexical and semantic, contextual — as are here adduced to construct its meaning in all its layers and dimensions. The logical consequence of this, turned into design, is that, typographically, the text forms merely a strictly circumscribed two-column inset, in the middle of the page's upper half, into the commentary's display of learning. This reversal of our sightlines gives us the essence of what an edition is, and what editorial presentation is all about: it is an achievement, often scholarly in nature, of networking texts and knowledge. It is this which, from the editor's intelligent pre-disposition, via the type-setter's intelligent disposition of his skill in typography, ultimately enables the intelligent reader and user to assimilate knowledge from an edition's design.

With such an understanding as our foil, we may penetrate to the considerable depths of knowledge and editorial argument underlying the typographical beauty of even a single printed page. Take the Catalogue page of the Shakespeare First Folio (Figure 5), that is: the volume's list of contents. It manifests in a nutshell the printers' skill in turning editorial argument into design. It does so by composing onto just that one page a survey of the contents to follow over the 900-and-something subsequent pages. The lay-out of the Catalogue is the work of an accomplished typesetter in the printing house. But the matter so to display was given him by the editors. For the Catalogue embodies an argument. What it proposes is that Shakespeare compartmentalised his writings distinctly into *Comedies, Histories,* and *Tragedies*. This is a conception of his oeuvre we are still dominated by. Yet it was thus decreed by the Folio editors, and it materialised at their instigation into typographic design.[8]

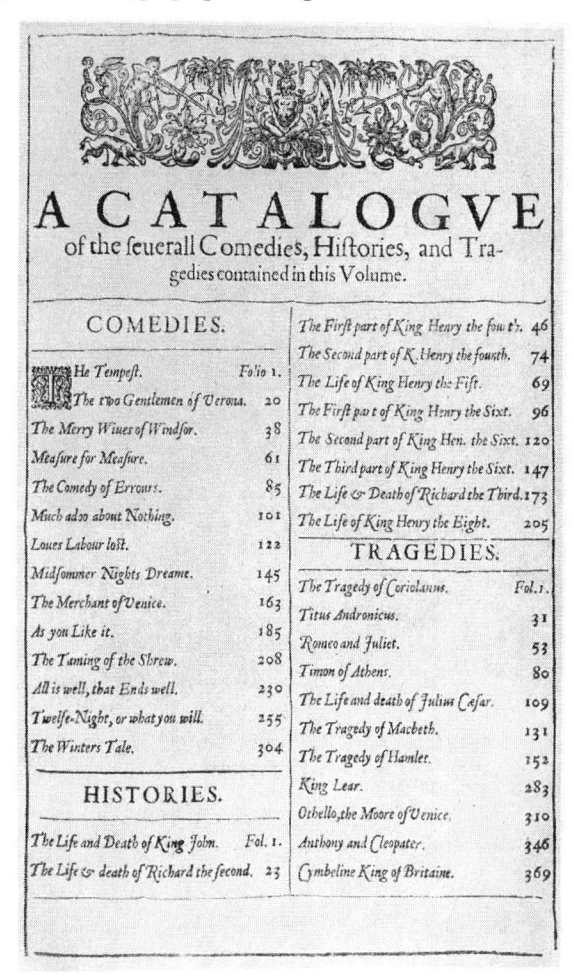

Fig. 5. The Catalogue page of Shakespeare's First Folio.

---

[8] The Folio editors thus established the canon of Shakespeare's dramatic oeuvre in terms of genre.

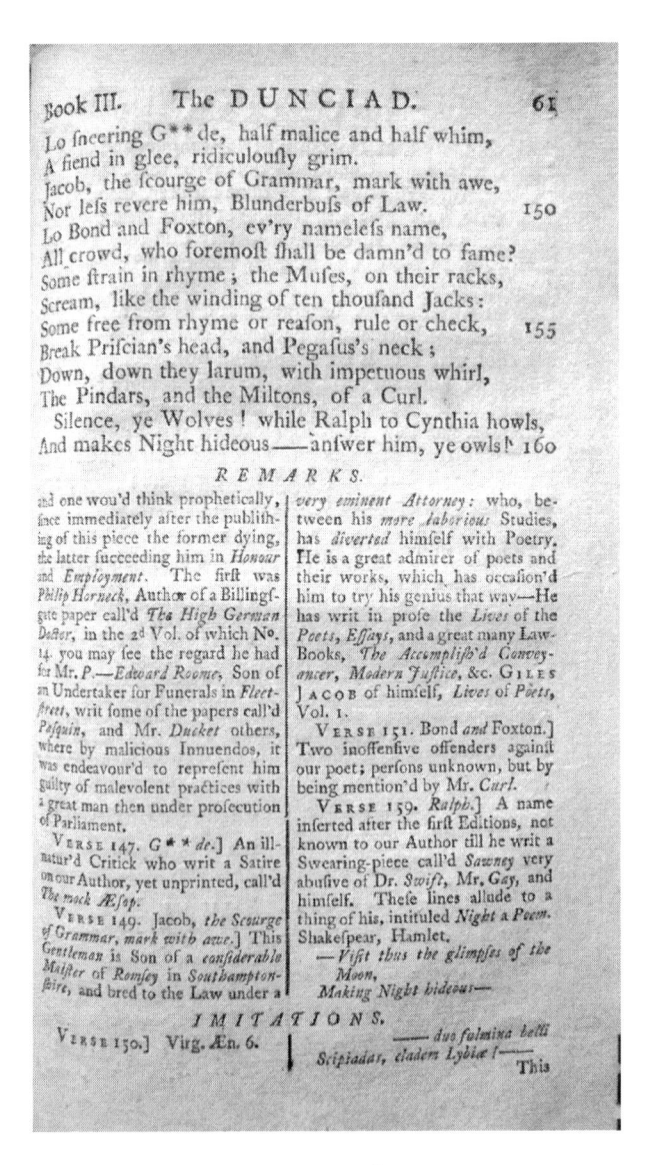

Fig. 6. A page from Alexander Pope's *Dunciad*.[9]

Beyond the Catalogue page, moreover, the interplay of editorial argument and typographic design permeated the entire First Folio volume. In

---

[9] From an early edition (printed in Dublin) of the *Dunciad* in Werner von Koppenfels's possession.

the volume, the plays are divided (with varying insistence) into acts and scenes. This was a conscious change from the practice in preceding quarto editions of individual plays. These were not edited and had no shaping argument behind them: they were what one might call the playtexts-in-typescript of the day. The introduction of act-and-scene divisions in the First Folio, by contrast, went together with the literary (and ultimately "classical") claim made for the Shakespearean oeuvre by compartmentalising it into the three generic categories. By the editorial arguments and fashionings designed into the volume of the First Folio, Shakespeare the playwright was transformed into an author under a literary rather than a theatrical dispensation. Materially, too, he became a writer containable in a book, and in book conventions of textual presentation.

＊＊

The format of learned editions as printed in books, developed as it had been for texts predominantly in the ancient languages in the course of the first couple of centuries since the invention of printing, had by the early 18th century become both so standardised and so notorious, that the century's greatest wit, Alexander Pope, could mercilessly use it as vehicle for his all-round satire on all the dunces of the age, the *Dunciad* (Figure 6). This was so, notwithstanding the fact that Pope, in another of his roles as leading intellect of the age, was one of the Augustan editors of Shakespeare, and not the meanest among them. With its internal references, as the image shows, the poetic argument of the *Dunciad* carries hypertextually, as one might say, from top-of-the-page text to footnote text, and back again — as, with its external references, it indeed carries out of the page, too. In this manner of presentation, the *Dunciad* is an eminently writerly, or should one properly say: printerly, work. Without the design matrix of editions in print, it would have been unrealisable, even unthinkable.

If Pope used the template of the scholarly edition with footnotes metaphorically, one might say, in the *Dunciad*, he used it according to rule in his Shakespeare edition. A culture of editing acquired in academic training on the example of ancient texts, combined with the typographical conventions developed by the printing trade in the lay-out of books, began in the 18th century to introduce the footnote into editions of texts in the vernacular. For Alexander Pope, sensitively, judiciously and normatively judgmental as he was, this combination provided the grounds to restyle, and (with the best of intentions!) often enough to rewrite Shakespeare (Figure 7).[10]

> Thou *Julia,* thou haſt metamorphos'd me;
> Made me neglect my ſtudies, loſe my time,
> War with good counſel, ſet the world at nought;
> Made wit with muſing weak; heart ſick with thought.
>
> ††† S C E N E   II.
>
> *Enter* Speed.
>
> *Speed.* Sir *Protheus,* ſave you; ſaw you my maſter?
>
> † *This whole Scene, like many others in theſe Plays, (ſome of which I believe were written by* Shakeſpear, *and others interpolated by the Players) is compos'd of the loweſt and moſt trifling conceits, to be accounted for only from the groſs taſte of the age he liv'd in;* Populo ut placerent. *I wiſh I had authority to leave them out, but I have done all I could, ſet a mark of reprobation upon them; throughout this edition.* † † †
>
> P*ro*

Fig. 7. Pope's note on page 157 of his edition of Shakespeare's *Two Gentlemen of Verona*

With footnotes characteristically entering editions of literature in the vernacular in the 18th century, the 18th-century gentlemen editors of Shakespeare in particular — for instance Theobald, Hanmer, Warburton, Samuel Johnson — engaged in discussions predominantly of meanings in their footnotes. The footnote space in their editions became the sparring ground for debate (with luck, spirited; frequently controversial; and sometimes, stimulatingly, both) for the benefit of the educated *dilettanti* of the age, chief among whom were the editors themselves. The footnote space in these editions was, as it were, the period coffee-house transposed onto the printed page. Yet who wanted (or could afford) to bring together the whole array, say, of contemporary Shakespeare editions on their bookshelves and desks? The difficulty was solved with the edition *cum notis variorum*: the Variorum edition. Samuel Johnson and George Steevens provided the first such assembly service for editorial notes and commentary at the very end of the 18th century.

To move forward in (as it were) the note space from the late 18th century to the late 19th and into the 20th century means to move from footnoting as the product of cultured communication to footnoting of mass provision. It means to move from the age of reason to the age of positivism. As a book form, the variorum edition was resuscitated towards the

---

[10] Savour especially Pope's note as co-authorial editor on p. 157!

end of the 19th century by Horace Howard Furness, father and son, in the United States. What they revived had mutated in its underlying conception since Johnson and Steevens; and as we know, it has continued to change as the edition has evolved into today's New Variorum under the auspices of the Modern Language Association of America. In terms of design, the edition's volumes are focussed thoroughly on the note space. The text may almost, or even entirely, be crowded out from the page. (Figure 8, left). The mode of design thus becomes what Stephen Dedalus, in James Joyce's *Ulysses*, satirises as: "Five lines of text and ten pages of notes about the folk and the fishgods of Dundrum." (*U*, 1,365-366[11]) — which suggests not an 18th-century coffee-house mode of socialising over the fine points of meaning of texts, but rather a drowning of text and work and author in heavily positivist scholarship. The *notae variorum* in the New Variorum edition assemble erudition generated in a professionalised field of academic pursuit — the Shakespeare industry. (Figure 8, right)

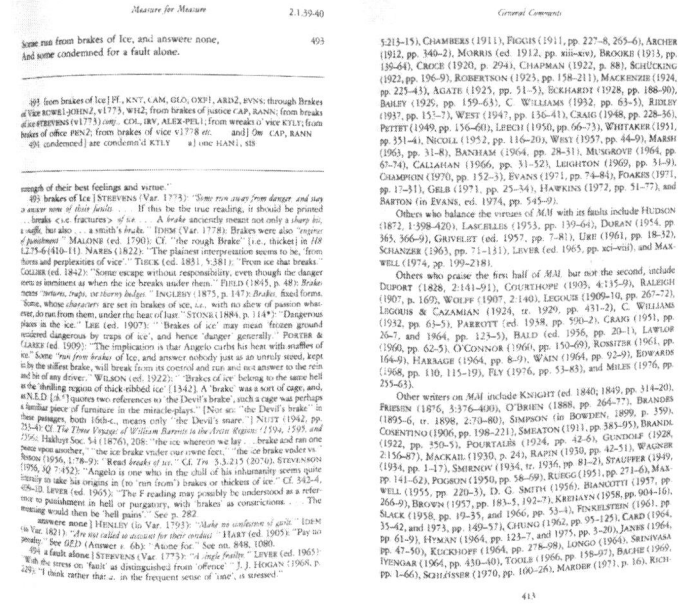

Fig. 8. A page from the Modern Language Association New Variorum Shakespeare.

---

[11] The reference — [James Joyce,] *U*[*lysses*], [episode, i.e. chapter] 1, [lines] 365-366 — is the one meanwhile generally adopted from the editions of *Ulysses* under my editorship since 1984/1986.

Hans Gabler From Argument to Design 171

There is a dark side to the positivist approach: it can appear, or become, thoughtless. And needless to say, the phenomenon is not confined to "the age of positivism". Alexander Pope, for one, castigated thoughtlessness in editions even in his day (witness *The Dunciad*). It becomes manifest always in effects at the surface, at the interface of the medium: that is, in the design, or lack of it, of the book pages. At the high-tide of a positivist conducting of scholarship through editions, it took form particularly in what cannot but be recognised as un-reasonable (because unreasoned and unreasoning) compilations of variants in apparatuses. In German, these are called "Variantenfriedhöfe" — "cemeteries of variants". The books and book-pages that display them are not designed: they are merely ugly. What they display is that editorial argument has lost a reasoned grip on variant materials. Conspicuously, too, a content-related, and thus meaning-related, commentary dimension has all but evaporated from the apparatus entries. Thoughtless editing issues in correspondingly thoughtless, typographically dead design. The making of editions as books has become reduced to routines of assembly-line production.

From the recent past, we know the popularly voiced reaction to apparatus-heavy editions: Nobody, it says, wants to read texts in editions with footnotes. In the United States from the middle of the 20th century onwards, Fredson Bowers was a main mover in turning this sentiment into a new look in book design for critical editions. Edited texts were provided as clear-text presentations on uncluttered pages; the apparatuses related to the textual editing went into appendices at the back of the edition volumes. Under the aegis of an otherwise militant rift between scholarship and criticism, the "new-look" editions were the gift of the scholars to the critics who, under the dispensation of the New Criticism then in fashion, were *a priori* apt to taking texts as given. The New Editors, on their part, set highest stakes on the establishment of texts and gave little or no attention to those traditionally fundamental critical endeavours of editorial scholarship, annotation and commentary. If not abandoned altogether, these became paratextual, in that they were rigorously relegated to the backs of volumes or into separate volumes. Even if so sequestered, it is true, these sections of the "new-look" editions are anything but thoughtless. In, say, Bowers's Dekker, or his Marlowe, his *Dramatic Works in the Beaumont and Fletcher Canon*, his Fieldings (both *Joseph Andrews* and *Tom Jones*), or his Stephen Crane, one invariably finds prefaces to the edited texts that rigorously argue the given edition's rationale and procedure; to them, in turn, the apparatus lists at the end of the edition volumes are systematically correlated. In the apparatus lists, argument is expressed through a shorthand of symbols which condenses, by its semiotics, the editorial reasoning following from the analysis of the textual transmission and its stemmatics; correspondingly, the apparatus symbols support and justify, too, the editorial decisions underlying the establishing of the edited text. The intricate meta-textual semantics of the apparatuses in Bowers-type editions deserve renewed attention today for their potential of re-implementation in the mode of relational links in the electronic medium. As yet, the intellectual substance of their stringent formalisations seems too little recognised, owing to a considerable degree, no doubt, to the relegation of apparatuses and commentary to the realm of the paratextual. At their clear-text surface, the "new-look" editions hearken to an ideology of scholarship erased. Yet in this manner, paradoxically, they too turn editorial argument into design, by endeavouring, as they do, to make a scholarly edition look just like any other book.

***

German editing in the 20th century similarly departed from the breadth and comprehensiveness inherent in the traditions of the scholarly edition through its networking, and thus mutually contextualising, of text and apparatus, annotation and commentary. Editorial scholarship here, too, focussed mainly on the establishment of edition texts. Yet the modes of doing so differed significantly from those adopted in Anglo-American editing. They sprang from a strong sense of the real history of texts and works and led increasingly towards a genetic orientation in editing. The postulate was that states of textual variation and processes of textual development, whether over stretches of distinguishable versions, or recognisable as layers of composition on draft manuscripts, deserved to be edited in their own right. A new type of edition entered the field, namely the *Handschriftenedition*, or "manuscript edition". Its pace-setters were Friedrich Beissner's Hölderlin edition of the 1940s, and Hans Zeller's edition of the poetry of the Swiss poet Conrad Ferdinand Meyer of the 1960s to 1980s.

Figure 9 is a sample of what Zellerian editing of the genetic development of a Meyer poem looks like on the printed page. Two features essential to Zeller's editorial conception inform the deployment of typography for his edited text presentations. One arises from the basic tenet that acts and processes of writing and revision always take place in context. This notion materialises on the printed page by way of what he terms the "integral apparatus": apparatus is no longer excerpted, reading by reading, from the edited text and placed, by reference and lemma, in footnotes or at the back of volumes. Its indications of change, rather, remain embedded in the flow of a text as a whole that provides the invariant context for advancing composition and revision. The mode of representation of textual flow and change within invariance is synoptic. Typographic patterning is deployed to indicate the acts and processes of writing and revision. Bold-face is resorted to, for instance, both to mark out invariance and to highlight textual states that, past initial fluidity, attain stability (in fair copy, say, and eventually in publication). Patterning is thus achieved, on the one hand, by means of type-face (for instance, lean as opposed to bold) and perhaps font, as well as by topographical positioning (a reading and its variants will form a column).

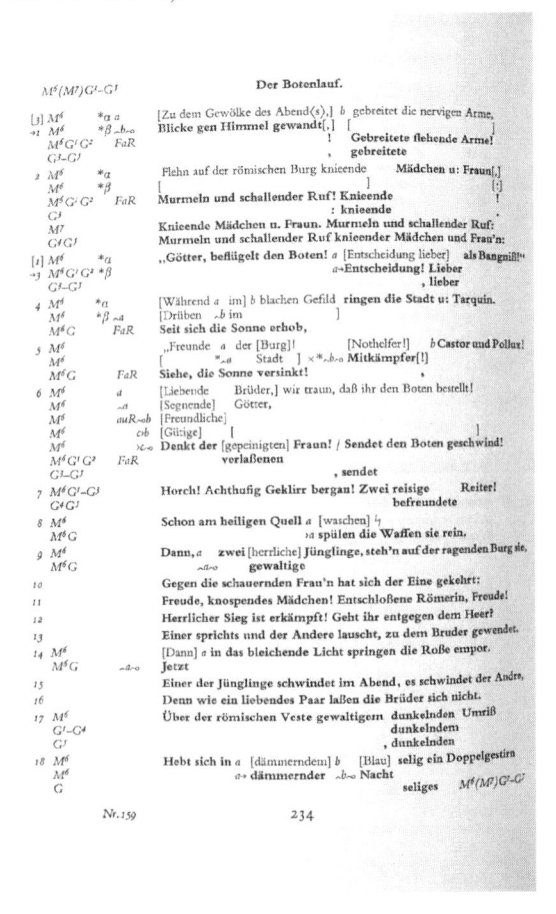

Fig. 9. A page from Zeller's Meyer edition.

Yet on the other hand, as the example shows, there is on Zeller's edition pages also a spread of symbols less obviously meaningful. These symbols, as a beyond-text extension of the "integral apparatus", represent, on the printed page, the second essential feature in Zeller's conception. What, he claims, the meta-textual semiotics on the printed page should have the power to do, is to allow the user of the edition to reconstruct the document of original inscription behind the editorial representation. Images of the actual documents, however, are not supplied — it was, at the time the Meyer edition was conceived, both technically and commercially prohibitive to reproduce them, save in very small numbers. Instead, it was the edition's grand achievement to abstract the documents into their meta-symbols. It was, at the same time, its great weakness. For in practice, the powers of re-imagination that these meta-symbols called for, were patently beyond the capabilities of both textual scholars and critics. It was thereupon the second significant Hölderlin edition of the 20th century, Dieter Sattler's "Frankfurt" edition, that offered an alternative by juxtaposing image and transcription, (Figure 10) as for instance for this multiple-layered holograph draft presented in facsimile, and face to face with a transcription, correspondingly layered typographically. Again, it was an altered concept and editorial argument that resulted in an alternative design for its presentation.

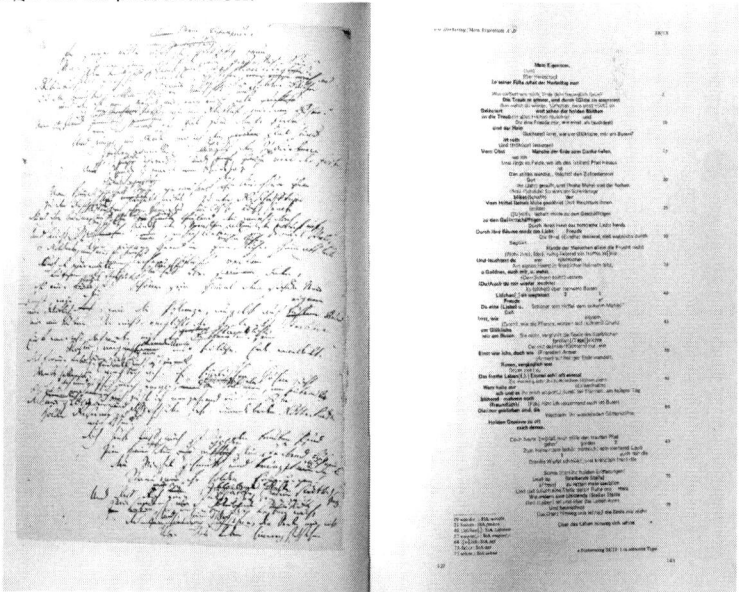

Fig. 10. Sattler's "Frankfurt" edition of Hölderlin.

Zeller's and Sattler's genetically oriented editions of Conrad Ferdinand Meyer's and Friedrich Hölderlin's poetry are, each in its way, grounded in the documents vouching for the texts inscribed in them and, at the same time, happening on them. Inevitably, too (for the time they were conceived and realised), they are editions in book form. They endeavour to represent, by editorial means and typographical design, three- and four-dimensional processes of writing and of textual development (three-dimensional by writing and over-writing on the manuscript page, and four-dimensional with respect to the time axis to be inferred from those writing and over-writing patterns). Even so, however, the representation remains tied to, and bound within, the static two-dimensionality of the book page. This constitutes a practical dilemma with weighty theoretical implications. In terms both of practice and of theory, writing and text are dynamic and processual: writing is so as the human activity in time that it is, and text is so since it simply is *not*, and is *nothing*, unless it constitutes itself in response, and construction of meaning, through reading. On such elementary premises rests, too, the conception and argument underlying the scholarly edition as a genre of learning. Logically, writing and text exceed by their very nature the limits of what, in the medium of the book, is capable of representation. Hence, the book (or codex, or scroll) has since time immemorial been a pragmatic compromise for the construction, or establishment, of editions. Editions have inevitably had to resort to representing again on the material of paper (or papyrus, or parchment) the objects for editing that they found transmitted on just such paper (or papyrus, or parchment), in the first place. This means that editions have always hitherto (and as it were, "naturally") been editions of texts. They have not been capable of presenting and representing writing processes other than from a perspective of their results as text, and texts. For the representation of writing in print can always only be the representation of a product, never of the process that is of the very nature of writing (as it is ultimately, too, of text, constituting itself meaningfully only through reading). Essentially, therefore, the two-dimensionality of the book page is incongruous not only with the third dimension established by the changes and revisions on, say, a draft page by its manifest over- and under-writings of changes and revisions, but all the more also with the fourth dimension, time, of which those changes and revisions are but the material traces. *Mutatis mutandis* the same goes for the processes of change a text undergoes over a series of documents, whether unpublished or published.

Hence, today's answer to the challenge of turning argument into design for scholarly editions is no longer, essentially, the book. As we are facing again a medial watershed — now from printing and the book to data processing — we may become aware of what opportunities data processing holds for designing scholarly editions. Don't misunderstand me, though: I am not doing away with the book. Books are and remain books, and it is books we read. Nor do I claim that the electronic medium can give us the processuality of writing and texts in reality — it can merely better illusion its interactive dynamism. For what in transmission physically exists and lives in the material medium of paper and ink, may henceforth yet be analysed and critically explored in and through the electronic medium. To switch media for editions, meaning: to situate scholarly editions in the electronic medium, opens horizons of a new order. It will be through advantages gained by the medium shift that the scholarly edition need no longer be misconceived as a mere provider of texts, but instead as a genuine knowledge site or knowledge space, through the dynamically relational contextualising of its several and diverse discourses that the electronic medium makes possible. Editions become designable, in the virtuality of the electronic medium, as genuinely relational webs of discourse. To conceive of the implementation of scholarly editing and scholarly editions in the electronic medium, of designing editions of books beyond the book, is an exciting challenge. We are only at the very beginning of taking it up.[12]

Bibliography

Gabler, Hans Walter. 2007. "The Primacy of the Document in Editing." *Ecdotica* 4: 197-207.

McGann, Jerome. 1990. "How To Read A Book." In *New Directions in Textual Studies*, edited by Dave Oliphant and Robin Bradford, 13-37. Austin: Harry Ransom Humanities Research Center.

McKenzie, D. F. 2002. "Typography and Meaning: The Case of William Congreve." In *Making Meaning*, edited by Peter D. McDonald and Michael F. Suarez, S.J., 198-236. Amherst and Boston: University of Massachussets Press.

---

[12] My own very first experiments of designing manuscript editing into the electronic medium may bee seen from following the links given towards the end of my article "The Primacy of the Document in Editing" (2007). Since I am utilising there, however, an IT infrastructure developed by others originally for an electronic edition of manuscripts — the first jottings of Nietzsche aphorisms — that differ in their nature and appearance from the James Joyce drafts I endeavour to present, the design at the user interface sometimes only mediately concords with the tenets of my editorial argument.

Ossian

The Book History of an Anti-book

Christian Benne

In the light of the scholarly *Ossian* renaissance of recent years, it seems hardly feasible to say something revolutionary about the Ossianic poems or the ensuing debate, or indeed its reception across various literatures (Gaskill 1991; Gaskill 1996; Gaskill 2004; Moore 2004; Schmidt 2003; Stafford 1988).[1] Yet the link between book historical findings, including some overlooked publishing peculiarities, and the wider aesthetic context is still missing. Where Ossian studies have re-established the centrality of *Ossian* for the poetical development of English and world literature, its influence can be shown to go deeper yet. Arguably, *Ossian* epitomizes a literary culture striving to transcend the book even when it was still very much bound to its limits, or better: within its limits, the book covers. The traditional notion of the book understood as a container of more or less stable entities[2] — as an object that turns its insides into objects as well –, did not first become destabilised with the advent of literary theory or new media or indeed modern bibliography and book history at the end of the last century. On the contrary, its destabilisation has been a process running parallel to the unfolding of (literary) modernity itself.

Since the historical details surrounding *Ossian* are well-documented, a short outline to put the argument into context will have to suffice. James Macpherson, native of the Highlands and young graduate of Aberdeen University with literary aspirations, was incited by John Home, one of the leading Edinburgh *literati*, to translate some early poetry from the Gaelic language. He did so, reluctantly at first, but, encouraged by Hugh Blair and other figures of the Scottish enlightenment, with increasing productivity and, it has traditionally been assumed: creativity. The first fruit of his labours were the *Fragments of Ancient Poetry, Collected in the Highlands of*

---

[1] Special thanks to Howard Gaskill for many useful hints and for sending me some of his fabulous papers on *Ossian*. Many thanks also to Rüdiger Singer. Likewise Gauti Kristmannsson's *Literary Diplomacy* (2005) has been useful.

[2] Questioned, in an Anglo-Saxon context, at least since Donald McKenzie's *Bibliography and the Sociology of Texts* (1999) and the work of Jerome McGann.

Scotland, and Translated from the Galic or Erse Language, published in 1760.[3] Printed in a relatively small number of copies for the *cognoscenti* of Edinburgh and London, they sold out quickly and saw a second edition in the same year. However, the *Fragments* only managed to whet the appetite: *Ossian* offered the obvious chance to recover the grand prehistory of a Scottish nation worried about becoming culturally marginalised after the Union.[4] Macpherson was almost pressed into finding and composing a bigger work, as a rival to Milton that would outshine the English example through its "national" subject matter, its sheer age and sublimity. An expedition to collect ancient poetry was financed, and when he indeed returned with the desired indigenous epic poem (*Fingal* was published in 1762, and the "sequel" *Temora* only a year later), it created a sensation.[5] Rapidly growing publicity and demand led to the publication of the *Works of Ossian* already in 1765, with a revised edition from 1773 that eventually became the standard reference in the Anglophone world. Rising scepticism regarding the Gaelic sources of the *Ossian*-material provoked Macpherson and some collaborators into a back translation from English into Gaelic that appeared posthumously in 1807. Experts today generally agree that it would be far to simplistic to qualify Macpherson's Ossianic compositions as mere hoaxes or fraud. After all, the Highland Society's famous report from 1805, which Henry Mackenzie had been in charge of and which had set out to answer all the questions raised by *Ossian* once and for all, had already tried to paint a complex picture of the authenticity debate even though it ultimately rejected *Ossian*. Clearly, something had got out of hand in the attempt of making oral tradition correspond to the literary standards of the Augustan Age.

The reception history of *Ossian* across Europe displays some marked differences. Most importantly, the oral substrate of *Ossian* was much more readily accepted in the homeland of Macpherson's most ardent admirers — Germany. The German preoccupation with *Ossian* compared to British efforts can even be quantified. No less than fourteen complete German translations of the Ossianic poems (from both English and Gaelic) appeared in the course of about 150 years. However, the number of translations

---

[3]   James Macpherson (1966) [Facsimile Edition of the 1760 edition].

[4]   This inaugurated a movement of discovery or invention of supposed national epic poems across Europe long into the 19th century (the *Nibelungenlied*, the *Kalevala*, the *Lāčplēsis* etc.).

[5]   Macpherson's source was the famous *Book of the Dean of Lismore*, consisting of late medieval manuscripts (cf. Stafford 1988).

is a consequence, not an explanation, of the differences in interest. The specific significance of Ossianism in the respective literary cultures, I will claim, did not just depend on linguistic aspects of the translations themselves, but equally on the paratextual ones of the bibliographical code. This thesis is supported by bibliographical research on Ossian editions in Britain and Germany; it will subsequently be tested with the help of book historical findings in Denmark, partly because of the manageable scale of Danish Ossianism, partly because in many respects it represents a cross between the German and the British development.[6] I will concentrate on the aesthetic implications of the more technical aspects of *Ossian's* book history that have been dealt with elsewhere.[7]

Where in Britain the debates surrounding *Ossian* were dominated by questions of authenticity, the aesthetic value of the poems was at the centre of interest on the Continent. The first readers of *Ossian* in Britain, such as the Scottish intellectuals and their English adversaries, were mainly interested in the historical and anthropological value of the Ossianic poems, less so in their literary merits; this is even true for Hugh Blair, despite the fact that he would later use Ossianic examples in his lectures on rhetoric and *belles-lettres*.[8] The 1773 edition of the *Poems*, instigated by Henry Home, justified a new chronological order of the poems accordingly, namely as "in the order of time, so as to form a kind of regular history of the age to which they relate".[9] By contrast, the translator of the first complete German edition of the *Works of Ossian*, notes in his preface that German readers can simply ignore the British authenticity debate and

---

[6] The Nordic slant of this comparison is explained by the fact that this paper was first presented at the SHARP-conference "Published words, public pages. A Nordic conference on international print culture" (Copenhagen, September 2008). Many thanks to my colleague Simon Frost for his organising skills.

[7] Cf. e.g. Uwe Böker (1991). Böker points out that Anglo-German book trade relations remained very weak long into the 1770s, not least because of the Holy Roman Empire's regional and political fragmentation.

[8] For Blair "that enthusiasm, that vehemence and fire, which are the soul of poetry" (Gaskill 1996, 345) comes only third place as far as the interest in *Ossian* is concerned, after the historical reconstruction of Celtic pre-history, and after general anthropological insights.

[9] Quoted after *James Macpherson's Ossian. Faksimile-Neudruck der Erstausgabe von 1762/63 mit Begleitband: Die Varianten*, ed. Otto L. Jiriczek (1940, 3:34). This is still the best edition from a book historical point of view, even though Gaskill (1996) is the more practical and readily available choice.

the attacks on Macpherson: "as they are of no interest for the Germans, who regard Ossian solely as a *poet*."[10]

The British focus on the epic poems as an important historical source was clearly reflected in editorial decisions. The *Fragments*, where the mythical Ossian did not even figure, is a slim volume, measuring only 17 x 9 cm; in fact the standard format of eighteenth century classical editions. It is thus presented as a minor find of genuine ancient remains, embellished by a classical quote implying that the bardic culture already known in antiquity had finally and miraculously resurfaced. It was remarkable only in the light of the cultural debate between England and Scotland. Yet Blair, who had ghost-written the preface and the advertisement to the *Fragments*, had larger ambitions. Hence *Fingal* and *Temora*, where Ossian is stylised as a single author of epic poems,[11] quickly replaced this all-too modest opening. They were launched in much grander quartos, including decorations on the title page in copper that depict "classical" scenes from the life of the bard in the style of Homer (Stafford 1988).[12] *Temora* even copied the style of the "arguments" from *Paradise Lost*, where every new scene and action is summarised and described as if it indeed was a carefully structured whole. Both *Fingal* and *Temora* included copious notes and learned introductions. It is these editions, now published in London rather than Edinburgh (and thereby claiming more than regional relevance) that readily attracted disbelief and charges of fraud.[13]

---

[10] *Die Gedichte Ossians. Eines alten celtischen Dichters*, aus dem Englischen übersetzt von M. Denis (1768, 3), my translation. In the 1773 English edition Macpherson notes: "The eagerness, with which these Poems have been received abroad, are a recompence for the coldness with which a few have affected to treat them at home" (Jiriczek 1940, 3: 31).

[11] Cf. the "Advertisment" for Fingal: "How far it comes up to the rules of the epopæa, is the province of criticism to examine. It is only my business to lay it before the reader, as I have found it." [...] "The story of this poem is so little interlarded with fable, that one cannot help thinking it the genuine history of Fingal's expedition embellished by poetry. In that case, the compositions of Ossian are not less valuable for the light they throw on the ancient state of Scotland and Ireland than they are for their poetical merit" (Jiriczek 1940, 1: x, xv).

[12] Jiriczek's *Ossian*-edition is the most useful in this respect as it is reproduced in the format of the original, including all of the illustrations etc., just short of a facsimile; in the introduction and critical notes of vol. 3 there is detailed information about size, illustrations, paper and other material aspects, also for the *Fragments*.

[13] Cf. Moore (2004, 1:xlvii and ff.) on the widespread belief that it was the "move from Gaelic ballad to neo-classical epic" that created problems for Macpherson. Moore does not follow up on the book historical differences that accompanied this process. Another reason why *Fingal* and *Temora* came to dominate the debate in Britain was the violent reaction of the Irish, who

The next, and arguably most important edition, *The Works of Ossian* from 1765 assembled all material of the *Fragments*, the two epic poems, and much more. It was meant to be a more popular and cheaper edition, and came out in a much smaller layout, on cheaper paper and in less costly bindings. Unlike *Fingal* and *Temora*, which were never published separately outside Britain, it was this edition that found its way to a larger audience on the Continent. Goethe's father possessed a copy of it; and Goethe together with his friend Merck produced a pirate copy in English.[14] It was even smaller than the original and measured only ca. 17,5 cm x 10,2 cm. Crucially however, it only included the naked texts of the poems, without the various dissertations and introductions by Hugh Blair and Macpherson.[15] In Germany, there have never been any grand editions of the epic poems alone. Unlike in Britain, these could never be conceived as Ossian's/Macpherson's "main works". On the contrary, the fragmentary character of Ossian's supposed creations was their most noticeable feature. In the German translations, the Ossianic poems were at first mainly distributed as a collection of smaller texts in literary journals and anthologies: as poems, songs or fragments or as groups of fragmentary poems. They were even incorporated as fragments in literary fiction, most famously in Goethe's *The Sorrows of young Werther*, by far the most important introduction to *Ossian* in Germany and perhaps on the Continent as a whole. Goethe, influenced by Johann Gottfried Herder, was not concerned with *Fingal* and *Temora* at all and only included the *Songs of Selma* in *Werther*, which had played virtually no role in Britain, having been hidden at the back of most editions and thus in a part of the book that few British readers ever opened.[16]

---

wanted to reclaim *Ossian* and *Fingal* for a paradigm of Irish prehistory and identity. See e.g. Groom (1999, 79 and ff.)

[14] Printing foreign books abroad was not considered illegal even by opponents and victims of pirate copying such as Goethe himself.

[15] Blair's Dissertation appeared in vol. 2 of the *Works of Ossian* (1765), but had already come out as a separate brochure in the same format as *Fingal* and *Temora* (without mentioning its author's name).

[16] Cf. Wolf Gerhard Schmidt, "Homer des Nordens" und "Mutter der Romantik" (2003), a near-complete overview, that leaves little to be desired, apart perhaps from the fact that some of the bibliographical, paratextual and material information included in Jiriczek's edition is unfortunately missing. For a concise overview of Goethe's *Ossian*-chronology see Dochartaigh (2004, 156-75). Goethe first really became interested in *Ossian* after meeting Herder in Strassburg in 1770. After returning to Frankfurt, he borrowed his father's copy of the *Works* (1765). Those passages

These editorial circumstances explain the mixed reactions to the first *complete* German translation of the *Works of Ossian* by the Austrian Jesuit Michael Denis. Trying to capture the epic flavour of the English version, he went far beyond even Macpherson's ambition and translated Ossian into hexameters, newly ennobled as the epic metre of German literature. (Macpherson had not used the metrical forms usually associated with the epos in English literature, blank verse or rhyming couplets.[17]) Not at all surprisingly, Denis' hexameters were criticised by the some of the most influential literary voices of the day, among them Herder. Significantly, Herder had come to his conclusions before he even had so much as looked at the English "original", let alone at some Gaelic specimen. To him, the characteristic expression of *Ossian* was "short, forceful, manly, fragmentary (*abgebrochen*) in images and feelings" (Herder 1993, 448; cf. Gaskill 2001). In fact, no scholar has said as clearly as Herder himself, what effect the publishing circumstances had had on these convictions. In *Homer und Ossian*, his essay of 1795 and the *summa* of his lifelong pondering of the subject, he writes:

> Many readers will remember the sweet astonishment with which Ossian's appearance was met in the years 1761 to 1765. First, some modest songs emerged as fragments, and perhaps the majority of Ossian's admirers love him the most in this guise in which they first came to know him. [...] The incoherent shape of these stories, their noble simplicity and, if I may say so, their low-hanging skies and their narrow frame, all contributed to the impression that they made on everybody, and in particular on youthful souls. As if from a distance, from a cave, over the sea, from a valley or from the hills of the misty island, one heard sweet voices and saw, as if in a dream, the cramped cottages of the noble-minded and beloved surrounded by clouds.[18]

---

that Goethe tried to translate from the Gaelic are the specimen from the first edition in *Temora* (1763) that had been reprinted in the *Works*-edition. They represent Macpherson's first attempt at publishing "originals": "They are certainly more idiomatic and less contrived than the 1807 full text of the supposed original Scottish Gaelic" (1765, 158).

[17] It was Macpherson's "measured prose" with its mesmerising rhythmical effects that sparked off a veritable literary revolution and that we still have to acknowledge as his lasting legacy. English, with its wealth of monosyllabic words, was of course much better suited to this then either Gaelic or German.

[18] Johann Gottfried Herder, *Homer und Ossian* (1998, 72), my translation.

Later in his essay, Herder remarks that Fingal and Temora seem rather unusual by comparison, having been announced as epic poems to compete or even better Homer.[19] They certainly do not embody the Ossian he approves of: if to him already Homer was a metaphor for the compilation of popular songs and verse of his age, this was even truer for Ossian.[20] To conflate these songs into artificial, book-length narratives in enormous volumes was a symptom of the preposterous nature of the soulless age of print and letters. Although Ossian appeared in countless translations in Germany, none of them ever managed to achieve the same effect as the fragments whose effect Herder recorded for posterity, published in Werther and elsewhere.[21]

An interesting response to support these findings came from Wordsworth. Heavily indebted to Ossianic imagery and moods in a way that recalls the German pre-romantic and romantic schools, especially in his early work, he levelled a deadening attack on the Ossianic heritage in the *Essay, Supplementary to the Preface* in the 1815 edition of the *Lyrical Ballads*. This is, incidentally, an overlooked text from a book historical point of view as Wordsworth produces a little book history of his own, using publishers' figures and records to prove that the best works of their times never have been the ones most purchased or read.[22] After singing the praises of Thomas Percy's *Reliques of Ancient English Poetry* (1765), in fact unthinkable

---

[19] "Sie wurden als Epopeen angekündigt, die mit Homer wetteifern, und ihn wohl gar übertreffen sollten. Dahin zielte in mehreren Anmerkungen *Mac-Pherson* selbst, Ossians unsterblicher Herausgeber; dahin *Hugh Blairs* kritische Abhandlungen; noch mehr *Cesarotti's* Anmerkungen zu seiner Italiänischen Übersetzung dieser Gedichte. Dem zu Folge sang Denis in wohlklingenden homerischen Hexametern, mit lyrischen Sylbenmaßen untermischt, sie den Deutschen vor, und gab ihnen dadurch noch mehr das Ansehen eines einförmig-fortgehenden Ganzen." (1998, 73).

[20] On the theory and history of popular song in this context cf. Rüdiger Singer, "*Nachgesang*". *Ein Konzept Herders, entwickelt an Ossian, der popular ballad und der frühen Kunstballade* (2006).

[21] Although Christian Wilhelm Ahlwardt's 1811 translation of the supposed Gaelic "original" was the bestselling Ossian-edition of the 19th century, this is not saying much: the edition of the *Works* from 1765, including the excerpts derived from it, dominated the hot phase of German Ossianism and therefore remains the most influential one. For an excellent overview see Paul Barnaby, "Timeline: European Reception of Ossian" (2004). It shows the extent to which fragments and single excerpts dominated the early phase in Germany. While the revised version of 1773 became the standard edition in Britain, the 1765-edition (which had incorporated many of the "original" fragments) dominated in Germany for a long time (cf. Schmidt 2003, 2:1134, and Jiriczek 1940, vol. 3).

[22] Surely, but I stand to be corrected, one of the first examples of literary history as the history of the technicalities and consequences of publishing.

without *Ossian*, and the ballad tradition, Wordsworth turns to the object of his scorn: "But from humble ballads we must ascend to heroics. All hail Macpherson! hail to thee, Sire of Ossian!" (Gill 1984, 654 and ff.) Note the ambiguity of "Sire": Wordsworth's undisguised sarcasm takes offence at the success Ossian once enjoyed. The context shows that Wordsworth has the epic ambitions of Macpherson in mind, less the other poetry: it is *Fingal* and *Temora* that are unfavourably contrasted with the lyrical tradition in which he places himself, and which according to him will never excite a similar interest. After quoting a typical passage from *Temora* he exclaims: "Precious memorandums from the pocket-book of the blind Ossian!" The claim to grandeur of *Fingal* and *Temora* was evidently incompatible with the cheap octavo bindings that had become the norm, whereas they were perfectly adequate for the more modest genre of the ballad. It is not the fact that Macpherson had applied his liberties as editor and translator somewhat freely that had prompted Wordsworth's criticism — this kind of creativity he praises in Percy — but the fact that he did not live up to expectations. According to Wordsworth, the best proof of *Ossian's* unnaturalness was his failure to influence the course of English literature — by which he can only mean that his *epic* poetry had failed do so, as it had not, unlike the ballad, suddenly become fashionable again.

Danish Ossianism, not previously considered in this context, offers some supplementary aspects. It has always been a mystery why in a country with such close cultural ties to both Germany and Britain, Ossian did not play a comparable role. Although this cannot be derived from the small numbers of translations alone (since Danish intellectuals generally read German and often relied on German sources rather than translations), there seems to be a curious indifference, which is also mirrored by the much more modest creative consequences of Ossianim. Not until the early 19th century, when most other nations were slowly turning away from Ossianism, did Danish Ossianism gain momentum, culminating in Niels W. Gade's overture *Efterklange af Ossian* (1840). Once again, there are two issues at stake: national identity and book history, both interlocked in an interesting fashion.

When Andreas Christian Alstrup published the first Danish translation of *Ossian* in 1790, he picked the worst possible moment. His translation was the off-shoot of Danish interest in German literature and culture generally, and specifically in the Klopstock circle of Copenhagen that had introduced so many German and Danish intellectuals to the mythical bard. Yet the years of 1789/90 was also the time of the so-called *tyskerfejde*, the violent reaction against German cultural influence at court and in the country that had been in the making at least since Johann Friedrich Struensee's execution in 1772; it is generally regarded as the birth of modern Danish nationalism. National-minded Danes who already knew *Ossian* in German or English translations were bound to have reservations already from the perspective of historical identity. On the one hand, the Germans had proclaimed *Ossian* to be among the forefathers of German culture; on the other, Macpherson's and Blair's prefaces and dissertations to the various English *Ossian*-editions had put the history and prehistory of Scandinavia, and specifically of Denmark into disrepute. Danish warriors and Scalds do not compare favourably with the Celtic and Bardic tradition; the description of how Fingal "expels the Danes from the country" (Macpherson 1966) p. viii, was hardly a recommendation.

Alstrup did not even touch upon this problem and, following his German sources, took Macpherson's and Blair's story at face value, defending *Ossian's* authenticity with some new, but at times hair-raising arguments.[23] The fact that Alstrup adorned his *Ossian* with a Klopstock-motto (instead of the original Lucan-quote Macpherson had chosen) did not exactly help, but this is not the only paratextual aspect that gave problems. The discrepancy between the dry and scholarly text devoid of poetical ambition and the attempt at celebrating its epic character was apparently too noticeable. It is as if Alstrup tried to combine not the best but the worst of both worlds of the English and German *Ossian* editions. The two modest octavo volumes without the ornaments and illustrations of the English Ossian, but including a long and rather dry scholarly introduction on the origin of the Bardic tradition could hardly inspire awe and are reminiscent of Wordsworth's jab at the pocket-book character of a work with claims to sublime grandeur.[24]

---

[23] One example: the bards, claims Alstrup, had been subordinate to the druids in the Celtic hierarchy and had been allowed to share their secrets and mysteries. This enabled them to create ideals in their songs which in turn made the chiefs want to conform to these ideals, thereby gradually refining their barbaric character. Flattered, the chiefs made sure that their glory would be transmitted to the next generations; even when the bards ceased to exist as a class, the individual families kept their songs alive (sometimes even writing them down) — and thereby their family tradition (Alstrup 1790, xii-xiv).

[24] The standard piece on the Danish *Ossian* reception is Anna H. Harwell Celenza, "Efterklange af Ossian. The Reception of James Macpherson's Poems of *Ossian* in Denmark's Literature, Art, and Music" (Celenza 1998). This is exemplary in many respects, but not without its problems.

The first popular Danish *Ossian*-translation was produced as late as 1807 by Steen Steensen Blicher, a transitional figure marking the shift from romanticism to a kind of poetic realism. Familiar with *Ossian* from his youth and especially taken by the landscape descriptions that he likened to his native Jutland, he was, like German writers of the period before, less interested in historical than poetic authenticity. As in the German editions of *Ossian*, Blicher published a poetical text without any critical notes and commentaries. A "Hater of all useless work", Blicher (1807, xxvi; my translation) wanted to leave all commentary to those "future scholars, who will comment on Ossian in quartos and folios." (!) His version can, on the other hand, perhaps best be described as a modernisation of the epic idea. In effect, the result is the first example of an Ossian-edition that almost reads like a novel. Blicher altered the sequence of the individual poems of the *Works*-edition in order to achieve a more natural and logical depiction of all the battles of Ossian. Instead of printing paragraphs in individual blocks like all previous editions in all other languages had done (thus indicating possible lacunae), Blicher and his publisher chose to link the paragraphs together, creating a type area that looked decidedly familiar to readers of contemporary novels. Combined with the octavo-format in a single book this was a cheap and easy-to-read pocket book suited to the tastes of the day, not an obsolete attempt at epos-making. This packaging seems to have contributed greatly to its publishing success.

Manifestly, Blicher's novel-like Ossian is far removed from the genuine findings of snippets of some old Gaelic songs from an oral poetry tradition around the middle of the century before, distinctly different from both the German and the English versions. Something other than a change in the bibliographical code must have occurred around 1800 that suddenly made *Ossian* acceptable in this format; and at the time of the British bombing of Copenhagen (1807), it was certainly not because of a new cultural alliance. Before this question can be properly addressed, another development has to be taken into account. If the Danish reception of Ossian is remembered at all today, it is through the medium of music (cf. Smith 2004) rather than literature. Niels W. Gade's ouverture *Efterklange af Ossian*, already

---

Curiously, there is no reference to the groundbreaking work of Howard Gaskill. Celenza also underestimates the extent to which Danish authors and intellectuals used German translations of *Ossian*. The Danish Ossian-reception certainly did not start, as she seems to assume, with the Danish translations. Moreover, intellectual Denmark was an extremely small society so that the number of translations is not a very good indicator of impact.

mentioned above, was actually based on Blicher's translation; musically, it is indebted to Mendelssohn (and related thematically to Schubert's *Ossian* compositions). As Anna Harwell Celenza (1998) has pointed out, there were over forty *Ossian*-compositions in Germany before 1850, but only two Danish ones — the musical reception of Ossian is primarily a German tradition that the late flowering of *Ossianism* in Denmark inherited long after the *tyskerfejde*. Already Alstrup (1790, xiv) had stressed the role of music for the preservation of the poems, a direct inspiration from his mentor Klopstock, who had been one of the first to become interested in an assumed original music to the Ossianic poems. Klopstock had even sent a letter to Macpherson (who never replied), enquiring about the rhythmical conditions of Bardic poetry in Scotland. Johannes Ewald, Denmark's most important writer of the late 18th century and a follower of Klopstock, was supposed to travel to Scotland and the islands of the North Atlantic on his behalf in order to research and recover those lost tunes. Only the political upheaval in Denmark and growing anti-German feeling in the aftermath of Bernstorff's and Struensee's fall stopped the project.

This affinity between romantic music and its language of *Stimmung* (≈ mood) on the one hand and *Ossian* on the other that reached its pinnacle around a century after the Macpherson's first *Ossian*-publications has a common root in the 18th-century discovery of the performative nature of oral poetry, especially in the German context. While the discussion on the British Isles went round in circles over the manuscript question, the fact that the *Ossianic* material could not be reduced to mere words on a page only added to its attractiveness for Herder and others.[25] Indeed, it was the awareness of performative, anti-literate aspects of literature that led to the interest in *Ossian* in the first place, a result perhaps of primitivism and Rousseausism gaining more and more ground. Herder, *Ossian*'s most important theorist and propagator on the continent advocated the collection of oral poetry like no one else before. *Ossian* for him was just

---

[25] In *Homer und Ossian*, Herder writes: "The original of these songs in their fragmentary shape, accompanied by the right metre and melody, whose delightful simplicity and variety several admirers of Ossian praise, would — even without any critical commentaries — have been a proof of their authenticity for all the world and for posterity against which no Englishman, no Johnson could have so much as uttered a single sound." (Herder 1998, 75; my translation) And in a footnote: "Was everything printed as it was found? Was it copied from living songs (*lebendigen Gesängen*) or from manuscripts? Are those manuscripts identical to each other? or to the living song? Can the songs' and manuscripts' diction be dated (*Aus welcher Zeit ist die Diktion des Gesanges und der Handschriften*)?" (my translation).

a primary example of the potential results if only one would look hard enough (Herder 1993, 481). Popular culture offered redemption from mere scholarship, the organic answer to the demands of artificial civilisation. The wilder, the less tamed a people, the freer, more sensual, fuller of life their song: "The further away a people is from artificial, scholarly ways of thinking, from language and letters, the less its songs have to be produced for paper." Herder celebrated the "living and dance-like song" of Ossianic oral poetry, its "living presence of images" (Herder 1993, 452). What poetry had lost by forming an exclusive alliance with writing, it could regain in the immediacy of oral tradition. Musical performance of Ossian only looks like the next logical step; Herder described his plans for travelling to Scotland in order to experience the songs of a vital, living people at close hand, to become a Caledonian for a while (1993, 455).[26] In his prized essay *Ueber die Wirkung der Dichtkunst auf die Sitten der Völker in alten und Neuen Zeiten*, heavily indebted to his work on *Ossian*, Herder categorically censures the modern culture of the printed book, aiming to revitalise it with the help of the bardic legacy.

This is a central point. Some 200 years prior to the groundbreaking work on oral literature by Milman Parry, Walter J. Ong, Paul Zumthor and others, a performative imperative that wants to transcend the book and transport the reader elsewhere is the defining characteristic of *Ossian*'s reception in Germany, precisely because Ossian was presented primarily as a collection of songs, not as a coherent epos. *Ossian* is not to be read at home in one's study, but outside, or in the very least in the middle of some emotional upheaval. Napoleon, a great admirer of Goethe's *Sorrows of young Werther*, is reported to have carried his edition of *Ossian* constantly with him on campaign, even on horseback.[27] While the editions of *Ossian* became physically smaller and more transportable, its contents seemed to outgrow the medium by way of readers' reactions. It looked as if the book could no longer contain *Ossian* — this was not mere "literature", meant for the book. Rather, it had to be memorised, sung aloud and taken along into wild nature. In his autobiography, Goethe describes the melancholy of a whole generation enthused by *Ossian* in the following terms:

---

[26] Herder also compares the ancient Caledonians with contemporary Native American Indians.

[27] Still unsurpassed: P. van Tieghem, *Ossian en France* (1981).

But so that an entirely appropriate locality would not be lacking in all this gloom, Ossian enticed us to follow him to the end of the world. In this place, while walking on endless grey heather, among jutting moss-covered headstones, we saw around us the grass blown by a terrible wind and above us the heavily overcast sky. It was first by moonlight that this Caledonian night became day; fallen heroes and wilted maidens floating around us. [...][28]

Ossian does not even need to be read anymore. He is always already there, almost as a pantheistic presence, animating the world.

Back in Britain, Samuel Johnson, England's fiercest *Ossian* critic, was not much for walking on heather. His own trip to Scotland left him famously underwhelmed. Oral poetry was a contradiction in terms: proper literature was bound to writing — and bound between two covers (preferably leather). This is the real significance of his thundering reaction to the "Caledonian bigotry" of Macpherson and the circle behind him: "Where are the manuscripts?" This urgent demand, as Johnson knew very well, could not be satisfied.[29] There could be no manuscript "original" of *Ossian* if the Ossianic poems really did start life as oral poetry. Written down samples of it would be little more than the equivalent to muscial scores because the mere linguistic sequence of written language cannot capture the somatic aspects of the *mise en scène* and the indispensable interpretative creativity of oral transmission. Macpherson was faced with the impossibility of recreating an artificial secondary orality out of his sparse findings.[30]

To be fair to Johnson, it was not so much the lack of transcription manuscripts, but the fact that Macpherson had claimed a written basis for the Ossianic poems himself, fearing they would not be taken seriously

---

[28] Johann Wolfgang *Goethe, Werke. Hamburger Ausgabe* (= HA), ed. Erich Trunz, (Goethe 1981, 10: 582; (my translation). Cf. Rüdiger Singer, "Ossian: Der 'Homer des Nordens' und seine Textlandschat" (2004).

[29] Samuel Johnson, *A Journey to the Western Islands of Scotland*, ed. Mary Lascelles (Johnson 1971), esp. p. 117ff, p. 118: "I suppose my opinion of the poems of Ossian is already discovered. I believe they never existed in any other form than that which we have seen. The editor, or author, never could shew the original; nor can it be shewn by any other [...]".

[30] Paul Zumthor, *La poésie et la voix dans la civilisations médiévale* (1984, 38): the *text* is nothing more than "la séquence linguistique", in contrast to the œuvre, which is formed through "la totalité des facteurs de la performance" (voice, rhythm, etc.): "[...] je désigne du mot de *performance* l'action vocale par laquelle le texte poétique est transmis à ses destinataires. La transmission de bouche à oreille *opère* littéralement le texte; elle l'effectue."

otherwise.[31] Already the preface to the *Fragments* opened with the following statement:

> The public may depend on the following fragments as genuine remains of ancient Scottish poetry. The date of their composition cannot be exactly ascertained. Tradition, in the country where they were written (sic!), refers them to an æra of the most remote antiquity: and this tradition is supported by the spirit and strain of the poems themselves; which abound with those ideas, and paint those manners, that belong to the most early state of society. (Macpherson 1966, ii)

Macpherson continued to call himself a *translator*, not a *recorder* of the fragments with their ancient pedigree. The very concept of the fragment usually implies some form of materiality, such as an incomplete written record: "In a fragment of the same poems, which the translator has seen, a Culdee or Monk is represented as desirous to take down in writing from the mouth of Oscian, who is the principal personage in several of the following fragments, his warlike achievements and those of his family" (Macpherson 1966, iv). Even though Macpherson notes that most poems had originally been handed down by oral tradition, implications of a strong manuscript basis unblemished by the usual problems of textual corrosion abound.[32] The advertisement to *Fingal* mentions "a design on foot to print the Originals, as soon as the translator shall have time to transcribe

---

[31] It is not clear why Nick Groom, in his otherwise remarkable book, claimes that "*Ossian* was presented as an oral phenomenon" (1999, 75). There is plenty of counter-evidence, especially in the early *Ossian*-publications and editions. Boswell records *in Life of Johnson*: "If he [Macpherson, C.B.] had not talked unskilfully of manuscripts, he might have fought with oral tradition (sic!) much longer." Cf. also Derick S. Thomson, *The Gaelic Sources of Macpherson's 'Ossian'* (1952); Gaskill (1991) and Gaskill's introduction to his *The Reception of Ossian in Europe*, (2004, 1-18) with a section on the so-called "manuscript myth" in the *Ossian*-tradition. Interestingly, Gaskill argues convincingly that the famous "originals" that are supposed to having been on display in Thomas Becket's bookshop in 1762 ("for the inspection of the curious") were Macpherson's own notes - Macpherson saw himself as a Gaelic poet and creative heir to his people's tradition; the claim in the *Advertisement* to *Fingal* to transcribe the originals was meant seriously, in contrast to *Temora*, which was a clear fabrication. In any case, the evidence presented here proves that a manuscript basis was important for Macpherson, too — oral tradition did not suffice.

[32] "Though the poems now published appear as detached pieces in this collection, there is ground to believe that most of them were originally episodes of a greater work which related to the wars of Fingal. [...] By the succession of these Bards, such poems were handed down from race to race; some in manuscript, but more by oral tradition." (Macpherson 1966, vf). Even the fact that this tradition is said to be "incorrupted" makes sense only in the context of traditional textual scholarship: the category of "corruption" is pointless in oral poetry.

them for the press." *Temora* claimed that "all the genuine remains of the works of Ossian" had come into the translator's possession.[33]

When Thomas Percy compiled the *Reliques*, later praised by Wordsworth, he had learned from the early mistakes of Macpherson (Groom 1999, 73) and made sure to point out his manuscript basis (the so-called Percy folio). The incorporation of manuscripts, that previously had been thoughtlessly destroyed, into the field literature, their complex juxtaposition with contemporary aesthetic problems, had finally begun. In Walter Scott's Waverley-novel *The Antiquary*, we find an overlooked repercussion of the Ossianic debates. First published in 1816, it is set in the mid-nineties, when the debate had already diminished in strength, shortly before the death of Macpherson. In episodes as amusing as telling, we learn that Oldbook, the aged antiquarian, is strongly opposed to Macpherson. As a defender and apologist of book and print, he hides his disgust with Ossian behind pedantic attacks on oral poetry in general while simultaneously trying to convince his protégé to publish a book that has been composed out of old collections in a very similar manner to Percy and indeed Macpherson.[34]

Howard Gaskill's insight that Samuel Johnson's insistence on manuscripts "is one instance, albeit perhaps the most significant one, of the way in which he has left his mark on subsequent criticism", is profounder than might be imagined at first glance (Gaskill 1991, 15). The period between Macpherson's *Fragments* and Scott's *Antiquary* might serve as a convenient bracket in which to place the birth of a new literary trend that I would choose to call modern manuscript culture. Manuscripts did not vanish with printing technology, on the contrary, they simply took on a different significance after having been freed from functioning as the main means of dissemination. The concept of modern manuscript culture, not to be confused with scribal culture of the 17th century, describes the fact, that individual authors began to collect, work with, and distribute various types of their own manuscripts, including scribbling pads, sketches, working papers, revised offprints etc. — not to mention letters and diaries — in a way that had not hitherto been the case. Print was losing its aura and

---

[33] Jiriczek (1940, 1:iii). Cf. also the *Dissertation Concerning the Antiquity, etc. of the Poems of Ossian the Son of Fingal in Fingal*: "All that can be said of the translation, is that it is literal, and that simplicity is studied. The arrangement of the words in the original is imitated, and the inversions of the style observed. As the translator claims no merit from his version, he hopes for the indulgence of the public where he fails." (xvi).

[34] Walter Scott, *The Antiquary* (1816), chapters 14 and 30.

exclusivity in terms of artistic creation; Literature (with a capital L) would increasingly be represented by a writer's *inédits* — this, of course, is also the problematic premise of modern editorial theory and practice.[35]

Roughly speaking, it is plausible to concede a key role to Ossianism in this development. There are two main reasons for this. Firstly, Macpherson's attempt to reconstruct Gaelic culture through literary fragments inspired the fragmentary constitution of individual authors' work and life. The authenticity debate that grew out of the debate around his manuscript basis elevated the status of manuscripts to the level of indispensability. *Ossian* demonstrated and demonstrates how hard it is even to define the subject matter of its book historical analysis. The book history of these "books" of *Ossian* reminds us, secondly, that for long stretches of its history, it was celebrated as an anti-book that transcends the medium of letters. The vanishing interest in the texts (not the music) of *Ossian* in the 19th century has to be read not so much as a reaction to the report of the Highland Society, but as a sign that it had served its purpose of both introducing a higher esteem for manuscripts and for performance into a literate culture dominated by print, thus contributing to creating an altogether more complex medium.

Just as diaries and letters became incorporated in literature proper, sometimes even forming new genres like the epistolary novel, the fragmentary contributed to a gradual transformation of traditional genres into a new literature that was not aiming for closure and perfection anymore. *Ossian* is arguably only the first example of a textual body in modern literature displaying both the performative aspects of oral literature and the aesthetics of the fragment.[36] Taken seriously, both aspects question the *telos* of

---

[35] "Ossian was Homerically blind, and so even in singing his pre-literate songs articulated the end of writing." (Groom 1999, 74). Groom goes as far as calling the antiquarian interest in the aura of the manuscript "a challenge to the mainstream ideological supremacy of print" (1999, 38). Not quite: admittedly, manuscripts created their own public sphere, circulating among the *cognoscenti* in the same way as the first print runs. This is also how Percy became aware of *Ossian*. Cf. Margaret M. Smith (1990). However, things are more complex and need to be further analysed. The concept of manuscript culture employed by me instead has otherwise only been applied to the pre-print era, with the exception of a phase of scribal production right into the early 18th century. Cf. Harold Love (1993); H. R. Woudhuysen (1996). My paper is an abridged sample of the analysis of a modern manuscript culture not so much different from than complementary to print culture. Its origins and consequences are the topic of a forthcoming book.

[36] "Without the hoax poems [i.e. *Ossian* and similar texts, C.B.], the fragment might have remained the province of the antiquarian, the metaphysician, and the connoisseur of sensation and sensibility" (Levinson 1986, 35). *Ossian* is a major prerequisite for the (artificial) fragment

literary production in the traditional rhetorical system. Instead of a final product, they focus on the *process* of composition. The point of writing is no longer to improve, but to edit effects. As a result, the author becomes less of a second-maker in the Shaftsburyan sense than a prism of all the phenomena that concentrate poetry in the scene of writing he is the director of.[37] The subsequent cult of the manuscript appears to be ideally suited precisely to combine performance and collection of fragments. Joining forces, they take over the function of documenting the perfomative process of the act of writing itself. Saving and continuing the manuscript becomes, from the end of the 18th century onwards, the means to saving the traces of the act of creation, demonstrating the authenticity of art.

In his early *Ossian*-Essay, itself published in fragmentary form, Herder distinguished two kinds of modern poets, namely those who, like Milton, plan and structure everything before the actual act of composition without changing much afterwards, while the others, like Klopstock, produce in fits and emotional outburst that need constant change and revision. Indeed, Klopstock was infamous for the changes to his poems and the countless different editions of his Milton-inspired main work, the *Messias*. It is the second type of poet that produces fragments. The aesthetics of the fragment is one of spontaneous production ("overflow of powerful feelings" in Wordsworthian diction). The fragment made superfluous the division of *res* and *verba* of rhetoric and was stylised as the opposite of artifice; like the ruin, literary fragments claim to be free of intervention. The form alone is transmitted, and the reader has to reconstruct what it was meant to express then — in contrast to its current meaning. Fragments are found, not produced: in history or in the history of an individual. Every book becomes a fragment of the work, every work the fragment of a subjectivity, "Bruchstücke einer grossen Konfession", as Goethe has it in his autobiography. That these *Bruchstücke* or fragments are worth saving even for modern, contemporary authors — and that they ultimately are the more authentic and interesting text — is the real shift to modernity, the very moment, when

---

poems of the romantic era. These "install in the work the figure of the poet, or the presence of an eternal, chameleon, authorial energy. The discontinuities that score the RFP [=Romantic Fragment Poem, C.B.] — suspension of the author's shaping spirit- underline the processual, dynamic, experiential nature of the artwork, its stable appearance at any given moment an optical illusion" (214) .Cf. also Ernst Behler (1985); Matthew Bell (1994); Thomas McFarland (1981); Franziska Schmitt (2005).

[37]   Cf. Rodolphe Gasché (1977) and Rüdiger Campe (1991).

les modernes at last manage to catch up avec *les anciens*. "Many works of the ancients", Friedrich Schlegel writes in the 24th *Athenäum*-fragment, "have become fragments. Many works of the moderns are fragments already at the moment of their creation." (my translation) For Wordsworth, as we saw, the intrinsic pretensions of the Ossianic poems went beyond the scope of the "pocket-book" (Stafford 1991). As a child of a mountainous region himself, he doubts the naturalness of the depictions of nature in particular: "It will always be so when words are substituted for things" (Gill 1984, 655). Yet literature has no other means for expressing phenomena that seemingly cannot be expressed by words at all. This is as true of *Ossian* as of Wordsworth: paradoxically, his topos of unspeakability is inextricably linked to the legacy of Ossianism, even in his own work. The poems of *Ossian* became a symbol for all the things one would have liked to say but were unable to. All one could strive to achieve was the creation of a mood with the help of their magical powers.

At the beginning of Goethe's *The Sorrows of young Werther*, the singular most important introduction of *Ossian* into modern literature, there is an episode that anticipates the hero's obsession with the celtic bard. In the middle of a summer thunderstorm, Werther and Lotte are standing in front of the open window admiring the natural spectacle: "[...] she looked to the heavens, and at me, and I saw there were tears in her eyes; and she laid her hand on mine and said, 'Klopstock!'" (Goethe 2006, 27; Goethe 1981, 30). Werther immediately recognizes the ode she refers to; there is nothing else to say — united they stand flooded in tears. The "cold, dead words on the page" (Goethe 2006, 58; Goethe 1981, 70) cannot convey sublime feelings; they can only, as in the case of Klopstock, conjure them up. Literature is captured in the memory of the initiated: Klopstock's ode first really comes into being at the specular moment of two people watching nature (in the Wordsworthian sense mentioned above), unfold (Wellbery 1996). The parallels of this foremost and arguably first lyrical disciple of *Ossian* in German literature to the treatment of *Ossian* are obvious. Literature can only ever evoke the whole; all poetry in this sense is fragmentary per definition. Klopstock started the tradition of distributing "fragments" of his work amongst friends — the so-called *Manuskripte für Freunde* (manuscripts for friends), a phenomenon of the second half of the 18th century. In the same way that fragments of ancient poems including Ossian were symptoms of a given culture illustrating a specific stage in its development, fragments of an individual œuvre began to illustrate the historical development of the singular mind.

As has been hinted at above, Goethe in his first novel steers clear of the epic form, which does not match the fragmented and fragmentary life of Werther that he is interested in representing. *The Sorrows of young Werther* stands at the threshold of the development sketched in the preceding paragraph, demonstrating the increasing impossibility of pressing a work and a subjectivity between two covers. It starts with the admission that the pages in the hand of the reader are but a shadow of the real story. The fictional editor has "diligently collected everything" (Goethe 2006, 1; Goethe 1981, 7) that he was able to discover — but this is evidently not everything; the story remains a fragment, a loose collection of letters and reports. Towards the end of *Werther*, shortly before the great passage with the translations of *Ossian*, the fictional editor comments once again: "I wish very much that we had enough of our friend's testimony, concerning the last remarkable days of his life, to render it unnecessary for me to interrupt this series of preserved letters with narration" (Goethe 2006, 125; Goethe 1981, 92). He vows not to have left a stone unturned, to have collected every little detail and to have attended to even "the slightest scrap of paper" (Goethe 2006, 125; Goethe 1981, 92) from Werther's pen.

The collections forming Werther's life — a collection of handwritten diary scraps and oral history of those who had known Werther — make an unlikely book in the light of the contempt with which the printed word is met in the novel. Werther's famous first sentence: "How happy I am to be away!" includes a self-distancing from books: "You ask if you should send me my books? — My dear fellow, I implore you, for God's sake keep the things from me!" (Goethe 2006, 5; Goethe 1981, 7). Lotte, too, does not care too much for books anymore. She has left behind the love for novels she indulged in her early youth (Goethe 1981, 6:22 and ff.) When she refuses Werther's love in all too eloquent a fashion, demanding his friendship instead, he snorts that she should have her words printed and recommended to all teachers of rhetoric (*Hofmeistern*; Goethe 1981, 6:103). The climax of the novel, Werther's and Lotte's reading of his translations of Ossian, their last meeting, is a reading from manuscript, ending in emotional overkill. Lotte, who does not keep books any longer, has kept Werther's manuscript of Ossian, but had waited for Werther to recite — to perform — it for her. No mere book could have had that effect.

I would therefore even suggest a rather simple solution to a problem that has puzzled generations of readers. Countless interpretations have been put forward to explain the open copy of Lessing's *Emilia Galotti* on Werther's desk after his suicide, described in the closing scene "He had drunk only a single glass of the wine. *Emilia Galotti* lay open on his desk" (Goethe 2006, 174; Goethe 1981, 124). The point here is that the half-read copy of *Emilia Galotti*, a solid book by one of the most canonical contemporary authors, and not a bundle of Ossianic fragments or translations, serves as the equivalent to the sip of wine. The scene is formed as a kind of semantic parallelism: neither alcoholic or literary intoxication led to Werther's deed (in any case: in the linearity of the text, Werther had not even reached the point of Emilia's suicide at the end of the book). It would be futile to look for further explanations in Lessing's *text* after the protagonist has performed the ultimate performance to end all other performances.

After the end of the *Ossian* craze it seems to have been the mission of the novel to take over some of its qualities. Goethe's *Werther* showed how to make books out of an anti-book, how to incorporate the performative and the fragmentary into a written, aesthetic whole within that new and most flexible of genres. In the 19th century, novels of the appropriate format became an important (and always mobile) source of performative identification with literary models — admittedly not always leading as far as to copycat suicides as in the case of *Werther*. On a more modest level, Blicher's Danish novel-like *Ossian*, mentioned above, could be interpreted as the logical transformation of the old content into an adequate modern book format building on new notions of what literature was and should accomplish.[38]

Finally, it has also been the novel that has produced the largest numbers of writers' manuscripts. Goethe himself was one of the first authors to systematically collect his own papers. The book history of Goethe is a history not just of books but of something infinitely more complex; the reason, incidentally, why there still does not exist a proper historical-critical edition of all of his writings. Yet the new difficulties that come with the ever-increasing collections of individual writers' textgenetic records demand new methods not just of editing but also of reading. Modern hermeneutics is born simultaneously with modern manuscript culture. The reflection of

---

[38] This topic merits at least a paper in its own right, starting from the observation that the theory of modern universal poetry in the early romantic movement (Friedrich Schlegel and others) is inextricably linked to a theory of the novel.

this fact presents perhaps the next challenge for *Ossian* studies, but arguably even more so for book history itself, be it as an independent research paradigm or as a subdiscipline of literary criticism.

Bibliography

Alstrup, Andreas Christian. 1790. *Ossians Digte. Oversatte af det Engelske*. Copenhagen: Sebastian Popp.

Barnaby, Paul. 2004. "Timeline: European Reception of Ossian." In *The Reception of Ossian in Europe*, edited by H. Gaskill. London: Thoemmes.

Behler, Ernst. 1985. "Das Fragment." In *Prosakunst ohne Erzählen. Die Gattungen der nicht-fiktionalen Kunstprosa*, edited by K. Weissenberger. Tübingen: Niemeyer.

Bell, Matthew. 1994. "The Idea of Fragmentariness in German Literature and Philosophy, 1760-1800." *The Modern Language Review* 89 (2):372-392.

Blicher, S. S. 1807. *Ossians Digte. Oversatte af S. S. Blicher*. Copenhagen: Reitz.

Böker, Uwe. 1991. "The Marketing of Macpherson: The international Book Trade and the first Phase of German Ossian Reception." In *Ossian Revisited*, edited by H. Gaskill. Edinburgh: Edinburgh University Press.

Campe, Rüdiger. 1991. "Die Schreibszene. Schreiben." In *Paradoxien, Dissonanzen, Zusammenbrüche. Situationen offener Epistemologie*, edited by H. U. Gumbrecht and K. L. Pfeiffer. Frankfurt a.M: Suhrkamp.

Celenza, Anna H. Harwell. 1998. "Efterklange af Ossian. The Reception of James Macpherson's Poems of Ossian in Denmark's Literature, Art, and Music." *Scandinavian Studies* 70 (3).

Denis, M. 1768. *Die Gedichte Ossians. Eines alten celtischen Dichters aus dem Englischen übersetzt*. Wien: Johann Thomas Edlen v. Trattnern

Dochartaigh, Caitríona Ó. 2004. "Goethe's Translation from the Gaelic Ossian." In *The Reception of Ossian in Europe*, edited by H. Gaskill. London: Thoemmes.

Gasché, Rodolphe. 1977. "The Scene of Writing. A deferred outset." *Glyph* 150-171.

Gaskill, Howard. 2001. "'Aus der dritten Hand': Herder and his annotator." *German Life and Letters* 54 (3):210-218.

———, ed. 1991. *Ossian Revisited*. Edinburgh: Edinburgh University Press

———, ed. 2004. *The Reception of Ossian in Europe*. London: Thoemmes.

Gaskill, Hugh, ed. 1996. *The Poems of Ossian and Related Works*. Edinburgh: Edinburgh University Press.

Gill, Stephen, ed. 1984. *William Wordsworth*. Oxford: Oxford University Press.

Goethe, Johann Wolfgang. 1981. *Werke. Hamburger Ausgabe* (= HA). edited by E. Trunz. München: Beck.

Goethe, Johann Wolfgang von. 2006. *The sorrows of young Werther*. London: Penguin.

Groom, N. 1999. *The Making of Percy's Reliques*. Oxford: Clarendon.

Herder, Johann Gottfried. 1993. "Auszug aus einem Briefwechsel über Ossian und die Lieder alter Völker." In *Schriften zur Ästhetik und Literatur 1767-1781*, edited by G. E. Grimm. München: Deutscher Klassiker Verlag

———. 1998. "Homer und Ossian." In *Schriften zur Literatur und Philosophie 1792-1800*, edited by H. D. Irmscher. München: Deutscher Klassiker Verlag

Jiriczek, Otto L., ed. 1940. *James Macpherson's Ossian. Faksimile-Neudruck der Erstausgabe von 1762/63 mit Begleitband: Die Varianten*. 3 vols. Heidelberg: Winter.

Johnson, Samuel. 1971. *A Journey to the Western Islands of Scotland*. Edited by M. Lascelles. Yale: Yale University Press.

Kristmannsson, Gauti. 2005. *Literary Diplomacy*. Frankfurt a.M: Peter Lang.

Levinson, Marjorie. 1986. *The Romantic Fragment Poem. A critique of a form*. Chapel Hill and London: University of North Carolina Press.

Love, Harold. 1993. *Scribal Publication in Seventeenth-Century England*. Oxford: Clarendon.

Macpherson, James, ed. 1966. *Fragments of Ancient Poetry, Collected in the Highlands of Scotland, and Translated from the Galic or Erse Language*. Los Angeles: William Andrews Clark Memorial Library

McFarland, Thomas. 1981. *Romanticism and the Forms of Ruin. Wordsworth, Coleridge, and Modalities of Fragmentation*. Princeton: Princeton University Press

McKenzie, Donald F. 1999. *Bibliography and the Sociology of Texts*. Cambridge: Cambridge University Press

Moore, Dafydd, ed. 2004. *Ossian and Ossianism*. 4 vols. London/New York: Routledge.

Schmidt, Wolf Gerhard. 2003. *"Homer des Nordens" und "Mutter der Romantik". James Mcphersons Ossian und seine Rezeption in der deutschsprachigen Literatur*. 4 vols. Berlin/New York: Walter de Gruyter.

Schmitt, Franziska. 2005. *Method in the Fragments. Fragmentarische Strategien in der englischen und deutschen Romantik*. Trier: Wissenschaftlicher Verlag.

Scott, Walter. 1816. *The Antiquary*. Edinburgh: Constable and Co.

Singer, Rüdiger. 2004. "Ossian: Der 'Homer des Nordens' und seine Textlandschaft." In *Imagologie des Nordens. Kulturelle Konstruktionen von Nördlichkeit in interdisziplinärer Perspektive*, edited by A. Arndt, A. Blödorn, D. Fraesdorff and A. Weisner. Frankfurt a.M: Thomas Winkelmann.

———. 2006. *"Nachgesang". Ein Konzept Herders, entwickelt an Ossian, der popular ballad und der frühen Kunstballade*. Würzburg: Könighausen & Neumann.

Smith, Christopher. 2004. "Ossian in Music." In *The Reception of Ossian in Europe*, edited by H. Gaskill. London: Thoemmes.

Smith, Margaret M. 1990. "Prepublication Circulation of Literary Texts: The Case of James Macpherson's Ossianic verses." *Yale University Library Gazette* 64 (3-4):132-157.

Stafford, Fiona J. 1988. *The Sublime Savage. A Study of James Macpherson and The Poems of Ossian*. Edinburgh: Edinburgh University Press.

———. 1991. "'Dangerous Success': Ossian, Wordsworth, and English Romantic Literature." In *Ossian Revisited*, edited by H. Gaskill. Edinburgh: Edinburgh University Press.

Thomson, Derick S. 1952. *The Gaelic Sources of Macpherson's 'Ossian'*. Edinburgh: Oliver and Boyd.

Tieghem, P. van. 1981. *Ossian en France*. Vol. 2. Paris: Rieder & Cie.

Wellbery, David E. 1996. *The specular moment. Goethe's early lyric and the beginnings of romanticism*. Stanford: Stanford University Press.

Woudhuysen, H. R. 1996. *Sir Philip Sidney and the Circulation of Manuscripts 1558-1640*. Oxford: Clarendon.

Zumthor, Paul. 1984. *La poésie et la voix dans la civilisations médiévale*. Paris: Presses Universitaires.

Reviews

Peter Beal, comp. A *Dictionary of English Manuscript Terminology 1450-2000*. Oxford: Oxford University Press, 2008. xviii + 457 pp., 96 ill. ISBN 978-0-19-926544-2.

A dictionary of English post-medieval manuscript terminology has been long overdue. John Carter's much-revised *ABC for Book Collectors*, the equivalent reference work for printed books, was first published as long ago as 1952. Before the recent expansion of interest in early modern manuscripts — a scholarly movement which Peter Beal's magisterial *Index of English Literary Manuscripts* (1980-93) did much to instigate, as well as to inform — there may perhaps have been an assumption that manuscript production and circulation in the print era was not a sufficiently important phenomenon to merit such attention. We know better now. Since the early 1990s, scholars such as Harold Love, H. R. Woudhuysen, Margaret Ezell and Beal himself have done much to trace the many complex roles which manuscript continued to play in post-Caxton literary culture. Yet to many students — especially those without ready access to literary archives and established communities of manuscript scholars — the study of manuscripts has remained a somewhat recondite and forbidding area, its language often inaccessible to the uninitiated. Experienced scholars, too, have felt the lack of an authoritative, comprehensive guide to the diverse and often arcane world of manuscript terminology. The scholarly lacuna in this area has been much remarked, and has no doubt discouraged many from entering the field.

No one is better qualified to fill this lacuna than Peter Beal, who, through his work on the *Index* — soon to be updated and translated into electronic form — has an unrivalled understanding of the world of post-medieval English manuscripts. (For the electronic *Catalogue of English Literary Manuscripts*, developed at the Institute of English Studies in London, see www.ies.sas.ac.uk/cmps/Projects/CELM/index.htm.) This understanding is evident throughout his new *Dictionary*, which provides just the sort of user-friendly, wide-ranging and knowledgeable guidance from which readers of all levels of experience and seniority should benefit. The many merits of the *Dictionary* begin with its structure, which is straightforward, accessible and unfussy. Following the compiler's preface, which outlines the book's methodology and terms of reference, the book follows the conventional dictionary format, with over 1500 alphabetised entries, from "abbreviation" to "year books", and extensive use of cross-referencing. The entries, which are typically short and concise, encompass both such expected topics as bookbinding and watermarks and more abstruse items such as "amatl" ("a type of writing material [...] made of crushed bark and leaves treated with lime paste" [14]) and "scrimshaw" ("a type of nautical artefact" comprising "carvings on whalebone, whale teeth or seal tusks" [364]). These prose definitions are complemented by some 95 high-quality photographs, each supplied with its own explanatory caption, and illustrating such manuscript phenomena as contractions and abbreviations, marginalia and historic scripts such as secretary hand. The six-page "Select Bibliography" — identifying key studies in areas as diverse as alchemy and graffiti, heraldry and writing manuals — will itself be a useful research tool for many readers.

No dictionary can hope to please everyone, and the *Dictionary of English Manuscript Terminology* will undoubtedly have its critics. Many readers will regret the exclusion of pre-1450 manuscripts, while scholars working in later periods may feel that Beal — an early modernist — has focused too much on pre-1700 material. Yet every dictionary has to define its limits somewhere, and the boundaries set by Beal — excluding not only medieval manuscripts but also the textual world of computers and the internet — are clear, methodologically justifiable and allow him, as compiler, to play to his strengths. Entries such as those on commonplace books, verse compilations and the role of scribes benefit greatly from Beal's own work on scribal culture and miscellany production, dating back over thirty years. On other exclusions and inclusions, opinions will differ. My own view is that the comparative lack of attention to palaeography is regrettable, while it seems odd that the *Dictionary* includes entries on "questionnaire" and "red tape" but none on "scribal publication" or "circulation". However, the entry on "author", which might seem to some to stray outside Beal's territory, to my mind provides an exemplary illustration of how textual scholarship at its most material can recast and inform one of the most rarefied topics in recent literary theory.

Both learned and accessible, *A Dictionary of English Manuscript Terminology* will be an indispensable resource to future manuscript scholars. With its clear format, copious illustrations, and exquisitely produced endpapers, it also exemplifies the highest standards of contemporary book production. Both intellectually and aesthetically, it will be a pleasure to use.

Gillian Wright

Paul Eggert, *Securing the Past: Conservation in Art, Architecture and Literature*. Cambridge: Cambridge University Press, 2009. xi + 302 pp. ISBN 978-0-521-89808-9

Paul Eggert's *Securing the Past: Conservation in Art, Architecture and Literature* points up ways in which we attempt to restore the past in tangible forms. To our society, "private pasts are one thing, but the past that is held in common must […] be looked after, be secured" (2). The study discusses concepts and practices of three different kinds of preservation: the restoration of buildings, the conservation of works of art, the editing of literary texts. The main merit of the book lies in its combination of these three disciplines. Eggert shows links in our approaches to these activities and emphasizes how we expect professionals to do the restoration of each of them for us. However, he usefully reminds us, in each discipline the practioner does not just represent but necessarily interprets the building, painting, or text in question. Additionally, and this is one of his main points, Eggert discusses the underlying philosophies of preserving the past in each of these areas, and how attempts to secure the past of paintings, buildings and literary texts can be theoretically unified.

He proceeds by giving examples of crises in each discipline, since he claims that it is here that the similarities between the underlying justifications for each form of preservation of the past become most visible. One such moment of crisis that restorers of buildings, art, and literary texts have repeatedly been confronted with is forgery — for example, Han van Meegeren's 1940s paintings that he sold as being by Vermeer, or Major George Gordon Byron's forgeries of letters by Keats, Shelley and Byron. The examples from each discipline then point to similar underlying approaches: the existence of the notion of forgery presupposes the existence of the notion of authenticity, which, according to Eggert, is asserted through authorship. Regarding authorship as central, however, has implications on the shift of interest that took place from the 1980s onwards from "origination to consumption" (76), from author to reader: Roland Barthes' notion of the death of the author, Michel Foucault's shift from historical explanation centred on individuals to one centred on the discourses of the period, and the reader-reception theories of Wolfgang Iser, Hans Robert Jauss and Stanley Fish, who see the reader as a co-creator of the text. The meaning of a text, therefore, constantly changes because it depends on the horizons of expectations of the receiving community. Eggert argues that even if the interpretation of the text changes, our confidence in the historical document has to remain, so that it is in fact our knowledge about the time it was produced which makes it authentic. Since the moment of the text's conception, therefore, is of greater importance than that of its reception, the crime of forgery consists in misleading us as to the period something was produced. While realizing the problematic notion of authorship — for example in his discussions of Rembrandt paintings, where Eggert points out that it often remains unclear where exactly authorship ends — he still criticizes "proponents of consumption models" for their tendency "to turn a blind eye to the empirical aspects of textual production, in particular to the documentary site of the reader's performance of textual meaning" (77). This criticism comes as somewhat of a surprise, since he himself is primarily concerned with theory, and does not look at actual readers but stays on the level of the implied reader.

To resolve this tension of, on the one hand, meaning being created by the reader, and on the other hand, authenticity residing in authorship, Eggert proposes that we need to distinguish between text and document levels: the text's physical dimension is the document, and this is where forgery takes place. On the level of the text, forgery is not possible because "readers' participation in textual meaning is an essential constitutive factor of text and if each instance of text is therefore a new one, it is not possible to forge it" (77). A forgery of text, therefore, would simply be another instance of the text. He then expands his concept of distinguishing between text and document, but always considering both these levels, and applies it to buildings, paintings, and literary texts. (Here, as well as elsewhere, we might wonder why for example music is excluded from his discussion.) Eggert's discussion of forgery is also a good example of how he stays on a theoretical level for most of the book, as he himself repeatedly tells us: "in practice — when, say, we are reading a poem or a novel — the textual and documentary dimensions are never fully distinct. The meaning we take from a reading derives in some part (sometimes large, usually small, never negligible) from the physical qualities of the document" (82). (Similarly, he later discusses editorial theories rather than practical solutions.) Several times in his book, Eggert promises solutions to then not really be able to offer any.

His argument, that we need to look at both the production and the consumption levels for texts, paintings, and buildings, is reiterated at the end of most of his major sections: authorship, "no longer puffed up with Romantic illusions, remains of crucial relevance because of its explanatory potential, as a form of agency" (153). Of course the idea that bibliographic codes affect the reading experience and that therefore a text's exterior needs to be considered, is not new, as occasionally becomes clear when Eggert refers to D.F. McKenzie and Jerome McGann, again to emphasize that bibliographic and linguistic codes are not always clearly separable.

Overall then, this is a very enjoyable book, which represents a fascinating read for anyone interested in the preservation of the past in art, architecture, and literature through conservation, restoration, and editing. Not everything Eggert discusses is new, nor can he suggest any real solutions to the problems he discusses, but he usefully offers various theories for us to consider. Not the least of its achievements is that the book again makes us aware that there is no representation without interpretation. The chief merit, however, lies in the study's pointing up the connections between the philosophies underlying the conservation of paintings, buildings and literary texts.

Annika Bautz

Olga Anokhina and Sabine Pétillon, eds. *Critique génétique: Concepts, methods, outils.* N.p.: IMEC Éditeur, 2009. 191pp. ISBN 2-9082-95-97-0.

In September 2004, I took part in a week-long summer school on genetic criticism organized by ITEM and IMEC in the Abbaye d'Ardenne, whose chapel now houses the collections of IMEC and which has been converted into a residence where researchers can stay and work. Rather than a training course, it consisted of lectures and workshops on the numerous aspects of genetic studies, which are now published in *Critique génétique: Concepts, méthodes, outils*. Although some of the articles retain a pedagogical focus, it does not purport to be a textbook, or an introduction to genetic criticism such as Almuth Grésillon's *Éléments de Critique Génétique*, but rather provides a panorama of the current prevalent approaches while describing the tools and concepts developed over the past 30 years. It thus illustrates the specificity of a discipline which, as Louis Hay underlines in his contribution, has not evolved from theory, but from empirical experience, open to interdisciplinary cross-fertilisation and very much alive. One might regret that the bibliography has not been better organized, as only two specific topics, codicology and the psycho-cognitive approaches to genetic criticism, are given their own sections. For other topics, the reader is instead referred to the online catalogue on the ITEM website at www.item.ens.fr.

Two complementary points of view open the book: that of Louis Hay, founding father of genetic studies, and Bernard Beugnot, a specialist of seventeenth century literature who plays the outsider. Louis Hay traces the history of the discipline, from the invention of new tools such as the application of codicology to modern manuscripts to the internationalization and popularization of genetic studies, while insisting on the need for specialization combined with a comparative mindset and pointing out that the advent of personal computers, indispensable tools for genetic critics, might mean the end of manuscripts for them to study. Bernard Beugnot then delineates some of the frontiers of genetic criticism: he questions the historical limits of the discipline, showing the wealth of discourses on the genesis of texts that preceded its invention as well as calling for the study of periods deemed "without drafts", suggesting that the time has come to write a history of genetic studies. He then reflects on the generic limits of the discipline and advocates a reflection on the terminology of genetic criticism, a suggestion since taken up by ITEM, which now runs a general seminar in preparation for a *Dictionnaire de critique génétique*.

The second part of the collection is devoted to the material aspects of the study of manuscripts. Claire Bustarret's informative article describes all the criteria for the codicological study of a manuscript and shows what information the genetic critic might gain from a description of the types of paper and writing instruments used by the writer — e.g., to establish chronology. Marie Odile Germain provides the point of view of the librarian and traces the history of the institutions' attitude regarding the acquisition of manuscripts, demonstrating how decisive the role of the archivists can be, as they often have to become genetic critics themselves to classify and number the documents, unwittingly affecting future genetic analysis even before scholars have access to the documents. She finally calls on Cixous and Derrida's writings to reflect on the real and symbolic import of the gift and acceptance of such documents. Jean-Louis Lebrave then presents the different computer programs developed by genetic critics since the 1970s, aiming both at automating the analysis of drafts as well as exploring ways of publishing genetic dossiers, before describing in detail MEDITE, a software program allowing the comparison of two versions of the same text.

Three case studies follow, each illustrating different types of approach: microgenetics, with Almuth Grésillon's close study of the drafts of a short poem by Ponge, "l'Ardoise"; macrogenetics, with Bernard Brun's analysis of the interaction between typescripts and proofs in Proust, showing how structural reorganization takes place in page proofs at stages first, wrongly, considered final; and exogenetics, with Catherine Viollet's study of the use of documentation by Thomas Mann for his short story "Die Betrogene" as well as the role played by his wife and daughter. Each case study is treated as an opportunity to give advice to future genetic critics.

The fourth part gathers together four theoretical essays. Daniel Ferrer explores the notion of "accident" in the genesis of a work, using the concept of "emergence" and "path dependency" to try and provide a model for the process of literary creation. Anne Herschberg Pierrot calls for a new definition of style as a series of processes and as a dynamic within the text rather than as a stable and homogeneous category, not only in genetic documents but in all texts, before reflecting on the characteristics of genetic styles, in particular on heterogeneity and incompleteness. Irène Fenoglio reads drafts from an enunciative perspective and suggests a typology of graphic accidents (corrections, erasures, second thoughts and Freudian slips) as enunciative events, single or repeated, reflecting, as A. Herschberg Pierrot does, on the necessity of combining singular and general approaches. Denis Alamargot's more pedagogical article presents the different psycho-cognitive models of writing processes which have been created since the 1950s. So far these models are limited in scope, covering for instance learners (such as children or teenagers) or limited tasks (such as reports or letters). However, Alamargot shows how the study of the writing processes of professional writers (or "super experts"), as they appear in the manuscripts, could provide insights about the psycho-cognitive processes of writing in general.

By way of conclusion, Pierre-Marc de Biasi's final essay in the volume outlines what work has already been done on the genesis of theatrical productions, films, music, art, architecture or science, what the main characteristics of each of those creative processes are and what particular problems they raise, to underline the importance of interdisciplinary exchanges, in particular the borrowing of terms and concepts from other fields.

This book provides a good introduction to genetic criticism, as it covers most current areas of research in the discipline and a valuable discussion of the fascinating processes at work in literary creation.

Christine Collière-Whiteside

Siân Echard, *Printing the Middle Ages*. Philadelphia: University of Pennsylvania Press, 2008. xvi + 314 pp. and 83 ill. ISBN 978-0-8122-4091-7.

The method of *Printing the Middle Ages* is that of reception studies approached through the medium of book history. Its argument is clear and repeatedly articulated: that the chief imperative for later reprinters or redesigners of medieval works — an imperative born of a constant need to "touch the past", to "communicate with a world long gone" (201) — has been to convey a sense of antiquity and, above all, to demonstrate authenticity. This notion is not in itself challenging or surprising, and with a book consisting of what are essentially case studies, as this is, there is a certain sense of arbitrariness in the examples chosen to make the point. But Echard's powers of detailed description are so great, her cases so varied, and her learning so extensive and well deployed, that the comparative lack of intellectual challenge matters less. She presents the reader with a series of analytical narratives that have great interest in their own right, and shows herself to be a skilled storyteller, interweaving the biographical and the material with ease. One of her recurrent themes is the importance of the visual in conveying "the mark of the medieval" (4), either through facsimile reproduction or by the refashioning of medieval visual forms, and numerous highly relevant monochrome illustrations support this contention.

After an introduction centring on post-medieval printings of *Piers Plowman* ("Plowmen and Pastiche"), the book's five main chapters are arranged broadly chronologically. The first of them is devoted to the representation of Old English mainly in the sixteenth century, the printers using Anglo-Saxon letter-forms to indicate antiquity. The exposition moves from typography to the use of engraving, noting the importance of the author portrait (or, it may be, the scholar portrait) in enhancing authenticity. The second chapter then examines the career, principally in the sixteenth and seventeenth centuries, of the English heroes Guy of Warwick and Bevis of Hampton. Among much else Echard demonstrates that the story of Bevis retained its medieval form for far longer than did that of Guy, partly because of the lasting influence of the illustrations used in Richard Pynson's edition of 1503. Chapter 3, based in the eighteenth and early nineteenth centuries, is an illuminating account of the attention paid to a manuscript of the works of John Gower — first through a magnificent scribal transcription, then through a Roxburghe Club edition — by two generations of later aristocratic Gowers who believed themselves to be descended from the poet's family. Here as elsewhere the discussion ranges into areas of reception studies other than book history, in this case the topic of Gower's tomb, but with no detriment to Echard's narrative. The following chapter ("Bedtime Chaucer") takes up the subject of nineteenth-century adaptations of Chaucer for children and/or other non-specialist readerships, with much attention to illustrations and to the way in which Chaucer himself is presented; one result is that he is "gradually separated from the rest of the medieval canon" (xiv). With more biographical information having survived, we also learn more now about the compilers of the works in question, particularly the artist and proto-feminist Mary Eliza Haweis (1848-98). Chapter 5 discusses the appropriation of Froissart's *Chronicles*, in the nineteenth and early twentieth centuries, as an essentially English work of national history. Here a sub-theme is the eventual return to popularity of Lord Berners's early sixteenth-century translation — as contributing to a sense of authenticity — in place of the modern English translation by Thomas Johnes which was first published in 1803-1805.

There is finally a coda that discusses that nature of modern digital representations of medieval works, concluding, very reasonably, that despite attempts by enterprises such as the Canterbury Tales Project to give prominence to text, it is still the urge to get close to the authentic material object — to find the aura of the medieval through the visual — that drives most digitisation projects. Echard reflects, too, on the consequential phenomenon that "the objects to which we are increasingly offered digital access are themselves all but untouchable" (214), involving a kind of disappearance. Referring specifically to the British Library's "Turning the Pages" technology, she writes evocatively that "the effect is sometimes strangely like a photograph of the dear departed, a reminder of what is lost as much as a comfort of some kind of continuing presence" (215).

The book under review does not, of course, teach us anything new about the production or reception of literary works during the Middle Ages themselves, and a traditionalist might regret that an established medieval scholar like Siân Echard should have been distracted (as it would be) into the now fashionable area of post-medieval studies. But one cannot argue with this author's mastery of the field, the interest it obviously holds for her, and the extent to which she clearly feels at home in it. Whereas once medieval scholars looked backwards, at sources or etymologies, now they look forwards, to what future generations thought. Herein, perhaps, lies the danger of the arbitrary — or the difficulty of choosing — when there is so much to go at. Different skills are also needed, and a lack of linguistic awareness may lie behind the double transliteration, on page 35, of the

Celtic place-name Penwith as printed in William Camden's *Britannia* — with an Anglo-Saxon *wynn* for "w" — as "Penrith". On the other hand, many of Echard's careful descriptions of post-medieval printed books or manuscripts would not be out of place in the introduction to a traditional scholarly edition, laying out later witnesses to the text in question. The difference now, following the rise in book history, is that such accounts have become studies in their own right (and there are fewer editions).

There are very occasional proofreading errors (e.g., "illustrations" for "illustrates" [179] and "whose" for "who" [200]), but overall *Printing the Middle Ages* is a very well produced and highly attractive volume, the main text underpinned with a hundred pages of endnotes, bibliography, and index.

Oliver Pickering

The 1671 Poems: "Paradise Regain'd" and "Samson Agonistes." Ed. Laura Lunger Knoppers. Vol. 2 of *The Complete Works of John Milton*. Oxford: Oxford University Press, 2008. ISBN 978-019-929617-0

Old-spelling editions of John Milton's works are making a comeback. Within the past three years, John Shawcross and Michael Lieb have published a diplomatic transcription of *Paradise Lost*'s ten-book first edition, Barbara Lewalski has edited a classroom-friendly, paperback text of Milton's twelve-book epic, and Stella Revard has published an original-language companion volume of Milton's complete shorter poems (Milton 2007a; Milton 2007b; Milton 2009).[1]

To this list of excellent old-spelling texts we can now add Laura Lunger Knoppers' superb new edition of Milton's *Paradise Regain'd* and *Samson Agonistes*, the first volume to appear in *The Complete Works of John Milton* from Oxford University Press. Knoppers' book is actually designated the second volume in Oxford's projected eleven-volume series, but the press was right to publish this book first because it so dramatically improves upon previous modern editions. *Paradise Regain'd* and *Samson* were originally published together in 1671, and Knoppers' edition is remarkable both for its fidelity to that first publication and for its detailed reconstruction of the 1671 volume's historical and bibliographical context. Rather than following the common practice of grouping these two poems with either *Paradise Lost*

---

[1] Forthcoming from Blackwell is also a third volume, this one containing selections of Milton's prose and edited by David Loewenstein.

or Milton's shorter poetry, Knoppers allows readers to experience *Paradise Regain'd* and *Samson Agonistes* as companion pieces.

The edition also preserves the most distinctive feature of the 1671 volume, the often overlooked *Omissa*. In 1671, ten lines wentmissing from the scene in which Manoa and the Chorus listen to Samson's off-stage destruction of the Philistines' theatre. The missing text, labeled *Omissa*, was printed at the back of the book with instructions for its proper insertion. While the omission of these lines might seem to be a compositor's error, a bibliographical examination reveals that the *Omissa* in fact contains an important authorial addendum. Milton, as I have argued elsewhere, uses the missing text to emphasize his poems' interdependence and to dramatize the need for readers to follow Jesus' and Samson's examples of active obedience (Dobranski 2005, 183-209). But whereas most modern editions of *Samson* silently fold in the missing lines, Knoppers includes the *Omissa* where it properly belongs, following the text of the two poems.

Knoppers also scrupulously reproduces other material aspects of the 1671 volume that might affect the works' poetic meaning. In addition to preserving the poems' original spelling, punctuation, capitalization and italics, she includes facsimile illustrations of the first edition's two title pages and images of various doctored and annotated copies. In editing the text, Knoppers collated 17 copies of the first edition and, by my count, examined an additional 52 copies; she also collated five copies of the second edition from 1680 and consulted 13 additional copies. While none of this research has yielded startling new variants, it allows Knoppers to correct minor errors in some previous modern texts and to equip readers with a thorough understanding of the poems' early publication history. Textual notes appear along the bottom of each page, while a concise critical commentary for both poems is printed at the back of the volume. The commentary mostly contains explanations of Milton's geographic or biblical references and brief definitions from the *Oxford English Dictionary* for Milton's sometimes obscure diction.

The volume begins with two introductions, one general and one textual. The underlying premise of these essays seems to be that Milton's two poems are "obliquely and allusively" political (lii). As Knoppers announces at the start, she believes that *Paradise Regain'd* and *Samson* "represent and reflect upon not only individual protagonist but nation" (lii). She thus focuses her introductions on the political circumstances of post-Restoration England and the publisher John Starkey's association with republican and non-conformist writers and thinkers. In this latter regard, Knoppers covers important new critical ground. If her claims for a seventeenth-century "radical print network" need a little more supporting evidence (xlvi), she nevertheless provides a compelling profile of Starkey as well as the first edition's likely printer, John Macock. In particular, Knoppers makes good use of Starkey's scribal newsletters to flesh out both the volume's print context and the publisher's political philosophy.

Admittedly, this religio-political emphasis crowds out other possible approaches to Milton's two poems. The book's two introductions have almost nothing to say about the poems' prosody, sources, or characters, nor does Knoppers attempt to address the wide range of interpretive traditions that continue to influence current critical discourse. It is not clear whether the edition's historicist emphasis, while certainly in keeping with Knoppers' own scholarly interests, will serve as a guiding principle for the ten other volumes of Milton's works forthcoming from Oxford or whether the subsequent editions will reflect a wide range of editorial approaches.

In the specific case of Knoppers' volume, her concern with the tumultuous political history of Restoration England remains broad enough for her to discuss the implications of genre for each poem, and she provides an especially useful overview of the controversy surrounding the dates of the two works' composition. She also includes a fascinating analysis of readers' holograph marginalia in the copies that she examined. While her use of the term "early readers" may be a little too general in this section (lxvi), Knoppers persuasively shows how readers who left marks in their copies of the 1671 book were engaging with the poems' versification, intertextuality and classical allusions (lvii-lxxiv). By comparison, I was not entirely convinced of the political significance that Knoppers detects in one reader's scribal index, but because she includes detailed information about this annotator's provocative notations, readers of the edition can draw their own conclusions about early modern reading practices and the poems' reception.

Ideally, Knoppers would have also provided a similarly full account of the orthographic inconsistencies in the 1671 volume. She proposes a correlation between differences in spelling in the first edition and differences in the book's formes — and she might be right. But while the individual examples that she discusses are instructive, her argument for a "high consistency" (lxxxii) would be more convincing if she were to have included a table listing all the differences in spelling and their corresponding formes.

These minor objections aside, readers of Milton have much to be grateful for in Knoppers' edition — and, it seems, much to anticipate in the forthcoming volumes of the *Complete Works*. In contrast to some new editions of early modern literary works that seem designed only to showcase the editors' interpretive annotations, Knoppers has created the most authoritative version of *Paradise Regain'd* and *Samson Agonistes* that is currently available. As the inaugural volume in *The Complete Works of Milton*, she has set the bar high.

Stephen B. Dobranski

Work cited

Dobranski, Stephen B. 2005. *Readers and Authorship in Early Modern England*. Cambridge: Cambridge University Press.

Milton, John. 2007a. *"Paradise Lost: A Poem Written in Ten Books": An Authoritative Text of the 1667 First Edition*. Edited by John T. Shawcross and Michael Lieb. Pittsburgh: Duquesne University Press.

———. 2007b. *Paradise Lost*. Edited by Barbara K. Lewalski. Malden, Mass. and Oxford: Blackwell.

———. 2009. *John Milton: Complete Shorter Poetry*. Edited by Stella P. Revard. Malden, Mass. and Oxford: Blackwell.

Janet Todd and Linda Bree (eds). *The Cambridge Edition of the Works of Jane Austen: Later Manuscripts*. Cambridge: Cambridge University Press, 2008. 742 pp. ISBN 978-0-52184-348-5.

Later Manuscripts is the last volume in *The Cambridge Edition of the Works of Jane Austen*, all produced under the general editorship of Janet Todd. The series as a whole was planned as "the definitive edition for the twenty-first century", to replace R.W. Chapman's magisterial edition of the twentieth. *Later Manuscripts* contains "Lady Susan", Austen's early epistolary novella featuring a wicked and glamorous anti-heroine, and the two major fragments "The Watsons" and "Sanditon". In a section entitled Jane Austen on Fiction, the editors include extracts from Austen's letters to her niece Anna Lefroy containing advice on writing fiction; her brief satirical "Plan of a Novel"; and the opinions of *Emma* and *Mansfield Park* that she collected from friends and acquaintances. The last section contains a small number of poems and charades that can be firmly attributed to Jane Austen. The Appendices to the volume comprise transcriptions of the manuscripts of "The Watsons" and "Sanditon"; the short skit "Sir Charles Grandison", sometimes attributed to Austen, but here discussed as the work of a juvenile Anna Lefroy; three prayers and two poems previously attributed to Jane Austen but now considered to be by others; and four family poems, two by Cassandra Leigh Austen, one by Cassandra Austen and one by Mrs Edward Austen (*née* Elizabeth Bridges), all in response to work by Jane Austen. The volume does not contain perhaps the most famous of her later manuscripts, the two cancelled manuscript chapters of *Persuasion*.

The editorial material is wide-ranging. Issues of provenance, dating and attribution, as well as the publication history and critical reception of all the material contained in the volume are elegantly and thoroughly covered either in the Introduction, or in the notes to each work. Major critical debates are discussed, and a valuable chronology of Austen's life is included in this, as in all volumes in the series. Missing, though, is a bibliography of the works consulted in the preparation of the edition. Though a general "further reading" bibliography (arranged thematically) is available in the *Jane Austen in Context* volume in this series, it does not contain several of the works cited in the introduction to the *Later Manuscripts* volume, and is, in any case, designed for a general readership rather than those interested in textual scholarship. A dedicated bibliography in the *Later Manuscripts* volume would therefore have been useful to scholars, particularly those concerned with issues of textual transmission.

All the works presented in *Later Manuscripts* are copiously annotated. The majority of the notes are helpful — scholarly without being pedantic — and supply useful literary, social, cultural, familial or historical background to the works. Those notes providing extra information about now-forgotten literary works, for example, are particularly valuable, especially when such works exist now only in unique or rare copies and are thus not easily accessible to most readers. The lengthy notes on the provenance and descent of manuscript material are invaluable, and fully deserve their place in the volume. The contextual notes on Austen's family and acquaintance, properly acknowledged as owing much to Deirdre Le Faye's research, are excellent.

A significant minority of the notes, however, are either redundant or repetitive. The editors appear to have assumed a readership with a very limited knowledge of Austen's works and the period, and only the scantiest general knowledge. Do readers of a "scholarly edition" of Austen's works really need definitions of satin, chaperons, cockades and muffins? Must we learn no fewer than three times, and twice within the notes to the same work (n. 14 and n. 116, "The Watsons" and Chapter 1, n. 14, "Sanditon") that "country" means "neighbourhood" or "local area", when it is obvious from the context that it does not carry its more modern meaning of "nation state"? Are the extensive and numerous (52 out of 418) notes on the geography of England really necessary? In particular, must we have Chichester not once but twice annotated for us? In fact, a number of words (including "address", "interesting", "lounge", "Town", and "post-chaise") are glossed more than once in the notes without any indication at the second appearance that they have previously been encountered. This is in contrast to excellent editorial practice elsewhere in the volume, where there is extensive cross-referencing between notes, both of single words ("dinner" and "academy", for example) and, more importantly, ideas or tropes.

Without doubt, there are readers, some within the scholarly community, who will find Todd and Bree's extensive annotations useful. And certainly the editors' concern with precise geographical locations and distances is reminiscent of Austen's own attention to these details, as shown in her letters to Anna Lefroy (collected in this volume as "Letters on Fiction to Anna Lefroy") and other correspondents. Nonetheless, such notes (and the unnecessary repetitions) take up valuable space that might have been used in other ways. While Todd and Bree's notes do often, and helpfully, make comparisons between the manuscript material under consideration and Austen's published works and letters, they occasionally fail to note both verbal echoes of other Austen texts, and thematic concerns that run through other examples of her writing. It would have been interesting, too, to hear more about the various "ambiguities in the manuscripts" mentioned in the Preface, and to have an account of how textual cruces were resolved.

The edition points to the inevitable difficulties of collecting scattered, disparate and diverse manuscript material. The editors of *Later Manuscripts* choose to provide "reading versions" of the two fragments, "The Watsons" and "Sanditon" which, they write, "have been discreetly edited to reflect basic publishing conventions of the early nineteenth century," thus ironing out Austen's idiosyncratic spelling, capitalisation and punctuation. They also supply line-by-line transcriptions of these texts, which reflect revisions, deletions, superscriptions, mis-spellings, and other idiosyncrasies. Bree and Todd "strongly recommend" readers to compare the reading text with the line-by-line transcription. This is a pragmatic solution to presenting texts that do not exist in a fair copy, but it differs from the policy adopted for "Lady Susan" and all the other texts, where Austen's peculiarities of spelling, capitalization and punctuation are kept, and variants are simply noted at the foot of each page. These editorial choices, though explained and justified in the notes, inevitably give the impression of inconsistency in editorial practice. For ease of comparison, too, providing the reading texts and transcriptions next to each other (as facing pages, perhaps) would have been advantageous.

These small quibbles aside, the Cambridge edition is unquestionably a useful critical edition, particularly valuable to its undergraduate readership. It interestingly raises much wider questions about the ways in which editions construct particular versions of authorial reputation. In their introduction, Todd and Bree rightly emphasize the ways in which manuscript material, in all its sometimes messy glory, provides us with an insight into the creative process. They present Austen as a writer who worked, and re-worked, her literary creations, honing, polishing, and perfecting them. She emerges both from their introduction, and from the extracts of letters included, as a writer preoccupied with even the tiniest details, obsessively concerned with accuracy and verisimilitude. This helps to correct a pervasive (and still current) nineteenth-century myth about Austen, begun in her brother's "Biographical Notice of the Author" (1817), which represented her as a gifted amateur, an instinctive writer who wrote for her own amusement, with great ease and spontaneous correctness. This edition, with its inclusion of material that demonstrates how seriously Austen took her writing, shows us, in contrast, not only Austen's work, but Austen *at work*: a consummate literary professional engaged in difficult labour.

Katie Halsey

Dirk Van Hulle. *Manuscript Genetics: Joyce's Know-How, Beckett's Nohow.* Gainesville: University Press of Florida, 2008. 256 pp. ISBN 13: 978-0-8130-3200-9.

> Mit Eifer hab' ich mich der Studien beflissen,
> Zwar weiß ich viel, doch möcht' ich alles wissen.
> — Goethe, *Faust* I.1, 600-01

Once upon a time, as the story is told, a Canadian university decided to invest some excess tar-pits revenue, and expand its holdings of Canadiana. A first step was to contact various aspiring (or expiring) writers, asking to buy notebooks, drafts and manuscripts, and sometimes offering more than the writers had made by legitimate sales. One destitute poet, it seems, having burnt all his drafts to keep warm throughout the long cold winter, realized that here was a god-send, an opportunity to re-invent his past — which he did, spending some months making old versions anew, with false trails, variants of what might have been, and enough inventive flourishes to keep the professors busy for years. All might have been well, were the story not too good to be restrained, and so the truth emerged, to the delight of the one who told me this tale, the Special Collections Librarian of another Canadian university.

Urban myth or cautionary tale, this might seem to vindicate Nabokov's fulmination, in his commentary on Pushkin, against the scholarly enterprise: "An artist should ruthlessly destroy his manuscripts after publication lest they mislead academic mediocrities into thinking that it is possible to unravel the mysteries of genius by studying cancelled readings" (Nabokov 1990, 15). Occasionally, I imagine the great modernist sceptics casting a cold eye over the contemporary critical scene: Flaubert shaking his head with an almost inaudible "Ça fait rêver" (a sentiment reserved for the more extraordinary instances of bêtise); Nabokov turning on the faucets of his scorn, as against the poor critic who exhibited erotic bits from Lolita and Ada: "like looking for allusions to aquatic mammals in *Moby Dick*", and who, seeking symbols, had claimed that Lolita's tennis balls represent testicles: "those of a giant white albino, no doubt" (Nabokov 1973, 304 and 307). Proust, in my imaginings, would share a glass of the Archduchess with Joyce, toasting the fact that their indifference to public opinion has been so universally celebrated, by manuscript critics in particular. As for Beckett: though he could be both generous and naïve in disposing his manuscripts (consider his exploitation by Jake Schwartz, dentist turned book-seller, and belatedly belabled "the great extractor"), and had long rejected the loutishness of learning, Beckett was at heart a scholar. His preservation of drafts and manuscripts, and their posthumous donation to the Beckett International Foundation, Reading, and Trinity College, Dublin, was, as Dirk Van Hulle says, "a well-considered choice" (2), and one that affirms the role of the scholar, and particularly the genetic critic, in the creative process.

For Van Hulle, "process" is the right word. Genetic criticism is less a reconstitution of authorial (or textual) intent than of a writing process; it acknowledges "the diachronic axis" (43), and the simple truth that literary texts are not only synchronic structures but are equally structured in time. Ferdinand de Saussure tried to keep the synchronic and the diachronic rigorously apart; the challenge of genetic criticism to the inhabitants of critical Flatland is to see texts as integrated within this further dimension. Van Hulle, by virtue of *Textual Awareness: A Genetic Study of Late Manuscripts by Joyce, Proust, and Mann* (2004) and a pleroma of articles and chapters of meticulous lucidity, is one of the most insightful and respected scholars in this emerging (united) field. This is not to be sycophantic, but to position myself in relation to any comments made in the course of this review that might imply otherwise. *Manuscript Genetics* has close affinities with *Textual Awareness*, but, intriguingly, Van Hulle offers a different intonation, with emphasis on the process as an integral part of the product, thereby enclosing what he calls "the fairly unexplored field of comparative genetic criticism" (5). The outcome is some wonderfully detailed readings that are precisely observed and justly considered; but as part of a "process" that itself raises some questions about its controlling metaphors.

The strengths of the study are unequivocal. Well written, with only a few minor blips (Rosemary Pountney as "Mary" [120]; a missing parenthesis [141]; but not an Ithacan fool stop [194]), and a turn of phrase that combines economy and wit, it is a worthy addition to the Florida James Joyce Series. The Notes are illuminating; and the "Works Cited" (some 450, which are all cited) not only testify to the extensive reading (in many languages) that has gone into this study, but also to how Van Hulle graciously engages with the work of fellow scholars. Part I offers a lucid exposition of Genetic Criticism, its methodology, strategies and typologies, the theory infused by fine readings of small details, such as the nodal power of "obscene" in Ian McEwan's Atonement. Part II is entitled "Joyce's Know-How"; and in his Foreword Sebastian Knowles pays tribute to the chronological survey of Finnegans Wake at its heart, as "a crowning demonstration of the benefits of the genetic approach" (xi). Part III, "Beckett's No-How", lacks any such core to the ideal onion; rather, the dissection tends to be that of various slices, circles that lack any centre. This leads to exquisite accounts of intricate modalities, but at the cost, perhaps, of a unifying syntagm (or field structure) that might bind the two writers together.

To clarify this comment: as he formed his own poetics, Beckett's contact was with the more "universal" Joyce of the *Wake* rather than the scrupulous realist of *Dubliners* and *Ulysses*. Despite what Sebastian Knowles calls the "parallel thematics" in the two writers' works (xi), and Van Hulle's clear insistence on the process of their writing as the focus of his genetic criticism (2), the Beckett and Joyce elements do not click together as well as they might. Van Hulle's choice to work with the contemporaneous *Finnegans Wake* rather than, arguably, the aesthetically more comparable earlier works, suggests (to me at least) that the common ties noted at the end of his Introduction (their shared standing as paradigmatic authors for genetic criticism and the role of the writing process in their works) bind the two parts of this study together rather too loosely. Beckett's "work in regress" neatly opposes the teleology implicit in Joyce's more familiar "Work in Progress" (3), but the overarching argument struggles to reconcile what Van Hulle rightly recognizes as the "quite divergent poetics" (3) of the two authors: the (late) Joycean impulse to universalize; and the (consistent) Beckettian principle of particularity.

As Van Hulle notes, literary modernism is the golden age of the manuscript, and the manuscripts of certain authors (including Joyce and Beckett) constitute "a considerable research corpus" (1), to which genetic criticism has responded with impressive results. Van Hulle's earlier work (to some extent replicated here) on *Stirrings Still* testifies to how a published text with nothing to indicate any intertextual reference can "from deep within" (45) contain echoes that only a genetic approach can detect, but which are nevertheless part of the text and not simply of its history. Yet the methodology embraced is not without its dangers. As Alan Sokal and Jean Bricmont convincingly demonstrated in "Intellectual Impostures" (1997), the cultural appropriation of one discipline by another (there, mathematics and physics; here, evolutionary genetics) can lead to "conclusions" raised upon metaphorical premises: the "genesis" and "evolution" of texts; "missing links" in the manuscript record; defective "genes" (or "memes") leading to defective (but in evolutionary terms, significant) lines of genetic text. Van Hulle acknowledges that the relationship is "merely metaphorical" (9), but he implies that such metaphors are useful, and discusses *The Dublin Helix* (2001) of Sebastian Knowles as a case in point (16-17). This is a delightful work, witty and insightful, but at times in danger (Joyce's scarlet letter "A" as messenger RNA, a carrier of [mis]information) of entangling itself in its own helicentricities. Sometimes, the Freudian from deep within me sceptically affirms, a misprint ("whether shit was a good thing" in the Calder edition of *Watt*) (165) is just a misprint, rather than a new departure (Beckett 1976, 225).[2] To be sure, to attribute a meaningful intention to a textual variant runs the danger, as Nabokov might say (see *Pale Fire*), of making a fountain out of a molehill.

For example, Van Hulle discusses the importance to evolutionary genetics (biological and textual) of the family tree, or stemma (18), comparing the writing process (as opposed to the public published text) to the roots of such a tree. Yet, as Van Hulle notes, this "radical" metaphor is "not quite adequate to visualize the processing of pretextual material in the drafts" (19); the "top down" compositional history can equally be considered as a "bottom up" process, to indicate the nutrient materials (my metaphor) that did not make it (above the ground) to the visible text. Serendipitously, as I was reading this section of *Manuscript Genetics*, I came across an article entitled "Uprooting Darwin's Tree", in which features editor Graham Lawton reveals that the concept of the tree that Darwin had used as an organizing principle and which has been a central tenet of biology ever since is not

---

[2] Compare "whether this was a good thing", Beckett (1953, 226).

a fact of nature, but rather a paradigm imposed upon nature to make the task of understanding it more tractable (Lawton 2009, 34-39). Instead, the evolutionary complexity of biology is greater than can be imagined, with a quantum-like complexity arising from a process of "horizontal gene transfer" (36) that indicates at all levels of evolution a considerable degree of hybridisation. This argument was foremost in my mind as I read what Van Hulle had to say with respect to the complex manuscripts of so many of the works of Joyce and Beckett, which feature details added not in arboreal sequence but at often random or indeterminable points in the process, notes on facing versos (written at various times) that might or might not enter the next stage of the evolutionary sequence, pretextual materials (the "Addenda" of *Watt*, for instance) that once were but no longer are…

This is not to belittle the meticulous and detailed work that *Manuscript Genetics* represents, but rather to lament, or perhaps to celebrate, the sheer impossibility of the genetic process (hence, my epigraph from Goethe, the irony directed not at his would-be scholar, Wagner, but at the enterprise itself). I very much enjoyed this book; I have learnt a great deal from it; and I admire the quality of the work and the thought that has gone into it. But I am left with another metaphor, this time from Borges: the sense of the textual node as an aleph, a point at which everything in the (textual) universe comes together to be apprehended as a whole. That Van Hulle can even intimate that possibility is a considerable achievement; but as imperfect scholars, Wagner's rather than Faust's, perhaps, what we are too often left with is a dazzling set of particulars that lack the universals to bind them together. Such is the modernist tragedy, with Joycean omnipotence and omniscience more commonly experienced as Pound's realization that real knowledge enters one only in dribs and drabs, or Beckett's nescience, his sense of the flotsam and detritus of particulars as the only straws that the mind might grasp. The final danger of Van Hulle's study is, perhaps, that it offers enough to create for its reader the delusion (which its author clearly does not share) that perhaps all can be known.

Works cited

Beckett, Samuel. 1953. *Watt*. New York: Gove Press.

———. 1976. *Watt*. London: Calder.

Lawton, Graham Lawton. 2009. "Uprooting Darwin's Tree." *New Scientist*, 24 January, 34-39.

Nabokov, Vladimir. 1973. *Strong Opinions* New York: McGraw-Hill.

———, trans. 1990. "The Structure of 'Eugene Onegin." In Aleksander Pushkin, *Eugene Onegin: A Novel in Verse*. Princeton: Princeton University Press, 1:15.

Chris Ackerley

Musisque Deoque: Un Archivio Digitale di Poesia Latina/A Digital Archive of Latin Poetry. N.p.: Progetto Ricerca di Interesse Nazionale, 2007. http://www.MQDQ.it.

The professional Latinist has been served by good electronic archives since the dawn of the electronic age. The researcher can freely use the many texts uploaded to the world wide web by adepts of Latin literature (e.g., on www.thelatinlibrary.com), and also access to paid services that provide authoritative editions of many Latin texts with convenient search options. The CD-ROMs of the Packard Humanities Institute and the Library of Latin Texts website (on http://www.brepolis.net) are just two outstanding examples. Recently, a new branch has been added to the tree of online archives for Latinists: *Musisque Deoque: A Digital Archive of Latin Poetry* (*MQDQ*). This new service offers a welcome new approach to the presentation of searchable Latin texts, but in execution far too little attention is paid to elucidating the scholarly and technical methods used for the archive.

MQDQ (as it will be referred to in this review) is an ongoing collaborative project between Latinists from several Italian universities and is available in two languages, Italian and English (although some of the translations are rather poor, e.g., "contatti" is translated as "links" instead of "contact us"). The website, which is accessible free of charge, offers a very complete archive of Latin poetry from before the third century B.C. until the seventh century A.D.[3] Although the website offers some texts that cannot be found anywhere else on the internet in digital form, this alone hardly warrants the scholarly labour of several esteemed Italian Latinists, let alone a review in *Variants*. However, the way variants are handled and presented in *MQDQ* does.

Since every trustworthy edition of a classical text that is intended for scholarly use contains a critical apparatus which records a selection of the variant readings and conjectures, it is remarkable that the principal electronic archives of Latin texts do not include any such apparatus. The important innovation of *MQDQ* is that it is the first large scale archive to include them for a growing number of texts, and that it also provides effective search tools for them.[4] It has an option to search text and apparatus at

---

[3] The older *Poeti d'Italia in Lingua Latina* archive, containing renaissance Latin poetry from Italy, now also available from *MQDQ*, will not be considered in this review.

[4] Since it is an ongoing project, not all texts in *MQDQ* are currently enriched with an apparatus. At the moment of writing this, in February 2010, one or more texts by 47 authors (out of 273) contain an apparatus. These authors are indicated on the website by an icon that resembles a feather.

the same time. The search results will display only the edited text. If the search term is found only in the apparatus, its corresponding emendation in the main text is highlighted; clicking on that word or hovering over it brings up information from the *apparatus criticus*. To give one example: the query "arido AND pumice" gives "Arida modo pumice expolitum" (Catullus 1.2, ed. Eisenhut) as a result; Arida (a reading based on a comment by the late-antique grammarian Servius) is highlighted, while the variant reading "arido" pops up from the critical apparatus. It must be stressed that this is a very simple search string; the advanced search screen offers many more possibilities for more elaborate searches and filtering of search results: even the place of a word in the verse can be specified and it is possible to automatically search on different orthographical variants of a word. For Latin poetry, it offers the most sophisticated search tool that I know of.

It will be clear that the fresh critical approach of *MQDQ* opens up many new possibilities to Latinists. To mention just a few, linguists will find evidence on grammatical matters that often remain hidden in the apparatus; literary scholars may trace allusions not evident before; and scholars of the classical tradition can reconstruct the reception of different versions of a given text in its tradition. For this reason, it is all the more regrettable that this truly innovative project is not accompanied by a solid explanation of its aims, methods and techniques. The website does not give any information about the way the electronic editions were created (were they scanned with OCR or typed out manually? were they closely proofread?), how the critical apparatuses were constituted (were they copied from authoritative editions, or put together from apparatuses from several editions, or (partly) based on new research of the manuscripts?), nor do we find any information on the mark-up of the texts. Furthermore, although the website lists for each text the manuscripts and its abbreviations, it would have been useful, or even necessary for the serious scholar, to present a stemma of the manuscripts as well. With all this information lacking, a professional Latinist will still be forced to go back to the print editions.

On the whole, the conclusion must be that *MQDQ* is pioneering in a new electronic presentation of Latin texts that hopefully will once be the standard for all archives of Classical texts. However, because of the inadequate presentation and the absence of a rationale for the project, every textual or literary critic would be wise only to consult this website with the greatest circumspection. It is to be hoped that this flaw can be remedied, but it would require a fundamentally different approach from the project leaders.

Werner Gelderblom

Contributors

Christopher Ackerley is Professor of English at the University of Otago, New Zealand. He has edited an edition of Beckett's *Watt* (Faber, 2009), and he is currently embarked on a project on Malcolm Lowry, *Under the Volcano: A Hypertextual Companion*.

Annika Bautz is Lecturer in English at the University of Plymouth. She is a specialist in Romantic and Victorian fiction, history of the book and reception studies, and the author of a *Reader's Guide to Essential Criticism of Jane Austen's Pride and Prejudice, Emma and Sense and Sensibility* (2009).

Christian Benne is an Associate Professor in the Institute for Litterature, Culture and Media in the University of Southern Denmark. He researches comparative literature and the history of ideas in Europe, with a particular interest in manuscript culture in Europe since 1700.

Christine Collière-Whiteside is a Lecturer in English at the Paris Est-Créteil University. She works on the manuscripts of Lewis Carroll and George MacDonald, and on Carroll's personal library.

Stephen B. Dobranski is Professor of English at Georgia State University. He is the author of *Readers and Authorship in Early Modern England* (2005), and has recently completed *A Variorum Commentary on the Poems of John Milton: "Samson Agonistes"* (2009).

Hans Walter Gabler is a retired Professor of English Literature and Editorial Scholarship from the Ludwig Maximilians University of Munich, Germany, and is Senior Research Fellow of the Institute of English Studies, School of Advanced Study, London University. He was editor-in-chief of the *Critical and Synoptic Edition of James Joyce's Ulysses* (1984), and the critical editions of Joyce's *A Portrait of the Artist as a Young Man* and *Dubliners* (both 1993). His present main research interests are the writing processes in authors' draft manuscripts, their critical interpretation, and their representation in the electronic medium.

Werner Gelderblom is a PhD candidate in the Department of Classics at the Radboud University Nijmegen (The Netherlands). He is working on the genesis of the Neo-Latin poetry of Johannes Secundus (1511-1536).

Katie Halsey is Lecturer in Eighteenth-Century Literature at the University of Stirling. Her publications include several articles on Jane Austen, and the co-edited volumes *The History of Reading* (2010) and *The Concept and Practice of Conversation in the long eighteenth century* (2008).

Paula Henrikson is Associate Professor and a Research Fellow at the Swedish Academy, appointed at the Department of Literature, Uppsala University. She has authored the books *Dramatikern Stagnelius* (2004) and *Textkritisk utgivning. Råd och riktlinjer* (2007), as well as numerous articles on editorial theory, the history of editing, and Romantic literature.

Luc Herman teaches American literature and narrative theory at the University of Antwerp. He is the author of *Concepts of Realism* (1996), the co-author of *Handbook of Narrative Analysis* (2005), and the co-editor of the *Cambridge Companion to Thomas Pynchon* (forthcoming).

John M. Krafft teaches English at the Hamilton campus of Miami University. He co-founded *Pynchon Notes* in 1979 and served as an editor of the journal until 2009. He has co-authored several other recent or forthcoming essays on Pynchon with Luc Herman.

Sharon B. Krafft taught English at the Hamilton campus of Miami University and directed the Office of Learning Assistance. After her early retirement, she did occasional freelance editing. She succumbed to pancreatic cancer in 2009.

Rüdiger Nutt-Kofoth teaches German literature at the University of Wuppertal (Germany) and works at the *Goethe-Wörterbuch* (Goethe-Dictionary) in Hamburg (Göttingen Academy of Sciences and Humanities). He has written and edited books and articles on German literature and on editorial theory and practice. He is the co-editor of *editio. Internationales Jahrbuch für Editionswissenschaft. International Yearbook of Scholarly Editing* and of the series *Bausteine zur Geschichte der Edition* (Elements of a History of Editing). Furthermore he is the secretary of the Arbeitsgemeinschaft für germanistische Edition (Association of German Scholarly Editing).

Oliver Pickering is Honorary Fellow in the School of English at the University of Leeds. He was formerly Deputy Head of Special Collections in Leeds University Library, and editor of *The Library: Transactions of the Bibliographical Society*. He has published widely in the field of medieval texts and manuscripts.

Peter Robinson is Professor of Digital Textuality at the University of Saskatchewan. He has developed several computer-based tools for the preparation and publication of scholarly editions, and is active in the development of standards for digital resources. He has published and lectured on matters relating to computing and textual editing, on text encoding, digitization, electronic publishing, and on Geoffrey Chaucer's *Canterbury Tales*. His current major interest is in the creation of online "textual communities."

Michael Stolz studied German and Romance languages and literatures in Munich, Poitiers, and Bern. Subsequently he was visiting scholar in Oxford, Vienna, and Munich. As Assistant Professor of Medieval German Language and Literature, he taught from 2001 to 2005 at the University of Basel, where he initiated the "Parzival-Projekt", before being appointed Professor at the University of Göttingen in 2005. He is currently professor at the University of Bern and has published books and articles on religious lyrics, the history of learning, medieval writing, relationships between text and illustration, and textual philology.

Paulius V. Subačius is associate professor of Literature at the University of Vilnius, Lithuania. He has published *Textual Criticism: Guidelines of Theory and Practice* (2001, in Lithuanian) and some critical editions of 19th-20th century Lithuanian authors. He is working on an edition of Antanas Baranauskas' poetry and is interested in the biographical, social and religious context of text production.

Mikas Vaicekauskas is a senior researcher of The Institute of Lithuanian Literature and Folklore in Vilnius, Lithuania. He is author of *Lietuviškos katalikiškos XVI–XVIII amžiaus giesmės* (*Lithuanian Catholic Hymns of 16th–18th Century*, 2005) and *Motiejaus Valančiaus užrašų ir atsiminimų rankraščiai Lietuvių mokslo draugijoje: 1911–1914 metų istorija* (*Motiejus Valančius Notes and Reminiscences Manuscripts in Lithuanian Society of Science: The History of 1911–1914*, 2009). In addition to articles on Motiejus Valančius, he has also published on the work of Mykolas Olševskis, Kristijonas Donelaitis and on the Lithuanian hand-written books in the period of the ban on Lithuanian press.

Nila Vazquez studied English Philology at the University of Santiago de Compostela and Teaching, specialising in Foreign Languages, at the University of Vigo. She has been a lecturer of Historical Linguistics at the University of Murcia since 2002. She was previously a lecturer of English Language at the University of Alcala de Henares (1999-2002). She has published mostly on The Canterbury Tales and on New Techniques on Textual Editing. She is involved in the Reasearch Project 'Variation and Linguistic Change' (University of Santiago de Compostela) and in the 'Canterbury Tales Project'. Her main current areas of writing and research are Historical Linguistics, The *Tale of Gamelyn*, Textual Scholarship, Electronic Editing and Corpus Linguistics.

Gabriel Viehhauser is Assistent at the German Department at the University of Bern. He is author of Die Parzival-Überlieferung am Ausgang des Manuskriptzeitalters. Handschriften der Lauberwerkstatt und der Straßburger Druck (2009). In addition, he has published various articles on the transmission of Middle High German literature and the materiality of manuscripts.

Gillian Wright is Senior Lecturer in English at the University of Birmingham. Her principal research interests are in women's writing in manuscript in the long seventeenth century.

Jesús Varela Zapata has held several posts at the University of Santiago de Compostela such as Dean of Humanities and member of the University Board. He is the author of *V.S. Naipaul: El retrato de la sociedad post-colonial* and has edited a number of books on applied linguistics and cultural studies. He has also published extensively on postcolonial studies.

Textual Cultures

The official publication of the Society for Textual Scholarship

EDITED BY H. WAYNE STOREY AND EDWARD BURNS

Textual Cultures brings together essays by scholars from numerous disciplines and focuses on issues of textual editing, redefinitions of textuality, the history of the book, material culture, and the fusion of codicology with literary, musicological, and art historical interpretation and iconography. It is the official publication of the Society for Textual Scholarship. Membership includes a subscription to the journal.

PUBLISHED SEMIANNUALLY
eISSN 1933-7418
pISSN 1559-2936

Available in electronic, combined electronic & print, and print formats

SUBSCRIBE
800-842-6796
812-855-8817
http://inscribe.iupress.org
iuporder@indiana.edu

ADVERTISE
http://inscribe.iupress.org/page/advertising

INDIANA UNIVERSITY PRESS
INDIANA UNIVERSITY

Indiana University Press/Journals

601 North Morton Street, Bloomington, Indiana 47404-3797 USA

Leichabdankung und Trauerarbeit

Zur Bewältigung von Tod und Vergänglichkeit im Zeitalter des Barock

Herausgegeben von
Ralf Georg Bogner,
Johann Anselm Steiger
und Ulrich Heinen

Inhalt
Vorwort
Ralf Georg Bogner: Die Totenklage der Frühen Neuzeit. Perspektiven der interdisziplinären Forschung
Misia Sophia Doms: Die 'Wirklichkeit' der Transzendenz. Überlegungen zur Magnetbildlichkeit in der Leichabdankung *Magnetische Verbindung des HErrn JESV/ und der in Jhn verliebten Seelen* von Andreas Gryphius
Johannes Birgfeld: Trauer(arbeit) auf Reisen. Wolfgang Jacob von Gera, Andreas Gryphius und der Tod sowie Neues von der Kavaliersreise Wilhelm Schlegels mit Gryphius (Mit einer Übersetzung aus dem Lateinischen von Ralf Georg Czapla)
Wilhelm Kühlmann und Lutz Claren: Heros und Skandalon: Zum poetischen Gedenken an den 'Ketzer' Giulio Cesare Vanini (1585–1619) in der deutschen Literatur. Von Johannes Bisselius SJ zu Friedrich Hölderlin
Ulrich Heinen: Stoisch trauern. Bewältigungsstrategien bei Peter Paul Rubens
Margit Thøfner: Material Time. The Art of Mourning in Early Modern Europe
Cordula van Wyhe: Death and Immortality in Rubens' Ildefonso Altarpiece
Christian Schmitz: Leichabdankungen als Quelle historischer Wissenschaften
Johann Anselm Steiger: Andreas Gryphius' Leichabdankung auf den Arzt Heinrich Fierling, Sigismund Pirschers Leichenpredigt und die theologia medicinalis. Ein Beitrag zur Geschichte der Parentatio zwischen 'weltlicher' und 'geistlicher' Redekultur

Amsterdam/New York, NY
2009. VI, 369 pp. (Daphnis 38 - 2009: 1–2)
Paper €75,-/US$101,-
E-Book €75,-/US$101,-
ISBN: 978-90-420-3028-2
ISBN: 978-90-420-3029-9

USA/Canada:
248 East 44th Street, 2nd floor,
New York, NY 10017, USA.
Call Toll-free (US only): T: 1-800-225-3998
F: 1-800-853-3881

All other countries:
Tijnmuiden 7, 1046 AK Amsterdam, The Netherlands
Tel. +31-20-611 48 21 Fax +31-20-447 29 79
Please note that the exchange rate is subject to fluctuations

Orders@rodopi.nl — www.rodopi.nl

Eulenspiegel trifft Melusine

Der frühneuhochdeutsche Prosaroman im Licht neuer Forschungen und Methoden

Akten der Lausanner Tagung vom 2. bis 4. Oktober 2008

in Zusammenarbeit mit
Alexander Schwarz

Herausgegeben von
Catherine Drittenbass
und André Schnyder

Die Ausschreibung der hier dokumentierten Tagung hatte den umfassenden Literaturbericht Jan-Dirk Müllers von 1985 als Ausgangspunkt genommen, an die Menge und die Vielfalt der seither geleisteten Forschung über den Prosaroman erinnert und zudem darauf verwiesen, dass in diesem Vierteljahrhundert wie wohl nie zuvor in der Fachgeschichte Forschungsparadigmen formuliert, diskutiert und propagiert worden waren; eine Vielzahl von ihnen betraf gerade auch den Prosaroman. Vor diesem Hintergrund steht die an der Jahrtausendwende getroffene Feststellung Müllers: "Eine Geschichte der Prosaromane, die sie nicht mehr nur vor dem Hintergrund ihrer mittelalterlichen Vorläufer betrachtet, ist noch zu schreiben" – ein Ziel, das weiter als je in der Ferne liegen dürfte. Insofern wollen die zwei Dutzend hier vorgelegten Tagungsbeiträge einzig neue Annäherungen an den ebenso vielfältigen wie reizvollen Gegenstand bieten. Günstig mag immerhin zu Buche schlagen, dass er in der Optik verschiedener Disziplinen (neben der Germanistik: Kunst-, Sprach-, Buchwissenschaft, Romanistik) betrachtet wird, dass ferner das Einleitungskapitel eine Tagungsbilanz erstellt und dass abschliessend eine Bibliographie die seit 1985 geleistete Forschung wenigstens als Titelliste fassbar macht.

Amsterdam/New York, NY
2010. 638 pp. (Chloe 42)
Bound €128,-/US$179,-
E-Book €128,-/US$179,-
ISBN: 978-90-420-3059-6
ISBN: 978-90-420-3060-2

USA/Canada:
248 East 44th Street, 2nd floor,
New York, NY 10017, USA.
Call Toll-free (US only): T: 1-800-225-3998
F: 1-800-853-3881

All other countries:
Tijnmuiden 7, 1046 AK Amsterdam, The Netherlands
Tel. +31-20-611 48 21 Fax +31-20-447 29 79
Please note that the exchange rate is subject to fluctuations

rodopi
Orders@rodopi.nl—www.rodopi.nl

Rodopi

From Recognition to Restoration

Latvia's History as a Nation-State

Edited and Introduced by
David J. Smith,
David J. Galbreath and
Geoffrey Swain

Taking its cue from the 90th anniversary commemorations of November 2008, this work explores the relationship between state and nationhood during the three phases to date in Latvia's existence as a territorial entity: the sovereign statehood of 1918–1940; the Soviet and Nazi occupations of 1940–1944 and the ensuing half-century within the USSR; and the post-1991 period, which has seen the restoration of independence on the basis of legal continuity from the inter-war period and — latterly — accession to the European Union. The aim in relation to all three eras is to go beyond the often essentialising contours of Cold War and post-Cold War debates and reveal the underlying complexities and ambiguities of political and social development.

Amsterdam/New York, NY
2010. 174 pp.
(On the Boundary of Two Worlds: Identity, Freedom, and Moral Imagination in the Baltics 25)
Paper €35,-/US$49,-
E-Book €35,-/US$49,-
ISBN: 978-90-420-3098-5
ISBN: 978-90-420-3099-2

USA/Canada:
248 East 44th Street, 2nd floor,
New York, NY 10017, USA.
Call Toll-free (US only): T: 1-800-225-3998
F: 1-800-853-3881

All other countries:
Tijnmuiden 7, 1046 AK Amsterdam, The Netherlands
Tel. +31-20-611 48 21 Fax +31-20-447 29 79
Please note that the exchange rate is subject to fluctuations

rodopi
Orders@rodopi.nl—www.rodopi.nl